NELSON'S PATHFINDERS

NELSON'S PATHFINDERS

A Forgotten Story in the Triumph of British Sea Power

MICHAEL BARRITT

YALE UNIVERSITY PRESS
NEW HAVEN AND LONDON

For information about this and other Yale University Press publications, please contact:
U.S. Office: sales.press@yale.edu   yalebooks.com
Europe Office: sales@yaleup.co.uk   yalebooks.co.uk

Set in Adobe Caslon Pro by IDSUK (DataConnection) Ltd
Printed in Great Britain by Clays Ltd, Elcograf S.p.A

Library of Congress Control Number: 2024938420

ISBN 978-0-300-27376-2

A catalogue record for this book is available from the British Library.

10 9 8 7 6 5 4 3 2 1

For Rosanne

Contents

List of Plates, Figures and Maps   *viii*
Acknowledgements   *xiii*
Note on Conventions   *xv*

Prologue   1
Introduction   5

Chapter 1: Pathfinding for Colonial Warfare   15
Chapter 2: Pathfinding for an Empire of Trade   35
Chapter 3: Containing the Enemy: The Mediterranean   59
Chapter 4: Holding the Centre: Home Waters and Invasion   81
            Coasts
Chapter 5: Sea Power Projection: Northern Europe   103
Chapter 6: Sea Power Projection: Iberian Peninsula   129
Chapter 7: World War: The Americas and the Pacific   151
Chapter 8: Securing an Uneasy Peace   169

Postscript: A 'Great Maritime Nation'   192

Appendix of Statistics   *200*
Glossary   *203*
Notes   *214*
Bibliography   *238*
Index   *251*

Plates, Figures and Maps

Unless otherwise specified, all images are sourced from the UK Hydrographic Office (www.ukho.gov.uk).

Plates

1. The track of HMS *Victory* on first entry to Agincourt Sound, 1803. UKHO m13 Ry.
2. Captain Thomas Hurd.
3. Admiral Sir John Knight. Private collection. The RiverRoyal Collection.
4. Sir Francis Beaufort by William Brockedon, 1838. NPG 2515(90). © National Portrait Gallery, London.
5. Captain William Henry Smyth by James Green, 1818. Photo © Christie's Images / Bridgeman Images.
6. Edward Columbine's *Resolution*, c.1794. NMM CMP/50/1/5a-18. © National Maritime Museum, Greenwich, London.
7. HMS *Griper*, from William Edward Parry, *Journal of a Voyage for the Discovery of a North-West Passage from the Atlantic to the Pacific* (London, 1821).

8. A survey and view made during the operation at Copenhagen, 1807. NMD 144 strodeskort. National Museum of Denmark.
9. Pathfinding in HMS *Ranger*, 1810. UKHO C280 Hn.
10. Reconnaissance survey in the rias of Galicia, 1809. UKHO m85 Hy.
11. George Thomas's front-line survey during the Walcheren operation, 1809. UKHO c53 13b.
12. Reconnaissance survey of Vieux Fort, Marie Galante, 1808. UKHO MP 44 (Ac6).
13. Martin White's front-line survey, 1803. UKHO 841 5k.
14. Peter Heywood's survey of the coast of Sumatra, c.1801. UKHO v4 Bb2.
15. William Mudge's plan of Porto Santo, 1819. UKHO B118 Cb.
16. Martin White's fair sheet, 1812. UKHO 841 5k.

Figures

1. The East Bossevin rock. UKHO OCB 2690.   2
2. The coast and off-lying dangers observed from the East Bossevin rock. UKHO OCB 66.   3
3. Detail of the survey of Hurd Channel, 1806. UKHO A 124/1 6a.   21
4. Edward Columbine, self-portrait, 1795. NMM COM 02 22. © National Maritime Museum, Greenwich, London.   23
5. Diagram from Edward Columbine's field report, 1803. NMM COM 02 63. © National Maritime Museum, Greenwich, London.   28
6. Extract from Edward Columbine's survey of the Bocas del Drago, 1803. UKHO E36 Ag2.   29
7. Detail from Alexander Briarly's 'An actual survey of the River Orinoco from the great mouth up to the   32

City of Angostura', 1803. John Carter Brown Library Call
Number Roll GA803 1. CC BY 4.0, Courtesy of the John
Carter Brown Library.

8. David Bartholomew's view taken during Popham's survey   39
of the Red Sea, 1803. NMM BAR B 8409. © National
Maritime Museum, Greenwich, London.

9. Peter Heywood's survey of the Typa anchorage, 1804.   42
UKHO L2013 Bb6.

10. Thomas Hayward's survey of Back Bay, Trincomalee,   45
1795. UKHO A112 Ba2.

11. Peter Heywood's sounding sheet, 1819. UKHO 164/1 Af2.   55

12. David Bartholomew's manuscript chart of the Plate,   55
1807. UKHO E990 Af1M.

13. Extract from Thomas Mann and John Hepburn's fair   64
sheet, 1807. UKHO 195 Rn.

14. Detail from a contemporary copy of Durban's survey of   70
the Skerki Bank, c.1804. NVP 12 15. © National Maritime
Museum, Greenwich, London.

15. William Henry Smyth surveying, 1823. UKHO AAC 4.   76

16. Detail from William Henry Smyth's survey of the Strait   77
of Messina, 1816. UKHO f35 Su.

17. Extract from James Johnstone's survey of the French coast,   83
1804. UKHO 139 Df.

18. Detail from a survey by John Murray, 1806. UKHO 615b   86
4 15n.

19. A station pointer in use. Author's collection.   88

20. Detail from Thomas Hurd's plot, 1804. NMM DUC   92
224 2 18 MS. © National Maritime Museum, Greenwich,
London.

21. Contemporary engraving of a sounding boat. Private   95
collection.

22. Extract from Chart 43 in Thomas Hurd's *Channel Atlas*,   97
1806. UKHO OCB 66.

23. Details from Alexander Briarly's plan of the battle of Copenhagen, 1802. BM 1891,0414.185. © The Trustees of the British Museum. — 105

24. Thomas Atkinson's survey, 1807. Vy 3/28. MOD Admiralty Library. — 108

25. Jeremiah Beltt's plan of the anchorage in Hanö Sound, 1810. UKHO MP 101 Dc1. — 112

26. James Reeves' survey of the approaches to Makilito Bay, 1809. UKHO h1 Hr. — 113

27. Extract from William Henry Smyth's survey of Cádiz and environs, 1811. UKHO H99 Hz. — 135

28. Richard Thomas's survey of Cadaqués Bay, 1812. UKHO p97 Med. Folio 1. — 139

29. Detail from Anthony Lockwood's survey of the roadsteads of Corunna, Betanzos and Ares, 1804. UKHO 156 Hy. — 144

30. Reconnaissance survey of a bay near Corunna, 1809. NLS Adv MS.46.10.1 number 40. Courtesy of the National Library of Scotland. — 145

31. Detail from Peter Ney's sketch survey at Santander, 1812. UKHO MP 104 De2. — 147

32. Detail from Anthony De Mayne's survey of the Patuxent, 1814. UKHO 303 Ra. — 155

33. Charles Morris's survey of Tangier Sound, 1815. UKHO MP 33 Ab2. — 156

34. Anthony De Mayne's Admiralty chart of Tangier Sound, 1814. UKHO OCB 305. — 157

35. Detail from William Hewett's survey of Pernambuco, 1815. UKHO t16 Af3. — 163

36. Detail of Patrick Brady's view from the anchorage at Callao, 1814. UKHO View Folio 8E 16. — 166

37. Extracts from Alexander Russel's survey of the bombarding units at Mocha, 1821. UKHO 499 Cu. — 172

38. Robert Hagan's survey of the Shoals of St Ann, 1820.   178
    UKHO B226 Ch.

39. William Finlaison's view of Fish Town, 1820. UKHO   178
    r46 Ch.

40. Detail from Martin White's survey of the English   184
    Channel, 1812. UKHO 807a Oi*.

41. William Henry Smyth's sounding collector sheet, 1822.   190
    UKHO f47 S.

Maps

1. West Indies.   14
2. East Indies.   34
3. South America.   50
4. Mediterranean Sea.   58
5. English Channel and Strait of Dover.   80
6. Approaches to Brest.   89
7. Baltic Sea.   102
8. Southern North Sea.   116
9. Iberian Peninsula.   128
10. Chesapeake Bay.   150
11. Great Lakes.   158
12. Africa and the Atlantic Islands.   175

Acknowledgements

The research for this book has spanned more than a decade. The lists of primary and secondary sources are testimony to the shoulders on which this study rests. I hope that the citations give due credit to the expert advice from which I have benefited. Particular thanks are due to Paul Barrow, Richard Campbell, Andrew Cook, James Davey, Andrew David, Barry Gough, Tony Jenks, John MacAleer, Michael Nash, Catherine Scheybeler, Richard Smith, John Sugden, Adrian Webb and Richard Woodman. Any solecisms which remain are my responsibility. Andrew Lambert has gallantly read intermediate drafts and I am indebted to him for encouragement and strategic perspective. With Roger Knight, Janet Hartley and Nicholas Rodger, he has provided vital counsel on presentation of the story of my hydrographic precursors for a general readership.

So too, at Yale University Press, has Julian Loose, whose wise and patient steering has played a crucial role in shaping the argument and telling the story. I am grateful to him and to his team of Rachael Lonsdale and Lucy Buchan for piloting me through the editing process. Rachel Bridgewater's copy-editing has smoothed out many errors. Frazer Martin has been an invaluable support throughout, not

ACKNOWLEDGEMENTS

least in the vital matter of illustration. I am grateful to Martin Brown for interpreting my rough maps so elegantly. Lucy Doncaster and James Williams have choreographed publicity.

I am greatly indebted to successive managers and staff for access to the rich seam of material in the UKHO Archive. Once again, as a visitor from the provinces, I am happy to pay tribute to the facilities and helpful staff of The National Archives, the British Library, the Guildhall Library, the London Metropolitan Archive, the Caird Library of the National Maritime Museum, the Foyle Library of the Royal Geographical Society and the library of the Royal United Services Institute. I have received similar assistance from the expert teams in the Naval Historical Branch at Portsmouth, the Map Room of the Bodleian Library and the Museum of the History of Science in Oxford. I am grateful to Michael Nash for access to some important papers in his collection.

I owe a considerable debt of thanks to those whose hospitality and logistic support have made my research possible: Philip Barritt and Sam Fox, James and Val Collett, Admiral Jayanath Colombage, Andy Fuller, Andrew and June Kirkwood, Jan Miller and Ruth Sutherland. The most significant support has come of course from my wife Rosanne, who has never faltered in patient tolerance of my sleuthing activity and in faith in the outcome. She merits the dedication.

Note on Conventions

Location maps have been included for the main theatres of operation. A good atlas will be needed to supplement them. Current orthography as used on British Admiralty charts is shown in brackets after old names in the text.

The simple but effective note on the rating of warships by my tutor at Oxford, Piers Mackesy, in *The War in the Mediterranean, 1803–1810* has been borrowed and expanded below. A final column has been added with an illustrative draught, the critical parameter for access and power projection, for a vessel of a standard class in each rate. For comparison, the draught of the *Queen Elizabeth* class battleships of the two world wars of the twentieth century was 30', of HMS *Belfast* 17' and of the workhorse *Leander* class frigates of the late twentieth century 13' 6". All these, of course, had the advantage of mechanical propulsion.

NOTE ON CONVENTIONS

Description	Rate	Armament	Example (no. of guns)	Draught
Ships of the Line	1st Rate	100 guns and above (3-deckers)	*Victory*	21' 6"
	2nd Rate	98–90 guns (3-deckers)	*St George*	17' 10"
	3rd Rate	80–64 guns (2-deckers)	*Captain* (74)	18' 10"
Intermediate Class	4th Rate	60–50 guns (2-deckers)	*Leopard* (50)	15' 8"
Frigates	5th Rate	40–32 guns	*Phoebe* (36)	15' 0"
	6th Rate	28–20 guns	*Crocodile* (22)	12' 9"
Sloops		18–16 guns	*Termagant* (18)	11' 10"
Gun-brigs, cutters etc.		14–6 guns	*Protector*	7' 0"

Those requiring more information on this topic should consult the standard works by Lavery and Winfield which are cited in the Bibliography.

Throughout the text numbers will be shown in brackets after ship's names to indicate the number of guns and hence the rate of the ship. It was standard practice to refer, for example, to a '74-gun ship' or '74' for short.

Prologue

How much longer? The launch had a full load of filled water casks, sacks of sand and piles of brushwood, leaving little legroom beneath the oarsmen's benches. It would be a stiff pull back to the frigate *Diamond* at anchor in the deep water outside the expanse of rocks and reefs. Their passenger was certainly a cool customer. They had glanced at him as they laboured to gather their cargo on Béniguet Island. Surely by now the French had spotted this lone figure who, since early in that month of July 1804, had been popping up on the islets along the inshore edge of the long Ushant archipelago? Yet he was utterly absorbed in his observations and measurements. They could not share his composure. Barely three weeks had elapsed since three French gunboats had swooped on *Acasta*'s launch whilst a party was gathering sand on Béniguet and they had been carried off into captivity before other boats could come to their rescue.

Now he had taken them even closer to the French coast. He was perched 15 feet above them on the top of the haystack-shaped East Bossevin (Bossemen Orientale) rock. It lies just over 2 sea miles offshore at the exit from the Chenal du Four, the vital inshore channel along which naval stores were passed into Brest, the base of the

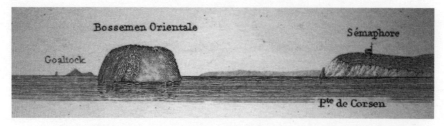

1. *The East Bossevin rock (Bossemen Orientale), Captain Thomas Hurd's nearest triangulation station to the enemy coast.*

French Atlantic Fleet. Captain John Knight's annotations on his chart, the best available to the Royal Navy, indicated that they were just out of range of shells from the heavy battery on Pointe de St Mathieu. But the boat's crew kept a careful watch on the entrance to the enemy small craft base at Port du Conquet from which those gunboats could emerge again.

Captain Thomas Hurd had explained what he was doing to the hand-picked sailors who helped to carry his tripod and the boxes containing his theodolite, sextant and miner's compass. Now he was training the telescope of his theodolite on the flagstaff which they had helped to erect on his station at the north-east end of Béniguet. They recognised the marks as he swept along the enemy coast, refocusing on the signal post at Le Conquet, the spire of Lochrist church and the lighthouse on Pointe de St Mathieu. With the angles between them recorded carefully in turn in his notebook, he swivelled out to westward, to extend the spider's web of his observations – his triangulation scheme – across the lurking hazards to the patrolling British warships: the pinnacles of Le Ranvel, Les Trois Cheminées, the Outer Black Rock. With this work complete and plotted he could probe in *Diamond*'s cutters, to find passages that the small craft of the Inshore Squadron could exploit to tighten the blockade, and to confirm that no other dangers to the supporting frigates and ships of the line had gone undetected. For beyond the Black Rocks lay the submerged reef of Le Boufoloc, and here Hurd's telescope picked up

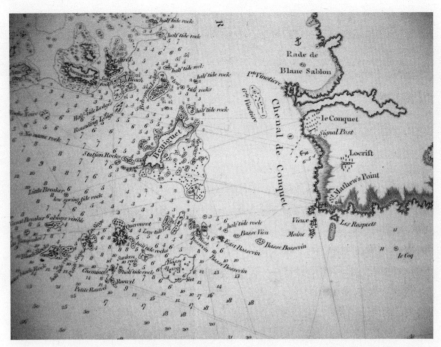

2. The coast and off-lying dangers that Hurd observed from the East Bossevin rock.

a protruding mast moving with the tide, buoying the resting place of the fine 74-gun *Magnificent*, which, unalerted by chart or pilot, had grounded and become a total loss.[1]

It was this incident that had brought Thomas Hurd onto the scene. Throughout the years of war with Revolutionary and now Napoleonic France, more than twice as many British warships had been lost to shipwreck than in action with the enemy. The application of British sea power took them into unfamiliar seas and into complex and dangerous coastal waters. Nowhere had the unsustainable losses been more onerous than off Brest, where Admiral Cuthbert Collingwood had confided whilst in command of the blockade: 'an anxious time I have of it, what with tides and rocks, which have more danger in them than a battle once a week'.[2]

Poor navigational data was a critical constraint on the effectiveness of British maritime strategy and tactics. As he worked, Thomas

Hurd pondered over the means of addressing this shortcoming in support for the fleet. In the present task his progress was hampered by his dependence on loaned boats, with fresh crews who had to be briefed on his requirements. He had no assistant for this work of establishing control for his survey – just the sailors to scramble ashore with his equipment. He had no one to help fix his boat's position or record the results as he directed the crew in sounding amongst the rocks, always alert for a break in the weather, the telltale onset of an Atlantic swell. It was here, on the very front line of the conflict, that Hurd formed a vision for the identification of men with higher skills to form a specialist cadre of pathfinders.

This book tells the neglected story of how he realised this vision and how his pathfinders made a vital contribution to the outcome of the Napoleonic Wars. By mid-century, Francis Beaufort, Hurd's wartime counterpart and eventual successor as head of that service, would urge his men on the front line in the Crimean War to be 'the Admiral's eyes'. Royal Navy hydrographic pathfinders would continue to play their part in the effective deployment of British sea power through succeeding turbulent centuries. Yet their past record and present worth are often forgotten, and the importance of their role has demanded constant explanation and advocacy. Serving in the Hydrographic Office in Whitehall, I took part in the fight to keep the capability alive through the cutbacks of the 1990s, with their mantra of delivery of a 'peace dividend'. The need for that advocacy is urgent today to preserve a key capability for the Royal Navy in ensuring the security of British citizens overseas, the safe passage of the seaborne trade that underpins this country's economic stability, and the protection of the networks of sub-sea pipelines and communication cables on which today's society depends.

Introduction

The purpose of this book is to show how Thomas Hurd made hydrographic capability a crucial enabler of strategic planning and front-line operations in the age that saw the classic application of British sea power. In the Seven Years' War in the mid-eighteenth century the Royal Navy and Britain's merchant marine had transported armies to seize the enemy's overseas possessions, extending the reach of British merchants and augmenting the commercial dominance of the City of London and other major British ports. The resultant financial dividends enabled the government to combat French ascendancy on the continent of Europe through subsidies to a coalition of allies. This strategy had been stress-tested but sustained in the War of American Independence, and it remained a foundation of government policy in the Great War of 1793–1815. Sea trade was the heart-blood of a commercial empire. Britain's navy was the priority for military expenditure. It is a stirring story, often told, of blockade and battle, capture of enemy trading posts and privateer bases, convoy protection and ultimately amphibious support as a small army was landed to play a proportionate role in the defeat of Napoleonic France on the continent of Europe. Sea power remained pre-eminent, for this was a global conflict that would near its bitter end as the US declared war on Britain.[1]

Victory came at a cost. Keeping the sea entailed going where others feared to tread: into uncharted seas, and into waters where guidance had been classified as a state secret of the coastal state. The Royal Navy was not helped by the fact that small government and reliance on the private sector were favoured in eighteenth-century Britain every bit as much as in recent times. In France a Dépôt des Plans, Cartes et Journaux de la Marine had been established way back in 1720. It was not until 1795, three years after the outbreak of war, that Alexander Dalrymple was appointed Hydrographer to the Board of Admiralty. His remit was limited to the custody and care of the manuscript plans and charts which had been submitted from the fleet, and the selection and compilation from them of information for printing and distribution by commercial publishers. He was moonlighting from his analogous post with the East India Company, where he had no title and not even an office but enjoyed much more latitude in his task.[2] By this time his French counterparts were systematically disseminating their products. British prisoners of war marvelled at the 'superb set of charts' issued to every ship in the French fleet.[3] By contrast, until Dalrymple could impose quality control, captains and masters in the British Royal Navy remained dependent on commercial sources. Inadequate charts were a major factor in the unsustainable ship losses.

The story of the emergence of the British Admiralty Chart to meet this need has been told. How the information for those charts was gathered by the Royal Navy's pathfinders has not – it is the uninvestigated thread in the narrative, now addressed in this book. Contrary to opinion at the time, and the verdict of some historians, the task was not neglected by the Royal Navy. Again, small government played a part. Systematic, high-quality data-gathering in British waters was commissioned from civilian practitioners. By contrast, work in Portugal was entrusted to engineers of the army and navy. Suitably skilled naval personnel were deployed in survey parties around continental Spain and her possessions in South

America and the Philippines. France had formed a cadre of highly skilled *ingénieurs hydrographes* with commanders such as Charles-François Beautemps-Beaupré, who continued their work in war-time, though their deployment was confined by British sea control. This book will show, however, that whilst the Royal Navy did not have a similar specialised cadre, British naval personnel were not idle.[4]

It first describes how experience of sea survey – hydrography – was accumulated as part of mapping for political and military control in North America and elsewhere in the trading empire. Similarly, experience was gained during eighteenth-century voyages of exploration, pre-eminently those of Captains James Cook and George Vancouver. Hence, practitioners with higher skills emerged from amongst the ship's captains, their commissioned officers and their navigational specialists, the masters, many of these drawn from merchant service and granted a warrant after examination at Trinity House. Over 200 personnel in the fleet conducted surveys of variable precision in the course of the wars. The significance of their path-finding is described as the Royal Navy achieved and sustained control of those sinews of trade that gave Britain decisive financial domin-ance, as enemy fleets were contained and as invasion was thwarted. Their skill became even more essential with the projection of sea power. Later chapters discuss campaigns in the Baltic and Low Countries to preserve the favourable balance of naval strength and to win the commercial contest with Napoleon by undermining his trade embargo, and the campaign in the Iberian Peninsula which would contribute to the emperor's downfall. Conflict with the US took the pathfinders into distant waters where Royal Naval presence would remain crucial for what Hurd described as 'a great Maritime Nation whose flag flies triumphant in every part of the World'.[5]

By the end of the wars in 1815 Hurd was issuing sets of charts, the mariner's maps, with the Admiralty stamp of approval. Some were just reproductions of pathfinders' sketch plans, many submitted as illustrations in the 'Remarks' which they were required to submit on ports and anchorages. These remarks were analogous to the directions which we give to someone visiting our home for the first time: 'Pass the pub on your left and a church to your right, go under the railway bridge then watch out for a postbox and take the next turning on the left.' Much higher skill and sustained effort are required to provide observations that enable an area of the Earth's surface to be expressed mathematically and hence to be used by a cartographer to construct a map or chart. As we set out on our Royal Naval career as hydrographic specialists, we were given an acronym to encourage us to keep in mind the essentials of a survey: POSS + D. This stands for: position, orientation, scale, shape – and detail. The detail of shore terrain (topography) and seabed (bathymetry) was built up by systematic recording of prominent land features and the sounding of depths. In the coastal waters that the pathfinders were probing, this last operation was achieved by casting a lead weighing 7 or 14 pounds at the end of a line marked at intervals down to 13 or 20 fathoms with cloth or leather strips or knotted twine. In covert night-time operations the skilled 'leadsman' required an instinctive 'feel' for those marks: blue serge at 13 fathoms, red bunting at 7 fathoms, white duck at 5 fathoms and serrated leather at 3 and 2 fathoms. He had to judge the intermediate depths: 'Deep 6, a quarter less 6, and a half 5, and a quarter 5, by the mark 5 . . .' An 'armed' lead, with tallow in a depression on its base, allowed him to report the nature of the bottom – hard, sand or mud. It was exhausting work. Thomas Hurd noted that he sometimes needed two men deploying the lead-line in his sounding boat in the approaches to Brest.

The first four elements of the acronym provide what is known as the 'control' for such examination. Procedures were described in contemporary textbooks. One of the most popular was John Hamilton Moore's bestselling *Practical Navigator*. Another was the *Elements of Navigation*, published in 1772 for 'use by Gentlemen of the Navy'

INTRODUCTION

by James Robertson, who taught at the Royal Mathematical School of Christ's Hospital London, and afterwards at the Royal Naval Academy, Portsmouth.

The observations for position and orientation are the most demanding and were the driver for Hurd's recruitment of a specialist cadre. His chosen Admiralty Surveyors had demonstrated understanding of astronomy and skill in careful observation, for which the Hydrographer now provided them with top-quality instruments. He also looked for command of the higher mathematics, especially spherical trigonometry, that were needed to compute the results. The effective use of chronometers, which were not issued to all ships, depended on the quality of the astronomical observation to fix the origin from which they gave difference of time and thus longitude. Scale was obtained by measuring a baseline laid out from a carefully observed position. In a rapid reconnaissance survey this might be done by timing the lapse between sighting the smoke and hearing the report from a gun fired at the other end of the line. For precise work a baseline was measured on flat ground using special chains. Shape was given by observing a network of angles from the marked positions at each end of the baseline to other marked stations, either natural objects, sometimes highlighted with whitewash, or flagstaffs. For their sketch surveys, ship's masters often had only a boat's compass with which to observe the bearings to and from the marks. In a flagship they might have a more sophisticated 'azimuth compass' with an integral sight. Some would achieve a more dependable result by measuring the horizontal angles between the stations with a sextant. Precise results required observation with a theodolite, as in Thomas Hurd's work off Brest. The resultant triangles would be plotted as a framework for the survey, and the whole process was called triangulation. How this worked can be seen in the illustrated detail from Captain Bartholomew's survey of Porto Santo (Plate 15). The sum of the angles in such a scheme could be used as a check on the precision of the observations, and practitioners who took this step would describe their results as a 'trigonometric survey'. All the marked stations could be used to fix the position of land features or a sounding boat, either by observing their bearings or, again, more accurately, by taking a horizontal angle fix with a sextant. More detail can be found in the Glossary, where some essential technical terms are explained.[6] Sadly, very few images have survived of survey work in this period.

The work had then to be plotted and rendered to the Admiralty, where the Hydrographer would have the whole survey engraved and printed, or would abstract data for incorporation in a smaller-scale chart. Most Admiralty charts were printed at Double Elephant or Half Double Elephant size (40" or 20" by 27"; 102cm or 51cm by 69cm). They were issued bound in atlases, or singly in boxes. There is some evidence of the smaller-scale charts being used to plot and plan tracks, but it seems likely that in general the charts were reference documents.[7] Indeed, some handy manuscript charts are preserved in the National Maritime Museum that were prepared for Rear Admiral Penrose so that he could hold them in his hand whilst superintending the entry of his flagship to the River Garonne (Chapter 6). The 'fair sheets' on which the surveyors recorded their results varied greatly in size. Hurd was able to arrange supply of stationery to his Admiralty Surveyors, but many other practitioners struggled to find paper on which to plot their work. They might resort to using the back of printed Admiralty forms. Some large fair sheets are formed of several sheets of paper glued together. Many are very substantial in size, which is why most illustrations in this book are of only a portion, to allow detail to be seen clearly. The fair sheet illustrated in Plate 16 is about 5 feet by 4 feet (148cm by 127cm), and even larger ones will be described below.

The evidence gathered during the preparation of this account challenges the verdict of contemporaries and historians that few personnel in the Royal Navy appreciated the tactical and strategic importance of hydrography. Hurd's eventual successor as Hydrographer, Edward Parry, had remarked as a young officer that:

> I have often taken great pains to make the inquiries you mention viz. the marks, shoals, dangers, and methods of avoiding them, and have been as often astonished to find that few, or none, seemed the least inclined to assist me in these occupations, though, thereby, they would be assisting themselves. The fact is exactly as you say, that they are too lazy to attend to this most necessary brand of sea-knowledge, because they are not expected to know it.[8]

In fact, the survey which he rendered from the Baltic was only one of over fifty made in that theatre during the wars. What Hurd appreciated was the need to identify those with aptitude, skill and application, and to endeavour to retain and maximise their output by forming them into an officially recognised specialisation.

Some of these practitioners were drawn, like Hurd himself, from the officer class, men who recognised hydrography as an element of their military seagoing skill set. Most entered as young gentlemen. As in Hurd's case, space in the ship's approved complement might dictate that their first appearance in pay books was as able seaman, but they 'walked the quarterdeck'. Edward Columbine, Francis Austen and Peter Heywood, who feature in the cast of this book, all came from this background. Others, like Thomas Hayward, were drawn from the professional classes and endured snobbery. Many, such as the merchant mariner David Bartholomew, won transition into commissioned status as a reward for obvious talent. Others, such as the masters Alexander Briarly and George Thomas, were denied this step.

Education was a really important enabler. A striking number of the practitioners hailed from Scotland and were beneficiaries of an educational system which gave everyone a grounding in mathematics.

Captain John Ross and many of the masters had studied astronomy and surveying in the schools of Scottish port towns. In England, the family or patron of an aspiring entrant to the Royal Navy might send him to one of a small number of academies set up as 'crammers' to provide the studies necessary for a sea career. A few of the officer practitioners, including Francis Austen, entered the service through the Naval College at Portsmouth, but there was much prejudice against a route that delayed acquisition of sea experience and deprived captains of early recruitment of protégés. Until the years after Trafalgar most products of the Royal Mathematical School at Christ's Hospital, the other source of an advanced programme of study, were apprenticed into the merchant service. Hurd kept an especially sharp eye open for any potential recruits who had entered the Royal Navy from that source. This book will show that there was a place for any talented man in Hurd's cadre, even in the post-war years of increased class-consciousness and discrimination. Skill mattered.[9]

This account draws on largely untapped sources. The archive of the UK Hydrographic Office preserves a treasure trove of remark books, surveyors' correspondence with the Hydrographer, original copies of Admiralty charts and the 'jewels in the crown', the original manuscript plans. Not all of these reached the Hydrographer, and examples have been hunted down where they have been scattered in other archives worldwide. The National Maritime Museum, part of Royal Museums Greenwich, holds a substantial series. We are indebted to curators there for some precious survivals, for example the rare original field records amongst Edward Columbine's papers described in Chapter 1. Fleeting glimpses in auction catalogues and press notices have also been exploited in forming a full list which will be published in a specialist volume. Some gems may well lie undetected in private collections.

INTRODUCTION

The narrative bedrock is provided by the Admiralty papers preserved in the National Archives of the UK. Like many researchers, I owe a debt of gratitude to the clerks in the fleet who compiled musters and pay books, and their counterparts in Whitehall, working under the direction of men, like John Wilson Croker, with a grasp of the vital importance of preservation of a public record. Their work on the massive volumes containing digests and indexes, with a systematic allocation of classes, assists the identification of correspondence, memorials and other sources of more detailed biographical information. Their effort is being matched in our electronic age by work by staff of The National Archives and the Hydrographic Office and other depositories to expand the *Discovery* catalogue.

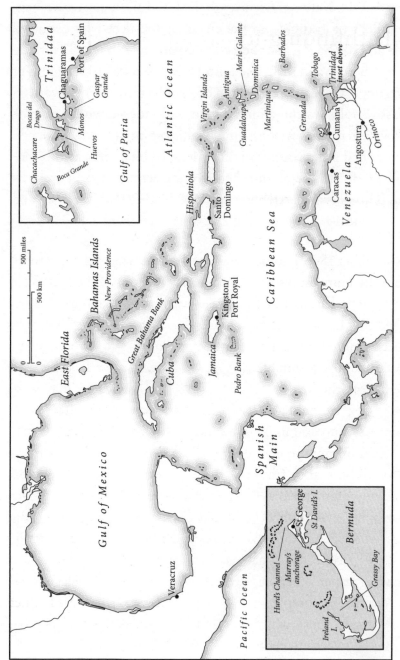

Map 1. West Indies.

Trinidad
Port of Spain
Chaguaramas
Bocas del Drago
Gaspar Grande
Monos
Huevos
Chacachacare
Boca Grande
Gulf of Paria

Atlantic Ocean

Marie Galante
Barbados
Antigua
Dominica
Tobago
Virgin Islands
Guadaloupe
Martinique
Trinidad inset above
Grenada
Cumana
Caracas
Angostura
Orinoco
Venezuela

Hispaniola
Santo Domingo

Caribbean Sea

500 miles
500 km

Bahamas Islands
New Providence

East Florida

Great Bahama Bank

Cuba
Kingston/ Port Royal
Jamaica
Pedro Bank

Spanish Main

Gulf of Mexico

Veracruz

Pacific Ocean

St George
St David's I.
Hurd's Channel
Murray's anchorage
Grassy Bay
Bermuda
Ireland I.

– 14 –

CHAPTER I
Pathfinding for Colonial Warfare

In December 1806 Thomas Hurd walked each day to the Admiralty from the home in fashionable Sloane Street where he had established his wife Elizabeth and thirteen-year-old son Samuel. He was busy plotting his work from a second season in the Bay of Brest and had been granted the assistance of a draughtsman for two months if he could identify a suitable person. On Thursday 18 December he wrote to seek the help of Rear Admiral John Markham, one of the Naval Lords: 'I should also feel myself obliged if you would procure me permission to examine those surveys for two minutes as I fancy I have rolled up my eye glasses in one of them.'[1] The documents in question did not arise from the Brest survey but from earlier work which had commended Hurd as the Board of Admiralty's chosen hydrographic practitioner. He could be forgiven for mislaying his glasses when consulting them. They comprised two manuscript charts, both over 6 feet square, each constructed from twelve sheets of drawing paper. They depicted the Bermudan archipelago, a sea area every bit as complex as the coast of Brittany, in detail which would astound those who compared his work with aerial photography in the twentieth century.

Hurd had taken the charts, 'the official survey of the Bermudas on a large scale', to brief the First Lord of the Admiralty, Thomas Grenville, as he mulled over a major challenge. Despite ongoing negotiations in London, there was evidence that the antipathy of Francophile President Thomas Jefferson towards Great Britain was hardening. Concern was growing over an increased threat to the security of the Royal Navy's logistic base at Halifax, Nova Scotia, on which all squadrons deployed in theatre from the coasts of Canada to the Caribbean depended. Hurd's earlier career had been inter-twined with the story of the British government's strategic concerns in that same vast theatre of colonial warfare. So too had the careers of two other characters in this story. It was here that all three had emerged as skilled hydrographic practitioners.

*

Rarely has there been a more acute appreciation of the importance of mapping to the implementation of government strategic policy than in Britain following victory in the Seven Years' War in 1763. Significant military and naval resources were committed to survey of the territory acquired in former French Canada, especially to encourage settlement there rather than through expansion into Indian lands to the west. The work onshore was conducted by men of the Corps of Engineers of the Board of Ordnance under Major Samuel Holland. They were skilled in 'triangulation', starting from the ends of a base-line carefully measured with surveyor's chains and using theodolites to measure angles to new stations on prominent positions throughout the area to be surveyed. The detailed mapping was built up from this framework. By the summer of 1771 the survey was reaching the deeply indented Atlantic coast, where settlers were moving into the river valleys of Maine and coastal areas of the Bay of Fundy.

Royal Naval personnel were called on to provide the nautical content for the survey. It was in North America that James Cook had built up his survey skills through contact with army counterparts.

Now Thomas Hurd was to follow a similar path. He had set out on a naval career at the comparatively late age of nineteen, joining the Plymouth guardship in September 1768.[2] He may have had some sea experience to commend him at a time when recruiting was getting underway in response to increased tensions in North America. He may have received some mathematical education and have developed an early interest in surveying, for he was born in Plymouth, a base not just for the navy but also for a division of the Board of Ordnance. Its citizens included a number of distinguished scientists and engineers, such as William Mudge, who began his military career in North America, later playing a major part in the trigonometrical survey of southern England. Hurd was quickly assigned to the sloop *Otter* (14) which deployed to Newfoundland, and in May 1770 joined Commodore James Gambier's flagship *Salisbury* (64). In August 1771 Midshipman Hurd was sent with a party of seamen to help to man the boats of the armed ship *Canceaux*, whose commander, Lieutenant Henry Mowat, was tasked to provide the nautical content for Holland's survey.

Hurd's aptitude was soon spotted, and in 1772 Holland sent him to assist in the survey of the outlets of the rivers St Croix and St John's, which provided the only overland communication between Quebec and Nova Scotia.[3] Hurd's role was to take the soundings and other 'naval observations' along the coast and into the inlets and rivers, which would then be absorbed into the large fair sheets favoured by military compilers. This work would occupy him for the next three years. It was quickly apparent that he had acquired higher survey skills. He was entrusted with astronomical observations along the coast. The extension of the main control network for the survey was a challenge because of the dense forest which covered most of the area. He compiled 'collector sheets' showing the detailed work which he achieved, fixing the offshore shoals by compass bearings. They carry careful notes of sunken ledges which would endanger a patrolling warship.[4]

Hurd brought his surveys back to England in 1775 and lodged them in the Admiralty. Here they may have come to the attention of Richard, Viscount Howe, for when he deployed in the following year as Commander-in-Chief North America in response to the outbreak of conflict in the American colonies, Thomas Hurd was one of the nineteen young gentlemen who secured a place in the gunroom of the flagship *Eagle* (64). Hurd would claim in later life that Howe took him because of 'his knowledge of the American Coast, and his talents as a Draftsman and surveyor'.[5] The tough ensuing campaign enabled Hurd to confirm his 'talents' as Howe issued instructions for the covert gathering of soundings, and other pilotage and navigational information to support the application of amphibious force.[6] By its close Howe had promoted him to the rank of lieutenant and secured him a prime appointment in a frigate which cruised against enemy trade with great success, making numerous captures after France entered the war. Hurd's performance in charge of the main deck guns of a 74-gun ship at the battle of the Saintes, the British victory known as 'the glorious 12th April', gained him further notice.[7] It was his hydrographic skill, however, which earned continued patronage from Howe, who secured him appointment as Surveyor General of the new colony of Cape Breton. This was short-lived, but Hurd's reputation for work with the land surveyors now opened up the task in Bermuda.[8]

The Bermudan archipelago presented a challenging scene on many fronts. The well-established island communities, trading in their famous 'Bermudan sloops', had complex relationships with the West Indian and North American colonies. Whilst they knew the channels giving access through the 64 miles of fringing reefs, the massive atoll with its 181 islands retained the fearsome reputation for other mariners which has persisted from Shakespeare's day to the 'Bermudan triangle' myth of today. Hurd's remit was therefore a practical and technical one. Was the archipelago a feasible option as a base for the deep-draught, square-rigged warships of the day? Were there practicable entrance channels for them and sufficiently commodious anchorages?

Lieutenant Hurd sailed from the Thames in March 1789, with an assistant, an outfit of instruments and equipment based on his experience in America, a six-oared cutter and permission to hire a local vessel. He arrived in the islands on 13 May 1789 and lost no time in getting to work at the very optimum season of the year. By August the lieutenant-governor was reporting that Hurd's observations had established 'without the smallest hesitation that the Roadstead and several harbours in the Somers Islands are the most secure and defensible of any in the West Indies'.[9] Both men were yet to grasp the time required to complete a rigorous survey and identify all dangers. Hurd had left behind his wife Elizabeth, whom he had married little more than four months before his departure from England. In December 1792 Mrs Hurd joined her husband in Bermuda, where Samuel was born the following year.[10] By the time that the survey was complete they would be established figures in the local community.

Hurd's first fair sheet showing his results was despatched to the Admiralty in the summer of 1792, a time of great tension when the British government mobilised the fleet in response to a clash with Spanish officials in Nootka Sound on the north-west coast of America. Tumultuous events with profound consequences had been unfolding in France whilst he laboured at his task. The outbreak of war with Revolutionary France highlighted the importance of the work of the far-off team. In November 1793 intelligence arrived in London that French forces displaced from Santo Domingo were operating from the US with considerable assistance from the authorities.[11] The British squadron which had patrolled off the coasts of Chesapeake Bay and the Carolinas throughout the summer needed a more convenient winter base than Halifax. In 1794 the squadron was reinforced and placed under the command of Rear Admiral George Murray. His ships encountered hostility at New York and whilst seeking water and provisions in Delaware Bay. As winter set in, the admiral picked up information that Hurd had identified a suitable fleet anchorage, and he lost no time in despatching *Cleopatra* (32), to get details. In November he received a chart and remarks provided by Hurd. In February 1795 *Cleopatra*, now under the command of Murray's protégé, Captain Charles Penrose, returned to Bermuda to pick up some prize crews. The captain's detailed report of the convenient anchorage, closer to the capital St George's, and of the available supplies to be obtained there, made the admiral 'more desirous than ever to visit' Bermuda.

Once again Hurd was benefiting from the support of an admiral with a clear awareness of the importance of operational hydrography. Murray had completed the course of study in mathematics and astronomy at the Royal Academy in Portsmouth, as had Penrose, whose important interest in an Admiralty Surveyor will be traced in a later chapter. Early in his career, whilst in command of the sloop *Ferret* on the Jamaica station, Murray had taken soundings for the surveys of George Gauld in the coastal waters of West Florida.[12] He now arrived in his flagship *Resolution* (74) on 17 May and found that *Cleopatra* was moored in the new anchorage. Embarking in a sailing boat, he traversed the channel surveyed by Hurd through the Narrows lying north-east of Saint David's Island and Saint George's Island, before agreeing that his ship of the line should be taken through by the local pilots working under Hurd's supervision. The Admiral had little hesitation in allowing his name to be given to the new anchorage.[13]

The worth of the native Bermudans was later noted by an astute observer who commented that they 'are accustomed to navigate in their commercial vessels; their lives are almost spent in boats'.[14] Hurd's close bond with them is shown by the careful record of local names. They manned his survey craft and helped him in his hunt for water deep enough to be navigated by large warships. The identification of the channel through the Narrows which was given Hurd's

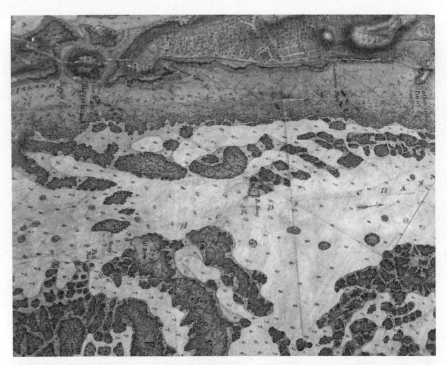

3. Detail of the survey of Hurd Channel, leading through the reefs to Murray's anchorage.

name was undoubtedly the most vital contribution of the naval team. Dalrymple noted that the precision of this work had been ensured by Hurd's use of his sextant to measure angles which would then have been laboriously protracted on tracing paper to plot each sounding. A sounding collector sheet for part of the work area has recently been identified in the archive of the UKHO. Pencil annotations indicate a network of intersected or resected positions on individual rock shoals, those at the extremity being marked with flags. Hurd is likely to have worked from these positions to sketch the detail of the reefs.[15]

Murray braved rough weather and ventured further with Hurd to inspect the North Channel leading to Grassy Bay, another big ship anchorage recommended by the local pilots. He lost no time in commending to the Admiralty a plan which Hurd proposed for a refitting basin on the adjacent shores of Ireland Island, which would provide a 'winter port independent of the Americans from which ships might cruise and refit without their motions being known'. A naval base would be established here which remained in operation into the twentieth century. Murray lauded Hurd's achievement, concluding: 'may I take the liberty to hint that six years services on the most arduous task of the Survey entitles him to some reward'.[16] This patronage secured Hurd's promotion in August 1795, but the small ships constructed in the Bermudan shipyards were taken from the eager commander as soon as they had completed their fitting-out for fleet duties.[17] By the summer of 1797 the field work, much disrupted by administrative duties related to the new base, was finally complete. All that remained was the laborious task of drawing the fair sheets. Hurd received permission to return with his young family to England. He arrived there in December and worked in his own house 'until their Lordships thought proper to appoint me to a room under the Admiralty Roof'. Even with the aid of one of the Hydrographer's draughtsmen, it was to be three years before Hurd could report that what the Hydrographer described as 'that admirable work' was complete.[18] Admiral St Vincent, the current First Lord of the Admiralty, was in no doubt of its strategic significance: 'I have been of the opinion – that is to say since Captain Hurd's accurate survey – that the arsenal should be transferred from Halifax to Bermuda.'[19]

As Thomas Hurd progressed his survey of Bermuda, another skilled hydrographic practitioner with benefit of the support of an enlightened senior officer came to the favourable attention of the Admiralty's Hydrographer. Alexander Dalrymple was a strict critic who was sparing with his compliments. He noted the 'elegant sketches', including diagrams of geological features and monuments, on two sheets of views, remarks and accompanying plans which were larded with references to Thomas Pennant and other antiquarians. These model reports came from Lieutenant Edward Columbine, a highly intelligent product of the King's School, Canterbury, with wide intellectual interests. He was in command of the cutter *Resolution*, patrolling the coasts of Northern Ireland and the Hebrides.[20] Hard work was an antidote to heartbreak. His appointment to the cutter in 1791 had followed close on the heels of divorce. He had married his childhood sweetheart just two months before deploying to the West Indies station in the frigate *Sybil* (28) in 1787. The subsequent three years' separation took their toll. Just six months before Columbine's return, she fell for another man.[21] He set aside the portfolio of beautiful watercolours which he had brought home for her, showing storms, jungle-clad islands and the palm-tree fringed beaches of Barbados. Nearly two centuries later, these would be spotted in a sale list by an alert curator who persuaded the National Maritime Museum to purchase them along with some most significant additional material.[22]

4. *A self-portrait of a pensive Lieutenant Columbine ashore at Staffa.*

Columbine's service record would commend him to Richard Bickerton, captain of *Sybil*. Entering the navy as a fourteen-year-old midshipman in 1778, Edward had been plunged into the thick of the War of American Independence. He was wounded in action barely four weeks after joining his first ship and spent six months as a prisoner of war in France. Thereafter, he served through the campaign on the coast of Virginia and gained his commission as lieutenant in 1782. Other attributes will not have gone unnoticed by Bickerton, whose acute awareness of the importance of hydrographic data-gathering would prove of immense importance at the opening of the Napoleonic Wars. He was only too aware of the shortcomings of published navigational information arising both from state secrecy and lack of hydrographic organisation in Britain, and lost no time in encouraging the talents which Columbine revealed in the course of the outward voyage. Once in the West Indies, as he gathered fresh data and drew up sketch plans, his superior skills in record-keeping and in higher-order astronomical and geodetic observations became apparent. In 1796 the commercial publisher William Faden would publish a chart showing Columbine's corrections to the plotting of a number of the islands in the Lesser Antilles chain.[23] Faden had already engraved and published Columbine's detailed survey of the approaches and harbour of St John's, Antigua. A separate sheet contained fine views to guide mariners clear of offshore coral, including the reef on which the ship of the line *Weymouth* had been lost in 1745.[24] Copies of this work had been rendered to the Admiralty, where they lay dormant, for it was not until 1795 that Dalrymple was installed as Hydrographer and given sight of incoming material. There had clearly been no incentive for Columbine to submit his considerable collection of surveys of other harbours. They remained in the portfolio which would be purchased by the National Maritime Museum. It contained a number of blank pages, headed 'Trinidad'.

Alerted by Columbine's 'elegant sketches', Dalrymple would ensure that Columbine's merit would not go unnoticed again when he returned to the West Indies in command of his own ship.[25] This was *Ulysses* (44), which deployed as guardship for Trinidad in 1801. The island was secured by Britain at the Peace of Amiens as a highly valued base and free port from which British influence might be extended into Spanish America. Merchants were eager to open new markets for their goods and return consignments of specie would prove to be a vital component in British conduct of the war with Napoleon.[26] Like the Bermuda archipelago, Trinidad presented challenges as well as opportunity. The north coast of the island is steep-to, rising to mountains clad with tropical forest. The terrain drops from there to a savannah fringed by further forest or swamp, and much of the east coast is hammered by ocean surf. Strong currents sweep round the headlands. Here, virtually on the equator and on the doorstep of a great continent, the surveyors did not have the advantage of the ocean breezes of Bermuda. Infection and fever were constant risks which the medicine of the day was inadequate to combat. Hence, amongst the 'zealous exertions to promote the interest [of the island]' which earned the praise of the local merchants was Columbine's hydrographic effort.

He had embarked a full set of surveying instruments. Work began in January 1803 'by order of Commodore Hood', one of the joint commissioners for the government of the island. Hood was another enlightened senior officer who had himself been charged with survey work in Nova Scotia earlier in his career.[27] He also knew the competence of Columbine's sailing master, Edward Strode, who had been with him in *Zealous* (74) at the battle of the Nile in 1798. Success depended on the higher mathematical and scientific skills and careful planning which are reflected in Columbine's records and correspondence. He commented on the dense vegetation covering much of the island which hampered the establishment of a major triangulation scheme – a challenge for surveyors well into the twentieth century. His observations were extended from a primary astronomical station at Chaguaramas, a bay to the west of Port of Spain. It was a bitter blow when Strode, who checked the computations and derivation of control, fell ill and was invalided.[28] Measurement of the dimensions of the island depended on carrying longitude along the coastal fringe by 'a well regulated time-keeper'. Observations for latitude were made with an astronomical quadrant: 'the instrument always being turned carefully round, with the same adjustment, after observing a star in one hemisphere, to observe another in the opposite. Several stars were observed for each latitude.' This practice of observing 'balanced pairs' of stars assures the precision in astronomical observation which is essential for hydrographic operations. Columbine compared his results with an earlier Spanish survey before confirming his choice of values for the length of a degree of latitude and of longitude. He realised that these were of the utmost importance for any cadastral work to determine the economic value of the colony. All his measurements were complemented with comprehensive and elegant written reports, which were copied carefully for the Colonial Office. Footnotes in his 'General Description of Trinidad' suggest that he had armed himself with a library of earlier accounts in Spanish, French and English.[29]

But it was his grasp of military significance and priorities which was of most importance. The deliberations of Commodore Hood and the army commanders on arrangements for the defence of Trinidad, including the best location for wooding and watering a fleet and providing careening and storage facilities, had been facilitated by Columbine's 'ability and great assiduity'.[30] Chaguaramas Bay and the coves of the island of Gaspar Grande had been examined with the senior Royal Engineer on the island. They had drawn up 'a larger survey [...] a report on the mode of fortifying it and plans for securing the ships in case of a siege; with drawings to illustrate the nature of the land'. The survey and accompanying report contained detailed assessments of vulnerability of the different roadsteads and bays to bombardment from adjacent heights, and showed recommended anchorage lines enabling a fleet to present its broadsides to an attacking force. Hood paid tribute to the military significance of survey skill, praising Columbine's perseverance and ability and concluding: 'I feel the greatest confidence in his aid'.[31]

Columbine paid particular attention to the approaches to the recommended anchorages from the Dragon's Mouths (Bocas del Drago), which give access to the Gulf of Paria. This can be assessed in a rare survival of field records from this period. Such documents are sadly ephemeral. Those rendered with the fair copies of surveys are generally disposed of once the work has been appraised. Some officers may retain their personal field books, but they are vulnerable to subsequent culling of family records if their interest to a researcher is not grasped. It is indeed fortunate that battered and yellowed clumps of Columbine's field sheets were amongst the sketches whose instant and compelling worth attracted the National Maritime Museum. They include diagrams showing his survey of the southern part of Chacachacare Island above an important anchorage on the flank of the Dragon's Mouths. He had taken astronomical observations to fix the position of two stations on a ridge of hills, measured a baseline between them and established their height above the low-water mark. At each of these stations in turn, using the other as a zero, he observed with his theodolite the angles to prominent features such as buildings, and to coloured flags distributed along the shorelines. When these secondary positions were plotted, they enabled him to lay down the detail of coastline and topography on his plan of Chacachacare Bay (Figures 5 and 6).

Though the climate of the offshore islands was comparatively healthy, three members of his party died during the work. The toll was heavier on the mosquito-ridden shores of the main island. Columbine records that *Ulysses* 'lost 3 Lieutenants, 1 Officer of Marines, Surgeon, Purser, 3 Midshipmen, the Carpenter, & 38 men out of a ship's company of 200 – and very few on board her escaped a serious fit of illness'. Eventually, Columbine himself fell sick, worn

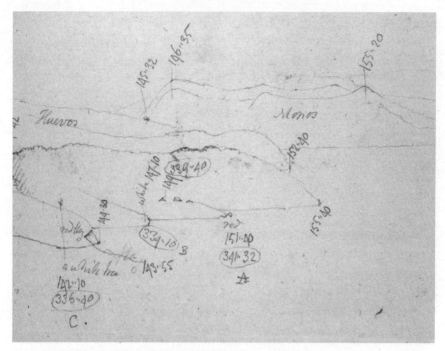

5. The diagram from Columbine's field record shows the angles measured from his two stations on Chacachacare Island. Circled figures distinguish one set from the other. Flags on salient points of the shoreline are sketched in with a note of their colour and their station letter. A skyline profile is included with angles measured to prominent peaks on Huevos and Monos islands and the mainland beyond them.

down by 'fatigue and exposure'. He returned to his ship at Port of Spain and was soon 'ordered on other duty'.[32]

Dalrymple bestowed another rare encomium: 'a very elegant Set of Charts of great part of Trinidada [sic] by Capt Columbine of H.M. Navy has been prepared for engraving at the Hydrographical Office. These charts are accompanied with <u>views</u> of the <u>land</u>, drawn in a masterly stile [sic].'[33]

But the work on engraving fell into abeyance as the focus of the war turned elsewhere. Probably with little confidence in timely action in Whitehall, Columbine turned again to William Faden to publish

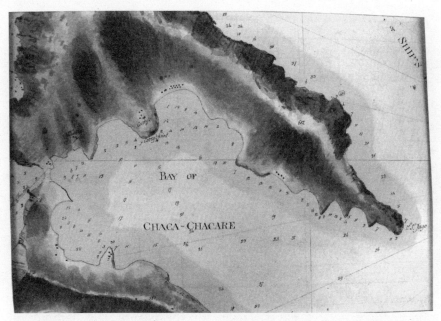

6. *The extract from his resultant survey of the Bocas del Drago shows his depiction of the same coastline with the three small promontories near the eastern headland.*

a meticulously graduated overview chart, entitled 'TRINIDAD as far as it has been survey'd by Capt. Columbine RN'.[34] It was eventually adopted into the Admiralty series in 1816, four years after Columbine's untimely death in the circumstances described below in Chapter 8. His survey covering the Dragon's Mouths finally appeared in the 1830s.[35] Thirteen fine survey sheets and accompanying views were only rediscovered in the Hydrographic Office in 1896.[36] Thomas Hurd was the man who would address such shortcomings in handling vital incoming data in the Admiralty. On the front line, commanders would rely on their hydrographic pathfinders until the Hydrographer could provide them with good charts. One of these pathfinders played his part in Trinidad.

Alexander Briarly was a happy man. He could enjoy his fine home in Port of Spain whilst the overseer managed the workforce of twenty-two slaves on his Terre Promise estate in Caroni County.[37] He enjoyed the favour of Lieutenant Governor Thomas Hislop, who had appointed him Lieutenant Colonel in the militia during a slave insurrection. Briarly had overseen the transportation of ordnance to batteries around Port of Spain during the alarm caused by the foray of Admiral Villeneuve's fleet to the West Indies in 1805. He also assisted the army engineers, contributing soundings and coastline for a survey of the new Fort George at the governor's favoured anchorage of Hislop Bay. On the plan he was credited as Midshipman Briarly, but he had now achieved a long-nurtured ambition, a lieutenant's commission, albeit a local one, from Rear Admiral Alexander Cochrane. The admiral was keen to exploit his skill. None of Columbine's larger-scale plans had been published, and so, in October 1805, Briarly was directed to examine the admiral's preferred option for a perfect naval station for the island: 'the harbour of Chicca Chicara' (i.e. Chacachacare). It was to be 'surveyed and a plan sent to the Lords Commissioners of the Admiralty'.[38]

Some of the backstory of this enigmatic Irishman will emerge in later chapters of this book. During the Peace of Amiens, like many other master mariners who had been serving in the Royal Navy, he had sought employment in the merchant service and had been taken on by the firm of John and Abraham Atkins, for whom he undertook voyages to Trinidad and other ports in the West Indies.[39] There were indications that he was also working for someone else. In October 1803 he had called at Falmouth at the end of his first voyage in Atkins' new ship *Edward Foote* with 'a cargo of tobacco, &c. from the River Oroonoco, bound to London'. It was reported that he had 'explored that river and the adjacent country, to a great distance from the main'. He had 'made a particular description of it' and 'has many plans and drawings of the parts he has examined'. This work had been done 'in pursuance of instructions from the First Lord of the Admiralty', Earl St Vincent, who, as we will see, knew Briarly well.[40]

It was this knowledge that Admiral Cochrane was keen to exploit. In 1806 General Francisco de Miranda, a Venezuelan revered as 'el precursor', the forerunner of Simón Bolívar, arrived in Port of Spain. His efforts to persuade the British government to join in the liberation of the Captaincy General of Venezuela had been frustrated by the counsel of Captain Home Popham of the Royal Navy, who regarded himself as an expert in prospects of gaining an opening in South America. Miranda had therefore acquired ships in the US, landed on the Caribbean coast of Venezuela and launched a botched attempt to foment an uprising. He had been rescued by the Royal Navy. He soon enticed Hislop and Cochrane to support fresh plans. These murky dealings would quickly involve Briarly.

In the preceding October Cochrane had reported to the Admiralty his agreement to Hislop's request to use Briarly's 'thorough knowledge not only of the coast, but the interior of the country' in command of a force of Sea Fencibles in an armed flotilla to combat enemy privateers based in 'the creeks and the mouths of the Orinoco'. This resulted in Briarly's commission as lieutenant. He was allocated two midshipmen, three warrant officers and fifteen men to deploy in small craft. They were based in a hulked brig which the Admiralty directed to be renamed *Orinoco*.[41] Briarly's credentials were not unfounded. His observations from the *Edward Foote* have been preserved in a huge fair sheet over 14 feet in length. A set of views of the low shoreline was annotated with directions for identifying the entrance and choosing the right stage of the tide at which to pass over the bar. He had taken careful profiles of soundings between the banks flanking the wide mouth of the river, recording them in feet for greater precision. Representative soundings in fathoms are shown in the recommended channel, all the way up to Angostura. The chart shows conspicuous hills rising above the flat landscape, and Indian villages, missions, redoubts and loading beaches along the shore.[42]

By the end of 1805 he had used his knowledge to descend on the indented coast and capture a small rowboat privateer with three of

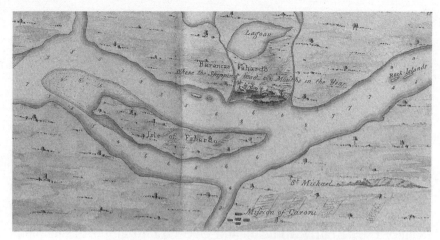

7. Detail from Briarly's chart of the Orinoco.

her prizes.[43] He was well connected on the mainland and able to gather substantial intelligence under a flag of truce. With Hislop he drew up a plan for an attack on Angostura, which he described as 'a most certain and sure key to all South America'. This was calculated to meet the approval of Cochrane, who had declared in similar vein: 'Trinidad [...] may be said to be the key of South America to the possession of which the River Oronoco [sic] offers a safe and easy passage'.[44] Miranda chose otherwise, descending once again on the Caribbean coast far to westward. He raised no local support, and after the arrival of a much superior Spanish force his party was evacuated by Cochrane's ships. Back in Port of Spain Miranda lodged with a troubled and touchy Lieutenant Governor tussling with the turmoil of Trinidadian society.

Part of his concern related to Alexander Briarly. The *Orinoco* served also as a prison hulk, and some of Briarly's subordinates abused their powers. Hislop would accuse Briarly himself of 'refractory and insubordinate behaviour' and connivance in smuggling. The Trinidadian writer V.S. Naipaul dismissed the slave-owning Briarly as 'a rogue'.[45] Though Briarly retained Cochrane's support, Hislop submitted damning reports to London, lobbying for his removal. He recounted that in 1807 he had committed Briarly to the Common Gaol for contempt of authority, and that the lieutenant was now detained in Trinidad on account of considerable debts.[46] In January 1808 Cochrane was directed to send Briarly back to England.[47] He would face a cold reception. The Admiralty and Navy Boards had not approved the formation of the Sea Fencibles, had queried the expenses of *Orinoco*, and noted the volume of complaints arising from Briarly's enforcement of the Navigation Acts, especially their ill-judged application to the East India Company ship *Fortitude*.[48] St Vincent, who might have spoken for him, was in retirement. In January 1809 Briarly would be refused both promotion and half-pay. He had meanwhile been struck off the list of masters.[49]

He had been preceded in London by Miranda, who at first fared better. A large military force was prepared in June 1808 for an expedition to Spanish America under the command of Lieutenant General Arthur Wellesley. It was metropolitan Spain, however, which proved to be the tinderbox, and it was operations in the Iberian Peninsula which would bring him fame. Earlier that same year Thomas Hurd and Edward Columbine had worked together under the brief chairmanship of Home Popham to address the deficiency of hydrographic intelligence for the Royal Navy, and the provision of charts for the Peninsular War would be urgent business for Hurd as he replaced Alexander Dalrymple as Hydrographer. That war would also provide an opportunity for the undaunted Briarly to reinvent himself, as a later chapter will show.

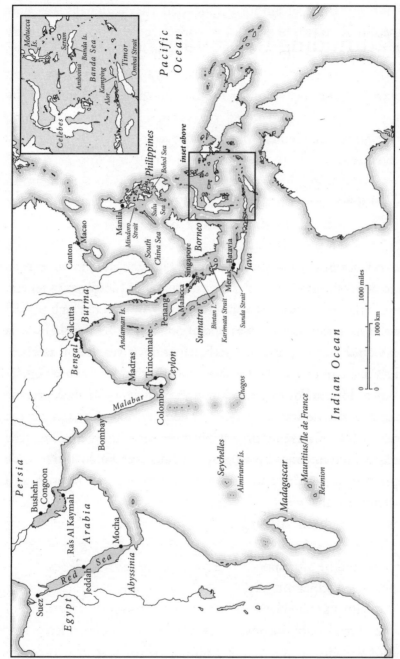

Map 2. East Indies.

Pacific Ocean

Molucca Is.
Seram
Banda Is.
Banda Sea
Ambonia
Celebes
Alor
Kamping
Timor
Ombai Strait

inset above

Philippines
Bohol Sea
Manila
Mindoro Strait
Sulu Sea
Macao
Canton
South China Sea
Borneo
Batavia
Merak
Java
Singapore
Malacca
Penang
Sumatra
Bintan I.
Karimata Strait
Sunda Strait

Burma
Bengal
Calcutta
Andaman Is.
Madras
Trincomalee
Ceylon
Colombo
Malabar
Bombay
Chagos

Persia
Bushehr
Congoon
Ra's Al Kaymah
Arabia
Mocha
Red Sea
Jeddah
Suez
Egypt
Abyssinia

Seychelles
Almirante Is.
Madagascar
Mauritius/Île de France
Réunion

Indian Ocean

1000 miles
1000 km

−34−

CHAPTER 2

Pathfinding for an Empire of Trade

It was doubtful if Thomas Hurd and Edward Columbine had time to miss Home Popham in the busy months after the completion of their first report on 29 February 1808. The three officers had convened as a committee to advise Alexander Dalrymple on the quality of published charts of waters with which he was not familiar. Popham had signed the report first, as senior officer. Now, whilst his colleagues continued with the laborious assessment task in the Admiralty attics, he was busy in the House of Commons, not least in defending his own reputation. Before many months passed, his expertise would be called on to plan a major amphibious operation in the Low Countries. He had, meanwhile, brought extensive personal knowledge to the committee from hydrographic effort on both shores of the South Atlantic and in eastern seas. Dalrymple was aware of work which Popham had conducted for the East India Company, and he also appreciated the hydrographic skills and effort of experienced adherents such as Joseph Edmonds, who had worked with Popham and had been usefully co-opted to assist the scrutiny of the commercial publications. Sadly, the energy, independence and operational focus of this 'Chart Committee' led to a breakdown of cooperation with the elderly Dalrymple, who was dismissed by the

First Lord. Three weeks later, on 19 June, the heartbroken work-aholic died. It was a bad business, and the sea officers on the Board of Admiralty who had worked with Dalrymple distanced themselves from it. John Markham had wished to appoint Hurd 'to bring out charts based on recent surveys, while Dalrymple continued his useful compiling labours', a solution which Dalrymple would never have accepted.[1] Hurd was appointed Hydrographer to implement the recommendations of the Chart Committee.

As Hurd established his regime in the Hydrographical Office during the following, high-paced year of 1809, the first lieutenant of the sloop *Sapphire* was putting the finishing touches to a manuscript chart which he had been fairing up during the long hours of a voyage home from a deployment in the Indian Ocean and Persian Gulf. The elaborate title with its cartouche contained words which illustrate the golden thread of enlightened patronage and interest that will be traced in this chapter. The identification and encouragement of talent by senior officers would be of significant assistance to Hurd in selecting a cadre of specialists. The draughtsman, David Bartholomew, would become one of Hurd's Admiralty Surveyors. The chart which he was completing was 'inscribed [...] as a tribute of respect [...] to Sir Home Popham Bart'.

The two men had much in common. Bartholomew, an accomplished merchant mariner from an extensive and established family in Linlithgow, was well educated, articulate, ambitious and genteel in manner. This had not protected him from the press gang in London in 1795. His experience and skills were spotted during operations in the West Indian and European theatres, and he was rated as master's mate. He had come under the patronage of Popham during an amphibious campaign in the Netherlands in 1799, whilst 'commanding a detachment of hired seamen attached to the army'.[2] It was the political interest and championship of military men and other influential figures outside their professional world that led naval contemporaries to view Popham askance. One anonymous memoirist would remark that 'he was not what is called one of Nelson's sailors [...] He had led a sort of miscellaneous life'.[3] They did not forget that he had forfeited his commission in 1791 by exceeding his leave of absence whilst trading in eastern waters under a foreign flag. The hydrographic and logistic expertise which he provided to the East India Company, and then to the army, had resulted in restoration and rapid advancement during the French Revolutionary War. Popham enjoyed the particular patronage of Henry Dundas, Secretary of State for War and President of the Board of Control of the East India Company.[4] This interest had secured him his first squadron command in 1801, escorting a force from India which landed at Suez and opened a second front against the French expeditionary force in Egypt. With this operation complete, he spent the next eighteen months pursuing a secondary task from Dundas and the Secret Committee of the East India Company, seeking to reopen commerce with the coastal Arab states.

Popham was an extremely talented product of Westminster School who, early in his career, had been trained in hydrographic work on the west coast of Africa. He had subsequently made skilful boat surveys during a search along the Namibian coast, notorious for fogs, swell and lack of fresh water. This work had informed government strategy, discounting the potential for a penal colony and strategic port of call on the route to and from the East Indies and turning attention to the much remoter option of Botany Bay.[5] Later surveys of the channels at Calcutta, the seat of British administration in the sub-continent, and at Prince of Wales Island (Penang), on the flank of a key route to China, would further commend him to the East India Company, to whom he now dedicated a large chart of the Red Sea, divided into a northern and southern sheet.[6]

In the descriptive legend on his manuscript copy, he had recorded: 'As I knew I was to traverse a tract of unexplored seas, I procured a Draughtsman in England at my own expense, and taught him, as well as numerous Quarter-deck, Hydrography and Practical Astronomy, which enabled me, with the assistance of eight chronometers, and some very expensive instruments, to form a chart.' He claimed that his outlay on his survey outfit was upwards of £1,200.[7] He took justifiable pride in the proficiency of his officers, including the midshipmen, whom he had drilled to observe for latitude by equal altitudes of a star crossing the meridian. He summed up the results of this training: 'I had in the *Romney* Eight Chronometers made by different Artists principally by Arnold which were constantly used in small Vessels under the direction of such officers who had qualified themselves by unremitting attention to this Science since we left England.'[8]

One of his pupils was David Bartholomew. He had clearly acquired a taste for surveying, as well as being anxious to please his captain. He produced a fine set of coastal views, and those on Popham's survey sheets are almost certainly also his work.[9] His navigational accomplishments are made clear in a track chart which he prepared from the record in his journal of the homeward voyage with a convoy of East Indiamen from Bombay in the spring of 1803.[10] This shows comparisons of observations for variation with different compasses, and regular observation of temperature. It also lists the sights which he took to compare with Home Popham's.

Back in England, Bartholomew made himself a dangerous enemy, no less than the First Lord, Earl St Vincent. He was suspected of writing a tract criticising the Board of Admiralty, and he had lobbied persistently for advancement. In a notorious incident, which was investigated by a Select Committee of Parliament, St Vincent had Bartholomew press-ganged once more, this time on the very threshold of the Admiralty. There were plenty of voices to protest at such an action. Bartholomew was soon released. Popham took him back under his wing in time to take part in attacks on Boulogne and secured his advancement to lieutenant.[11] Bartholomew was aware that he was viewed askance by some on account of his association

8. *A view taken by David Bartholomew during Popham's survey of the Red Sea.*

with Popham.[12] Both would be pleased to depart on another deployment into eastern and southern seas.

Enlightened encouragement of officers with a talent for surveying had been a consistent attribute of commanders-in-chief in the testing theatre of the East Indies throughout the wars, for hydrographic factors loomed large in their strategic deliberations. Which base would best ensure communication with the government in Calcutta at the head of the tortuous River Hooghly, enable support to the scattered British possessions around the Indian sub-continent and facilitate convoy escort along the trade routes? Commodore William Cornwallis, a bluff bachelor seaman who detested the society of Calcutta, escaped to sea as often as possible, which is where he thought that it was best for his officers to be, preferably for the 'purpose of exploring'. He himself took part in boat-sounding in the Andaman Islands.[13] Cornwallis's schooling shaped Jane Austen's brother Francis and others who would distinguish themselves in hydrographic data-gathering during later ship commands.

His successor, Commodore Peter Rainier, another fine seaman and navigator, sustained the encouragement as he took steps to counter any combination of the forces of France and Tipu Sultan, and as he moved swiftly to mop up Dutch possessions in the east after the French invasion of the United Provinces. The resultant operational survey and chart-making belies the unfavourable comparison which has often been made with the output of the East India Company's Bombay Marine.[14]

Amongst the officers whom Rainier encouraged were two men who had taken part in the under-resourced expedition of HMS *Bounty*, the outcome of which is possibly only fully understood by those who have served in Royal Navy ships on lone tasking in remote waters. William Bligh judged that the mutiny was prompted by departure from the life of Tahiti and farewell to 'female connections'. Though studiously avoided in the court martial proceedings and suppressed in hagiographical biographies, this factor most certainly applied in the case of sixteen-year-old Peter Heywood, a youngster in his first ship who was close to the older Fletcher Christian.[15] Both had been commended to Bligh through family links, and their place at the head of the list of mutineers which he composed during his open boat voyage reflected his acute chagrin. He recorded that he had given them special regard and attention since they 'promised as professional men to be an honour to their country'.[16] The description of Heywood in Bligh's list of mutineers included the note that 'at this time he had not done growing', and perhaps this should apply to his character as well as his physique.[17] The professional and intellectual development of the young man could not be unaffected by his early encounter with a fine seaman and skilled hydrographic practitioner. Influential family contacts earned him a pardon and re-entry to the Royal Navy. He served with a succession of sympathetic captains, including Pulteney Malcolm of *Fox* (32), which deployed to the East Indies in 1797. In the following year Heywood transferred with his captain to Rainier's flagship, and the door was open to a sequence of commands culminating in his advancement to post captain in *La Dédaigneuse* (36).

His hydrographic reputation was made in these ships.[18] His skill in astronomical observation is clear in track charts made during patrols in *Fox* in the South China Sea and north-west Pacific. In *Suffolk* he worked alongside the master, Duncan Weir, an accomplished surveyor. Both men would render surveys of harbours and hazards on the coasts of India and Ceylon. He appears to have purchased two chronometers which enabled him to calculate meridional distances and compile an impressive list of more accurate geographical positions in the theatre. A remarkable running survey in the bomb-vessel *Vulcan*, made during gales whilst escorting a convoy, identified dangerous shoals in the Timor Sea in an area which is still not fully surveyed. His reports were akin to those made from *Hydra* in the south-west Pacific in the mid-1970s, as we used a first generation SATNAV system to provide the Hydrographic Office with precise positions of islands and dangers.

The standard that Heywood could achieve in a regular survey was demonstrated whilst *La Dédaigneuse* waited as part of the escort of the homebound China convoy in 1804. His depiction of the Macao Roads and Typa anchorage is based on a control scheme of observed positions enabling thorough sounding coverage. His superior skill in draughtsmanship resulted in fine topography and views, as on his survey of the north coast of Sumatra with a panorama including the dramatic volcano Seulawah Agam. Dalrymple published no fewer than ten charts and plans by him in the East India Company series. His lunar and chronometric observations were prized by Dr Maskelyne at the Board of Longitude and were included in the famous *Directions for Sailing to and from the East Indies* produced by James Horsburgh, Dalrymple's successor as Hydrographer to the East India Company. Unlike a number of his former fellow-midshipmen in *Bounty*, Heywood would survive to play a part in major expeditions of the Napoleonic Wars, as will be illustrated later in this chapter.

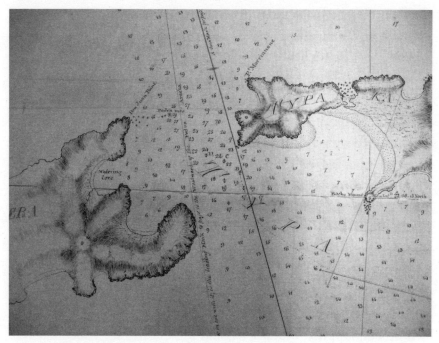

9. An extract from Heywood's survey of the Typa anchorage, showing thorough sounding and the network of control stations including that at which he observed for latitude and longitude.

William Bligh is not alone in having his competence and character repeatedly maligned by writers as a result of bias and snobbery in publications favouring the Fletcher and Heywood families. Their local standing in country society gave them 'illusions of superior gentility'.[19] The nineteenth-century editor of Sir John Barrow's account of the mutiny would note with approval the author's judgement that Bligh had not had the advantage of education 'among young gentlemen'. So too Barrow had quoted in full the letter in which Peter Heywood dismissed his fellow midshipman, twenty-year-old Thomas Hayward, as a 'wordling [...] raised a little in life'.[20] Hayward's background was in the urban professional classes. His father, Francis, was an eminent physician in Hackney. He may have secured his son a place as midshipman in the frigates *Aeolus* (32) and *Thisbe* (28) with

Captain George Robertson, another doctor's son. Robertson was one of the four captains who would provide Thomas with certificates for his examination for lieutenant after his return from the *Bounty* expedition. Hayward presented the examiners with journals from three years' service on the Newfoundland station which would have commended him to Bligh.[21] His selection to serve in *Bounty* had also been helped by a representation to Sir Joseph Banks from William Wales, astronomer on Cook's second voyage. Hayward's uncle, Charles Green, had been astronomer on Cook's first voyage. This background may indeed have spurred Hayward to apply himself to hydrographic work. Like Bligh, he was refused permission to take his instruments and charts into the launch when they were cast adrift.[22]

He appears to have been a somewhat isolated figure in *Bounty*. He was taunted by his fellow officers as the captain's 'lackey'. Although he had experienced Bligh's tough discipline, he showed him respect and would support him at a critical juncture in the arduous open-boat voyage after the mutiny. Bligh would speak favourably of his conduct.[23] He could not bear, however, to take any memories with him on his successful return voyage to procure the breadfruit trees. Hayward, promoted lieutenant, would instead return to Tahiti with Captain Edward Edwards in *Pandora* (18). When the accounts of Captain Edwards and Surgeon George Hamilton were eventually published by a colonial administrator in 1915, the apparatus followed established convention and dismissed Hayward as 'a time-server' sent on the voyage purely to assist in identifying and apprehending his old companions. It is clear, however, that Edwards respected the knowledge of the Pacific which his second lieutenant had acquired, including familiarity with the local craft, in which Hayward was despatched on a number of reconnaissance missions. Hayward was also recognised as a skilled navigator and observer. The departure from Rio de Janeiro on the outbound voyage commenced after he returned on board with the time-keeper and his instruments having finished astronomical observations.[24] He produced track charts of the voyage, and information from them on the approaches to the Torres Strait was included in an East India Company chart published by Dalrymple and in the atlas produced by Matthew Flinders. The track ends where *Pandora* was lost on the Great Barrier Reef in 1791.[25] Thus, Hayward endured a second boat journey through the tortuous waters of the Torres Strait, watching for the clouds of birds whose movements alerted them to the low reefs and islets covered with bush and scrub.

He was to experience another shipwreck. In October 1793 he was appointed second lieutenant of *Diomede* (44) a few days before she sailed as the first reinforcement for the East Indies station on the outbreak of war. On arrival on station in 1795 Rainier sent her into waters very familiar to Hayward to see the homebound China trade safely through the Sunda Strait. She then joined the force which the admiral assembled to persuade the Dutch garrison of Trincomalee to accept British troops to defend the strategic port from the French. Whilst standing alongshore at 8 knots in strong land breezes with a baggage transport in tow, *Diomede* struck a rock which still bears her name. Regular soundings had been taken, with a report of no ground in 19 fathoms just before she struck. Bearings were 'instantly taken' indicating 'distance offshore about 2½ Miles'. Today's chart, which bears the warning 'Uncharted dangers', indicates that distance offshore had been overestimated by a factor of 50 per cent. Pumps kept the frigate afloat until she anchored with the squadron in Back Bay, where she finally foundered.

Hayward was with the substantial party of *Diomede*'s sailors and marines who were landed to assist to storm the Dutch citadel. Seamen had also helped to haul guns across 2 miles of sand from the landing place to form the battery whose fire prompted the enemy to surrender. Hayward plotted all the details of these land operations in a sketch survey based on bearings taken from the frigate. His rough sheets indicate that, once ashore, he measured a baseline assisting him to lay down the coast and topography. Further observations with

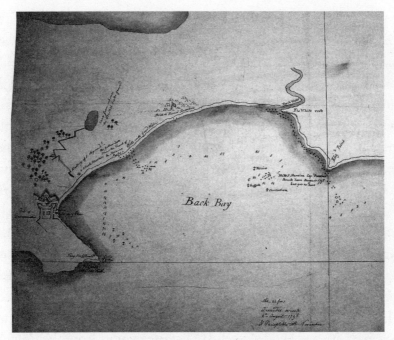

10. *Hayward's survey of Back Bay, Trincomalee, showing the land operations, the wreck of* Diomede *and the rocks on which* Heroine *grounded.*

the assistance of the admiral's nephew, John Spratt Rainier, enabled him to show the anchorage of the squadron, soundings and dangers, including the foul patch where *Heroine* (32) touched on a rock without suffering apparent damage whilst providing close support for the landing.[26]

Both men would be advanced by Rainier and encouraged to make further hydrographic observations. Shortly after the operations at Trincomalee he appointed them to the ship-sloop *Swift* (16), with Hayward serving as first lieutenant.[27] Hayward succeeded to command of *Swift* in December 1796.[28] He was despatched back into the region where he had served with Bligh and Edwards. Rainier had tasked Captain Edward Pakenham of *Resistance* (44), the senior officer on station at Amboyna, to conduct surveys to check the position of dangers shown on the Dutch charts. Hayward rendered two sheets showing corrected positions for a number of islands and shoals, which were published by Dalrymple for the East India Company. A later track chart by Heywood in *La Dédaigneuse* would show 'Koko shoal according to the late Capt Hayward'. Hayward refined the positions of the islands north of Timor, and *Swift* penetrated into the Ombai Strait, where scattered huts showed settlements on the mountainous islands of Kamping and Alor.[29] French frigates and privateers were suspected of frequenting these remoter waters before descending on convoys in the major straits through the Indonesian archipelago. Rainier's slender resources made it difficult to monitor the local rulers around the Banda Sea. A second published chart showed Hayward's survey of the harbour of Sawai on the north coast of the island of Seram, which was a base for a long-standing regional rebellion against the Dutch.[30]

In April 1797 Rainier learned that Spain had entered the war on the side of France. He despatched Hayward to the Strait of Malacca, where he was to open secret orders. These sent him to Macao, where he was to obtain any intelligence of Spanish forces in the Philippines before joining Pakenham at Amboyna. Rumours that a Spanish squadron had been formed at Manila caused the Secret Committee of the East India Company to order the convoys of homebound ships to head into the Pacific and make for the easternmost passages through the East Indies. In June, Hayward sailed from Whampoa, the anchorage of Canton, as part of the escort. Rainier was planning to advance him, like his old shipmate Peter Heywood, to post captain, and issued an appointment to relieve Pakenham in *Resistance*.[31] It was not to be. In September, Pakenham wrote a series of letters following arrival of the East Indiaman *Taunton Castle* with news of the dispersal of the convoy in a violent typhoon. He feared that the little *Swift* 'was not able to stand it'. By the following spring, Rainier was compelled to conclude that there was 'every reason to fear her total loss'.[32] The ocean of his earlier adventures had finally claimed Thomas Hayward's life.

His fate was shared by Lieutenant Daniel Whittle. He had been given a commission by Rear-Admiral Sir George Keith Elphinstone, later Lord Keith, after service as master of his flagship *Monarch* (74) at the Cape of Good Hope. As master and commander of the brig *Euphrosyne*, he was able to prosecute more thoroughly an investigation of breakers which he had spotted in False Bay.[33] He relocated the shoal on 23 November 1796 and on 19 December found a least depth of 12 feet at low water. In the following May the new flag officer on station, Rear Admiral Pringle, forwarded Whittle's chart of False Bay to the Admiralty, showing the rock which bears his name to this day.[34] It is a real hazard to ships approaching Simon's Bay, and the local authorities took further measures to promulgate the information. Pringle directed that Whittle was to continue on the survey of False Bay, where other unknown dangers were likely to be found. He considered that 'the whole eastern coast of this country may be said to be unknown, I do hope their Lordships will think proper to send out vessels fit for surveying, there are none so much so as cutters, since it is highly necessary they should be able at all times to work off a lee shore'.[35] During the coming months Whittle would struggle to keep a buoy in place on the shoal, breaking off from his survey to rendezvous with new arrivals on station and guide them past his rock.[36] In the winter of 1797 the *Euphrosyne* was despatched to carry French prisoners of war to Port Louis, Île de France, where Whittle may have picked up early intelligence that the governor was planning a proclamation of French support for Tipu Sultan.[37] On 7 April 1798 Rear Admiral Christian sent Whittle with an urgent update for Admiral Rainier. Whittle was sailing under American colours in a purchased American cutter that had been repaired after grounding on Robben Island and established as a tender to the flagship *Tremendous*. Named *Caroline*, she was said to be a 'staunch, strong vessel [...] coppered to the whales'. Having succeeded in his mission, Whittle sailed from Clappenburg Bay in Trincomalee harbour on 17 June. The following January Rainier wrote: 'am anxious to learn whether the little *Caroline* has joined you'. She had not. Whittle and his companions were presumed drowned.[38]

Another Keith protégé on the station was destined to play a longer part as a pathfinder. A contemporary described William Durban as a 'distinguished officer with first rate abilities' and noted the unusual cachet for a naval officer of LL.D.[39] He had been educated under the mathematician Isaac Dalby, who had been employed during the first great trigonometrical survey of England and Wales. When he had been appointed as a midshipman to the *Sphinx* (24) in the Mediterranean, his computational skill had come to the attention of a commanding officer who was a pioneer in promoting lunar observations in the fleet. His efforts had earned him promotion to lieutenant in 1790. He had been actively employed from the outset of the French Revolutionary War, deploying to the West and East Indies and to the Cape of Good Hope, where he served in Keith's flagship. After the capture of a Dutch squadron, Durban was included in the promotions and appointed by Keith to command one of the prizes, the *Saldanha* (40).[40] Durban was much aggrieved when the Admiralty only confirmed him as a commander rather than a post captain. He had participated in the detention of a valuable prize during a cruise off Cape Agulhas, and in April 1797 he was detached to convoy it to St Helena. When offered the option of proceeding to England on leave in order to attend the prize court proceedings, Durban had no hesitation in doing so, for the young officer had fallen wildly in love with a married lady who had landed at the Cape whilst on passage home to England, and had taken her with him in his frigate to St Helena. From there they returned together to England in the less comfortable surroundings of the whaler *Sally*. Durban's career appears to have been on hold until May 1799, when the lady's husband secured a divorce with damages against him.[41] In the same month Durban was appointed to commission and command the sloop *Weazle*. John Ross, the polar explorer, who was a midshipman on board, would later recall their inshore operations on the Dutch and French coasts.[42] The biographical details which Durban supplied to John Marshall claimed that he attracted their Lordship's attention by using his initiative to establish marks along the inner channels which would assist the interception of French coastal convoys moving between St Malo and Brest. Keith kept his eye on Durban, and would later request that he be allocated to his anti-invasion forces in the Downs in 1804 so that his surveying skills could again be used on the enemy coast.[43] It would be in the theatre discussed in the next chapter that those skills would be deployed to great benefit to British operations.

The Cape of Good Hope was returned to the Netherlands at the Peace of Amiens and reoccupied by a British expeditionary force in 1806. The naval commander was Home Popham. Though he had not supported Miranda's proposals for British intervention in Spanish America, Popham had not abandoned his own ideas. He now persuaded his army counterpart to release most of his force for an attack on the Spanish cities on the River Plate. This in due course necessitated the diversion of further naval assets under Admirals Stirling and Murray, the latter outward bound with a convoy of troops which had been intended for a descent on the coast of Chile. All these deployments, which reflected pressure for the opening of new markets for Britain, would offer opportunities for hydrographic practitioners, for not the least testing part of this campaign was the navigation.[44]

The unstable seabed of the huge, shallow estuary of the Plate (Map 3) is constantly changing, and the contemporary charts were of ephemeral value. The coastline is low and often obscured by haze. Modern commerce depends on efficient management of long, buoyed channels. In 1806 great difficulty was experienced in maintaining seamarks to guide new units arriving on the scene, especially in winter, when the offshore banks presented a very real hazard. The

Map 3. South America.

transport *Walker* was lost on the English Bank on 25 September 1806. Sailing ships were extremely vulnerable to the strong currents and to the unpredictable local gales blowing from the Andean chain across the plains, and thus known as *pamperos*. Admiral Murray recorded that the men of war 'always bring our anchors home in the gales that set in with the full Moon, whilst the transports held even less well'.[45] It would take some reinforcements a fortnight to work up from the mouth of the estuary to Montevideo. Frequent groundings were reported during the transit of the main force to Buenos Aires, where Popham's smaller vessels struggled to get close enough inshore to provide gunfire support for the landing and assault. The troops had to wade a considerable distance to the shore, finding their way with the help of one of Popham's adherents, Captain William King of *Diadem* (74), who stood in the shallows and acted as a marker throughout the disembarkation.[46]

Given Popham's hydrographic awareness, it is unsurprising that the struggles in the Plate stimulated an unprecedented amount of survey effort. A collection of sounding sheets from the squadron contains contributions by William King and other commanders with a bent for hydrography such as Francis Mason, another veteran of Popham's Red Sea survey, and Ross Donnelly.[47] Arrowsmith published a chart with the latter's soundings, which was carried by ships on later deployments to the station to supplement the Spanish chart supplied by the Admiralty. Another of Popham's men was Joseph Edmonds in *Diomede* (50), who had caught his eye whilst commanding a gunboat during the descent on Ostend in 1798. He would lead the squadron inshore to bombard Montevideo. Survey work in the Mediterranean had commended him to Dalrymple, and when data from the Plate was examined in the Hydrographical Office, particular weight was given to his products. He had been especially active, making sketch surveys around the island of Gorriti off Maldonado, which was garrisoned by the British, and of the anchorage at the Isle of Flores. He also took many soundings all the way up to Buenos Aires, enabling the production in the Hydrographical Office of a comprehensive manuscript plan of the estuary.[48] On the strength of this performance, Dalrymple urged that he be employed as an Admiralty surveyor in home waters, and Popham would enlist his help with the work of the Chart Committee.[49]

These sketch surveys would be supplemented by more rigorous work as the campaign dragged on. Dalrymple had been busy compiling information as reinforcements were drawn together for despatch to the Plate.[50] In October 1806 he commended accomplished surveyors for employment to produce a chart of the river and estuary.[51] One was Edmonds, the other was Peter Heywood, now Flag Captain to Rear Admiral George Murray in *Polyphemus* (64). The admiral had gathered vital hydrographic intelligence in the Baltic earlier in his career, and he clearly respected Heywood's advice as a front-line practitioner. He wrote to Captain Markham at the Admiralty: 'You would be much pleased with Captain Heywood's surveys. He has never gone anywhere without making very particular remarks and taken regular surveys when he has had time. Dalrymple is very much indebted to him for many of his plans and surveys.'[52]

On arrival in theatre, Heywood was critical of many of the efforts of his counterparts to improve on the Spanish charts: 'they appeared to be bad copies of it: with the addition of some ship's tracks laid down by log run only'. This would not do in an estuary which he declared 'on the whole is dangerous, and not calculated for ships of this class to be groping about in, blindfold'.[53] He would work hard to build up an adequate picture during this and a subsequent deployment to the Plate. An abstract of his journal was promulgated by Dalrymple, and a chart by John Warner, master of *Polyphemus*, would be published by Faden.[54] Warner included and acknowledged work by two other significant contributors.

One was the newly promoted Lieutenant David Bartholomew, serving under Popham in *Diadem*. He was entrusted with reconnaissance survey and installation of buoys and beacons in the river. He noted on a fair sheet that he had 'placed the Beacon on the west end of the Chico in 12 feet 3 inches water – by the mean of 12 stars [...] and by a meridional altitude of the Sun [...] Longitude per chronometer'. His comprehensive remarks would be endorsed and issued by successive commanders, and they were reproduced in a published memoir by one of the Royal Marine officers in the force, who described Bartholomew as 'a scientific naval officer, whose exclusive duty it was to sound all its bounds, to explore minutely around its shoals and dangers, and who recorded every remark at the moment it was made'.[55] Bartholomew rendered to the Hydrographer copies of Admiralty editions of Spanish and Portuguese charts, liberally annotated with soundings, remarks and the results of astronomical and chronometric observations.[56] Notes attached to the chart of Colonia, a harbour on the north shore occupied by the British, contain the following comment, which surveyors in every age might note with benefit: 'Near to this building is a bushy tree which brought on and kept a little open with the east corner of the Governours House is a good leading mark to carry you clear between the reef and the Fisherman's bank into the Harbour; but as trees and bushes are liable to be cut down I have not placed their situation on the chart.'

Bartholomew remained in favour and in post when Popham was recalled to England. Buenos Aires had been recaptured by local forces. During a second attempt to secure the city, Admiral Murray would state in his despatches that: 'Lieutenant Bartholomew of the *Diadem*, who was strongly recommended to me [...] for his knowledge of the river, embarked with me; and I feel it my duty to state to their lordships, that he was of infinite service.'[57]

Extracts from Bartholomew's remarks are amongst the papers of Captain Henry Bayntun of *Africa* (64), who was responsible during this operation for embarkation of the infantry at Colonia and their landing at Ensenada de Barragon. His sounding plots of the channel through the sand bar which was found during the landing are annotated with a record of the leading line recommended by Bartholomew.[58]

The other practitioner recommended by the Hydrographer was Commander Francis Beaufort of the store-ship *Woolwich*. He was known to Dalrymple as a 'very excellent observer and draughtsman' who had sought his advice before undertaking a voyage to India and had been supplied with a chronometer and sets of East India Company charts and publications.[59] The passage observations which he rendered to the Hydrographical Office had confirmed his calibre, and Dalrymple had secured him the allocation of an additional chronometer before redeployment to South American waters.[60] Heywood was delighted to have Beaufort's assistance to improve control of the survey work with astronomical observations at Montevideo after its capture. He then persuaded his admiral to allocate a gun-brig for a survey of 'the English Bank, and that to the Westwards of it on which the Spanish ship *Archimedes*, and *Diomede*, had struck' and to entrust the task to Beaufort, declaring him to be 'from his thorough scientific knowledge of his profession, more competent than any officer in the river, to perform such service with correctness and dispatch'.[61]

Heywood had groped across the uncharted Archimedes Bank 'rather nearer the ground than the sky, having many casts of 4 fathoms and the ship drawing 23 feet 8 inches'.[62] Time and weather would limit Beaufort's work, but his command of appropriate techniques enabled him to delineate the banks more precisely. The challenge is clear in the detailed notes on his survey sheets: 'Hereabouts the *Protector* gun brig was 20 hours beating over a hard sand in 6 feet water'.[63] Closer inshore, he completed sketch surveys of Montevideo and the nearby islets of Flores, both with detailed annotations.[64] His efforts, and the endorsements of Heywood and others, reinforced his reputation with Dalrymple, who repeatedly brought his ability to the notice of the Admiralty Board.[65] Dalrymple was working on a chart reproducing Beaufort's surveys during his last, turbulent, days in office.[66]

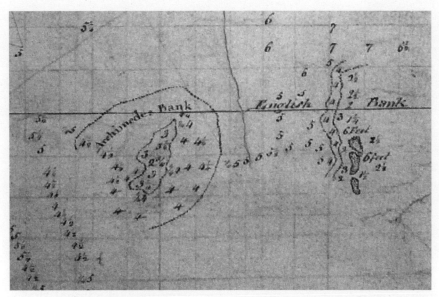

11. *Heywood's sounding sheet including Beaufort's work on the Archimedes and English banks.*

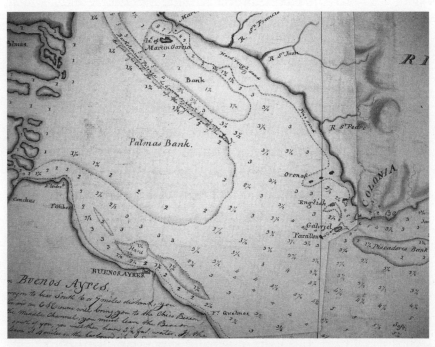

12. *Bartholomew's manuscript chart of the Plate showing 'Bartholomew's Passage'.*

The campaign would end as an embarrassing debacle, with the withdrawal of British land forces under the terms of an armistice, prompting several courts martial, including that of Home Popham. Naval support had been blunted by the challenges of weather and geography, but the critical factor had been underestimation of the spirited resistance of the local population. The economic gains which Popham had used as a justification and a lure would eventually emerge, not through 'liberation' of the provinces of South America, but through the expansion of commerce in response to Napoleon's European conquests and introduction of the Continental System.[67] This expansion would be aided by the establishment of a South America station and, as further north in the Americas and in the East, a pattern of enlightened interest in and promotion of front-line hydrographic skills would result. The operations in the Plate Estuary had also shown that a network of the 'Naval Officers of science' was falling into place. A marine officer recalled the 'kind feelings' which prevailed amongst the officers of all services during the testing campaign, and gave as example a letter from David Bartholomew reporting that the writing desk and clothes of an army officer in Spanish captivity had been saved and sent to England with Captain Heywood in *Polyphemus*.[68] A fascinating indication of this interplay, and a reminder of the worldwide operations covered in this chapter, would come to light nearly a quarter of a century later. In 1829 Francis Beaufort, newly appointed as Hydrographer, took custody of a large manuscript chart. Mr Whidbey, veteran of Vancouver's voyage and now superintendent of the construction of the Plymouth Breakwater, had found it in a press in a hotel in the town. It was entitled 'Rio de la Plata from an actual survey taken in the years 1806 and 1807'. It is the chart which Bartholomew had signed in London on 27 June 1809, just a fortnight before he would take part in another amphibious operation in the Dutch estuaries. It is a fair copy of all the information from the Plate originally submitted in rough to the Admiralty.[69] A note in what is now called Canal Buenos Aires proclaimed his pride as a pathfinder: 'Bartholomew's Passage, he having explored it and was the first Englishman who went up the Uruguay south of the island.' He would be followed by others in succeeding decades as South America loomed larger and larger in British foreign and economic policy. Meanwhile, his skills forged in the front line would place him amongst the first recruits for Hurd's surveying cadre.

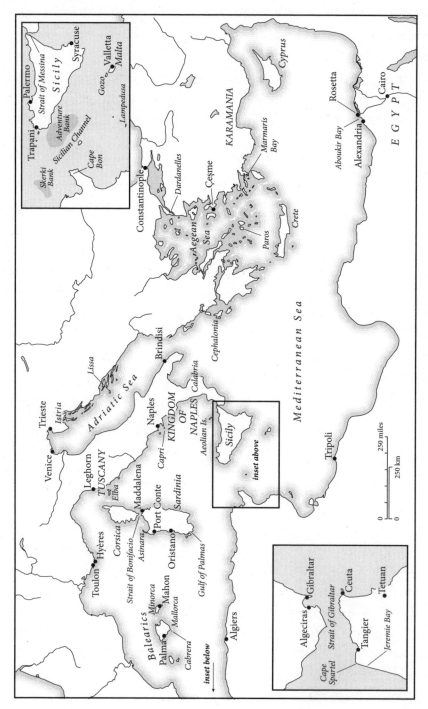

Inset (top left):

Trapani
Palermo
Strait of Messina
Sicily
Syracuse
Gozo Valletta
Malta
Lampedusa
Adventure Bank
Sicilian Channel
Skerki Bank
Cape Bon

Main map:

Constantinople
Dardanelles
Çeşme
Aegean Sea
KARAMANIA
Cyprus
Marmaris Bay
Rosetta
Cairo
E G Y P T
Aboukir Bay
Alexandria
Crete
Paros

Mediterranean Sea

Cephalonia
Brindisi
Lissa
Calabria
Adriatic Sea
Trieste
Istria
Venice
Naples
KINGDOM OF NAPLES
Aeolian Is.
Capri
Leghorn
TUSCANY
Elba
Maddalena
Sicily
inset above
Tripoli
Port Conte
Sardinia
Asinara
Oristano
Corsica
Strait of Bonifacio
Gulf of Palmas
Toulon
Hyères
Balearics
Minorca
Mahon
Palma
Mallorca
Cabrera
inset below
Algiers

250 miles
250 km
0

Inset (bottom right):

Gibraltar
Algeciras
Strait of Gibraltar
Ceuta
Tetuan
Tangier
Jeremie Bay
Cape Spartel

Map 4. Mediterranean Sea.

CHAPTER 3

Containing the Enemy
The Mediterranean

Returning from my first experience of the life of a pathfinder to
undertake basic hydrographic training, I was entrusted with the
latest fair sheets of *Hydra*'s work in the south-west Pacific. These
were to be delivered to the Assistant Hydrographer in Whitehall,
and I was advised that at some stage in my call he would ask where I
would next like to serve. So it happened, and I requested and received
an appointment to a surveying ship bound for the West Indies. In
the opening weeks of 1813, a young officer called on Thomas Hurd
in his office in Whitehall. Together they examined surveys that the
young man had brought from recent front-line operations around
the Iberian Peninsula. There were also sheets from a voyage in the
Pacific that had arrived in the Admiralty without attribution. The
Hydrographer, eager to identify front-line practitioners with higher
skills, could see ability which had gone unrecognised.[1] His ears
pricked up when the young man told how, on return from sea, he had
conferred with officers of the Trigonometric Survey to improve his
grasp of geodesy and triangulation. He had purchased a comprehensive set of astronomical and other instruments, one refined to his
own precise requirements by Troughton, the most renowned maker
of the day. Now the visitor, William Henry Smyth, volunteered to

gather further hydrographic information if sent back to the Mediterranean. Poring over material in the Hydrographical Office, Hurd explained the challenge which he faced in equipping the fleet with vital navigational information in that theatre.

It was in the Mediterranean Sea that the European chart had first evolved, giving warning of the dangers around the fringes of its two great basins and in the central constriction. The coastal states had produced extensive portfolios. Yet, as Smyth would show in a classic study produced later in life, many of the hazards they showed were missing from the products offered in the chandleries of London and other British sea ports. Until Hurd established an official system of chart supply to the fleet, Royal Naval captains and masters were responsible for forming their own portfolios from what was on offer. The consequences had been brought home throughout the campaigns in which the British Mediterranean fleet sought to contain French military expansion on the southern flanks of Europe. As demonstrated in the campaigns leading up to the battle of the Nile in 1798 and Trafalgar in 1805, if the French fleet in Toulon emerged undetected, a watch could generally be kept for a foray through the Strait of Gibraltar. But what if it vanished to eastwards? Would it threaten the Kingdom of Naples and the strategic island of Sicily, or descend on Egypt or elsewhere in the Levant to open up a land route to India? The British response was hampered by poor navigational information. In 1798, with his ship dismasted and under tow in the western basin, Nelson had no charts on board to help with identification of a safe anchorage on the coast of Sardinia. When he entered the eastern basin during the hunt for the French fleet in 1805, Mr Thomas Atkinson, the master, was plotting progress on an old French atlas taken from a prize after the battle of the Nile.[2]

This chapter will show how senior officers in the Admiralty and afloat addressed the problem. They had stimulated the production of sketch surveys by front-line practitioners. Nowadays such work would be termed 'rapid environmental assessment'. They had also pressed for their swift submission and publication. Pointing to the array of 'detached surveys' rendered from the fleet, which he and his colleagues on the Chart Committee had assessed and approved, Hurd commented that he had enough data with which to construct a chart of the Mediterranean Sea, 'but was greatly at a loss for latitudes and longitudes to dress it by'. He would secure the employment of Smyth to address this urgent requirement as 'their Lordships' maritime surveyor in the Mediterranean'.[3]

The encouragement which had been given to data-gathering had often stemmed from bitter personal experience of inadequate navigational intelligence. Captain Thomas Troubridge could not forget that all the accounts of Nelson's famous victory in Aboukir Bay recorded how his ship *Culloden* (74) ran aground during the approach, depriving the admiral of his support and leaving him a spectator of the action. This was a galling outcome for a man who throughout his career had taken great care to gather and share navigational information, including coverage of the Mediterranean theatre.[4] He vented his spleen on a man whose later naval career we have followed in Trinidad. Troubridge dubbed him 'Audacious Briarly'. He had made a first appearance on the books of the Royal Navy with a warrant as master of the fireship *Comet*, which deployed with reinforcements for the Mediterranean in May 1795. He would lose little time in securing patronage and a rapid rise. He was present at Admiral Hotham's action off Hyères on 13 July and a fortnight later was given a major advancement as acting master of a 74-gun ship, the *Terrible*. By September he had a warrant as master of *Audacious* (74), under Captain Davidge Gould, with whom he would serve at the battle of the Nile.[5] Troubridge was highly critical of the performance of Gould and his people in the battle. Briarly was already marked out as 'a person of some talent and much scheming', and the nickname which Troubridge gave him reflected the loquacious Irishman's reputation for spinning tall yarns in the wardroom after dinner.[6] In a later incarnation, he would certainly allow a story to circulate that he was alongside Nelson in *Vanguard* during the evacuation of the Royal Family from Naples.[7] At that time, *Audacious* was in fact part of the squadron blockading Malta.

Briarly's logs record how he broke the tedium by deploying in the cutter to take profiles of soundings along the coast, through the Comino and Gozo channels, in the bays of St Paul and Marsaxlokk and over the hazards of the Secca il-Munxar and the Benghajsa Reef, significant hazards for the vessels on watch close inshore.[8] Nelson extolled this work as 'of the greatest utility, both to British trade in these seas, and to vessels of the Fleet'. Briarly also produced a 'Chart of Bequis Bay', designed principally to show the 'situation of the English and French Fleets' at the battle of the Nile, but with an adequate depiction of the coastline and the shoals and a note of depths. Nelson urged Briarly to include it with a set of six charts of Maltese waters which he agreed might be dedicated to him.[9] They were published commercially in London in 1800.

This was the sort of outcome which had infuriated Alexander Dalrymple as he endeavoured to achieve effective liaison with the fleet and gather in data. He complained that 'Notwithstanding the many Men of War that were on the Coast of Egypt during the last War There is no compleat Chart of That Coast received in the Hydrographical Office, nor even an exact Plan of Aboukir Bay.'[10] Thomas Atkinson, then master of *Theseus* (74), was credited with a chart, again issued by a commercial publisher, no copies of which have survived. He supplied a list of latitudes and longitudes which was rejected by Dalrymple, who pointed out that lack of information on how they had been observed prevented him from using them, especially since they did not match well with the astronomical records of the French. The startling lack of information was underlined during the subsequent campaign of 1801 to expel the French from Egypt, when Admiral Keith's flagship broke an anchor and chafed her cables on the wreck of *L'Orient*.[11]

Keith had been careful to consult with captains with experience of the eastern basin. Benjamin Hallowell was a veteran of Aboukir Bay, who was acutely aware of the limitations of hydrographic information before that battle and of the scant time which was available to remedy this in the hectic aftermath. He had a copy of the remarks which the competent Edward Strode, destined to be Edward Columbine's assistant, had compiled when *Zealous* (74) was left to blockade the French.[12] Those rendered to the Admiralty included firm cautions on dangers in Aboukir Bay 'which we have not been able to explore'.[13] Back in Egypt in 1807, Hallowell would encourage two masters, Thomas Mann and John Hepburn, who conducted one of the most comprehensive surveys of the period. To their chagrin, they were obliged to show on their fine fair sheet the block-ships which had been sunk to deny the harbour of Old Alexandria to an enemy.[14]

As at the Cape of Good Hope, Keith encouraged gifted practitioners under his command. Joseph Edmonds had been promoted on the strength of Home Popham's report of his part in an attack on Ostend in 1798, and was now captain of *Pallas* (38). He made a fine survey of the anchorage in Marmaris Bay, where the 175 ships of the expeditionary force assembled and exercised beach landing. The skills which Edmonds would deploy later in the River Plate were also exploited in Aboukir Bay and the adjacent lakes. Other officers and mates were despatched to sound the channels leading to Alexandria and the bar and mouth of the Rosetta Branch of the Nile.[15] Master's Mate William Little served in *Dgerm No. 3*, a shallow-draught local boat taken up under Sir Sidney Smith's command to carry supplies and the siege train upstream. As the river fell steadily to summer levels, he produced a manuscript track plot of their progress from Rosetta to within sight of Cairo and the pyramids of Giza.[16]

Keith also prized the work of an assiduous gatherer of hydrographic data in the Mediterranean, whose published charts he gathered in a fine binding endorsed 'Knight's Mediterranean'.[17] John Knight had served as Flag Captain to Admiral Hood in the theatre in 1793–95, and

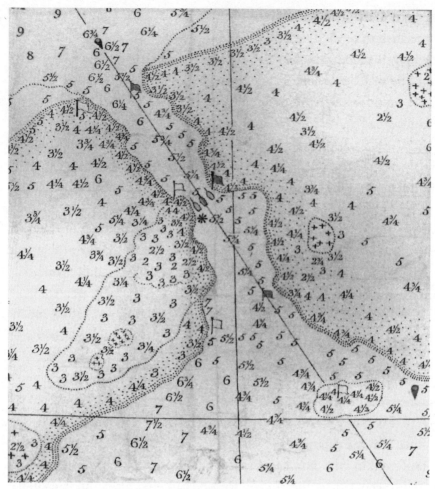

13. *Extract from the fair sheet prepared by Thomas Mann and John Hepburn showing the sunken block-ships in the entrance to Alexandria Old Harbour.*

his productions included invaluable small-scale charts for campaign and passage planning. He will have used them himself when, appointed as Flag Officer Gibraltar, he sailed in *Queen* (98), in command of the slender escort of a vital convoy of 45 transports carrying 5,000 troops, some for the defence of Gibraltar, the remainder bound for Malta. The safe arrival of this force in the central Mediterranean was of crucial importance. The Russians were pressing for a joint campaign in southern Italy, whilst the British Cabinet wished to see a garrison established in Sicily. The transit of this force coincided with the emergence of Villeneuve's fleet from Toulon and the breaking of the blockade of Cádiz. Knight's judgements were watched closely as he shepherded the convoy through the Strait of Gibraltar.[18] He sheltered it in the roadsteads of Ceuta and Tetuan, which he had surveyed in 1799.[19] This part in securing the main strategic objective of the Trafalgar campaign earned no praise from Admiral Collingwood. Indeed, when Knight then responded to intelligence that Villeneuve was bearing down on Cádiz and used his initiative to bring the four ships watching Cartagena in reinforcement, Collingwood's antipathy was expressed in an ungracious quip related to Knight's hydrographic bent: 'where have you been with your Admiral? What could possess him to go off and leave me in my poverty? I thought you were gone to survey Jeremie Bay'.[20] In fact, Knight's charts already showed this rendezvous anchorage on the Moroccan coast outside the Strait, which had been surveyed in 1798 on St Vincent's orders. Knight was delighted when a change to command boundaries placed him under Nelson.

On arriving in the Mediterranean on the outbreak of the Napoleonic Wars, Nelson had benefited from the astute planning of the second-in-command in the theatre, Sir Richard Bickerton, formerly the supportive frigate captain who had encouraged Columbine in the West Indies. He had been left in the theatre throughout the 'Truce of Amiens'. Acutely conscious of the fragility of the ongoing peace process and the diminishing prospects of secure bases in British hands, he had used his initiative and set in hand a remarkable campaign to assess the potential of Sardinian anchorages. Anticipating Admiralty interest in the vicinity of the strategic Bonifacio Strait, he despatched three men to the area: Captain George Frederick Ryves in *Agincourt* (64), Mr William Kirby in *Termagant* (18) and Keith's protégé, Commander William Durban, in *Weazle* (16). The anchorage which they surveyed in 'Agincourt Sound' in the sheltered Maddalena archipelago became a strategic base, with a store-ship with a complement of caulkers and artificers to repair calling ships. Nelson was particularly keen to assess this perfect base for his 'open blockade' of Toulon – tempting the French to emerge, but able to keep track of them and ready to get on their trail. When his fleet first entered the anchorage, Thomas Atkinson, now master in *Victory*, plotted the track on a copy of Ryves' survey (see Plate 1). Nelson himself kept a record of every alteration of course in a little notebook, which is preserved in the British Library. He was delighted with the anchorage and was back there at the outset of the Trafalgar campaign. The entrances at west and east ensured no delay in the pursuit when news arrived that Villeneuve's squadron was at sea.[21]

By now, the reception and handling of navigational information were on a decidedly better footing thanks to the Board of Admiralty headed by St Vincent. His own awareness of the importance of hydrography had been sharpened by personal experience of groundings in the Mediterranean.[22] He had persuaded two like-minded men to join his board. John Markham had early experience of front-line survey operations gained during the War of American Independence under Keith's command. In 1799, as captain of *Centaur* (74), he lost no time in passing to Dalrymple surveys of the Egyptian coast found on board a French squadron which he had intercepted and captured.[23] Markham's counterpart was Thomas Troubridge, a firm supporter of the young Hydrographical Office, supplying over fifty documents, twenty-nine of which related to the Mediterranean. He encouraged Dalrymple to search for other useful information amongst the holdings in the Admiralty and to publish it. All was of high import as the Napoleonic conflict loomed and intelligence came in of the build-up of forces in Toulon and the activity of French agents in Italy, along the Adriatic coasts and in the Levant. Troubridge's most significant contribution was now made during the Trafalgar campaign, spotting and selecting the most important of the new surveys coming in from Bickerton and passing them to the Hydrographer without delay. The rapid turnaround which Dalrymple had adopted with East India Company charts to encourage feedback on deficiencies was well suited to meet war-time demand.[24] The simple manuscripts needed little tidying up and adjusting to fit a standard engraved sheet. Short runs of about twenty copies were then produced on a press which had been purchased in 1800 for proof printing.[25] The understanding between Troubridge and Dalrymple is illustrated in the stream of messages which the former would send to his old friend Nelson: 'My Lord, I have sent you a few Charts of what we have finished, and by giving them to intelligent men with directions to make remarks and correct any errors we shall in time make them good [...] it is a great thing to know any information you may send me. I will add to our collection.'[26]

Nelson responded with enthusiasm. His alertness for hydro-graphic intelligence is reflected in his letter books, which include comprehensive notes on logistic resources in Port Conte by Captain Richard Moubray of *Active* (38), who had served with Bickerton and Columbine in *Sybil*.[27] Nelson would forward a survey of the Gulf of Palmas, which he declared to be 'without exception the finest open road-stead I have ever seen'.[28] It had been conducted by Thomas Atkinson, with the assistance of Charles Royer, a gifted young man who drew up a fair sheet of their soundings which Nelson judged to be 'a very correct and well-executed plan'. Nelson secured Royer's promotion to lieutenant and he would submit two more plans during subsequent service with two captains who were active hydrographic practitioners.[29] Dalrymple would recall the visit which Nelson made to the Hydrographical Office before his departure from England in 1805 and remark to the Admiralty Board that: 'Many pieces of the Mediterranean were sent to the Hydrographical Office, by the ever to be lamented Lord Nelson, and have been engraved'.[30] These 'pieces' were commendable, but as Thomas Hurd noted with frustra-tion as he showed them to William Henry Smyth, their usefulness depended on whether a commander knew where the anchorages or ports lay or could find them on a smaller-scale chart.

✳

This need for accurate smaller-scale chart coverage would be brought home dramatically on the 'clear moonlight night' of 20 October 1806.[31] HMS *Athenien* (64), commanded by Captain Robert Raynsford, was bound for Palermo with despatches for Rear Admiral Sir Sidney Smith and £30,000 of specie for the British Army, which had been landed in Sicily during the Trafalgar campaign. Proceeding at 9 knots with a fair wind, during the first watch she drove onto the notorious danger of the Esquerques or Skerki Bank, far out in the western approaches to the Sicilian channel. How could this happen? The existence of this danger had been attested since classical times, and it had been clearly marked, in remarkable detail, on the medieval portolan charts.[32] So too had many spurious shoals in deep water, and the evidence had been doubted by more recent chart-makers.[33] It was reported that, moments before the ship struck, the captain had remarked 'If the Esquerques shoals do exist we should now be upon them'.[34] The ship broke up and 347 lives were lost. Alexander Dalrymple would draw a lesson for the Board. The expense of providing every ship in the Royal Navy with a chronometer would be less than 'the loss of this one ship has occasioned, not to mention the inestimable lives lost to this country by that event'.[35]

Sir Sidney Smith sent search parties to the west coast of Sicily, where the despatches were found in a beachcomber's hoard. The specie was never recovered. Thomas Longstaff in the transport *Ellice*, with smaller local craft and divers, did locate the wreck and fixed its position before bad weather set in. His result tallied with the position of the Esquerques established in a survey which Keith had ordered some four years previously.[36] The court martial following the wreck would reveal that Captain Raynsford had a copy of this very survey. The verdict of the court was that, whilst a current might have caused some offset, the courses steered in *Athenien* were insufficient to carry her clear to the north of the reported position of the reef.

This had been established by William Durban in *Weazle*. He had arrived in the Mediterranean in February 1802 after a flying passage of fourteen days from Plymouth with despatches relating to the

Peace of Amiens. His old patron, Admiral Keith, swiftly employed him to assess the suitability of the harbour of Lampedusa as a base for the fleet should the British be forced to relinquish Malta. His report earned the acclaim of Sir Alexander Ball, veteran of Aboukir Bay and now governor of Malta, who rated him 'one of the most scientific officers in the Navy'. Durban's 'trigonometric survey' was controlled by sextant angles, with distances determined trigonometrically, and baseline and rays to stations shown on the sheet. It was passed promptly by Troubridge to Dalrymple, who had been awaiting it eagerly and had held back a compilation of earlier surveys so that it could be included in his Admiralty chart.[37]

Durban's higher accomplishments came fully into their own when Keith tasked him to locate, fix and sound the Esquerques.[38] He sailed from a point on the west coast of the island of Maritimo where he had made a careful observation for longitude, and ran out until he found himself on the bank. Having anchored, he sent 'all boats away sounding between sunrise and sunset' starring out from the sloop. He was assisted by Lieutenant Swiney in the cutter *L'Entreprenante*. After a call in Trapani for water and provisions, the local knowledge of the Sicilian fishing community was brought to bear to narrow down the hunt, and Durban returned to the task with a pilot embarked. On 25 August, *Weazle* was sounding when 'at 3.20 saw a rock on the lee beam, close to, rounded to and lowered the boat down to sound'.[39] They had located a breaking reef, the very shallowest part of the great Skerki Bank, and it retains the name they gave it: Keith Reef.

The comprehensive data which Durban rendered to the Admiralty was pored over by Dalrymple and his staff. Their efforts to compile it were still in hand when the alert Troubridge left the Admiralty, and publication of the resultant Admiralty chart in 1805 was further delayed by corrections by the Hydrographer.[40] He was discomfited when Lord Nelson reported, during his visit to the Hydrographical Office, that another shoal area on the bank had been discovered. The admiral deplored the fact that it had been named after him, 'as new

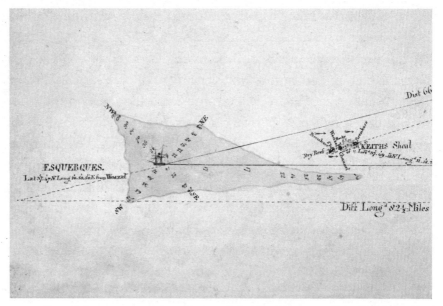

14. Detail from a contemporary copy of Durban's survey of the Skerki Bank, showing sounding starred from Weazle *and the dangerous Keith's Reef which he subsequently examined.*

names only tended to produce confusion'.[41] 'Nelson's Reef' would be disproved by later surveys and was almost certainly the result of similar inaccuracies in dead reckoning to those that had led *Athenien* to disaster. On his return to England, Durban set about promulgating all the work which he had carried out, and in 1810 Arrowsmith published *A Chart of the Dangers in the Channel between Sardinia, Sicily and Africa.* It was a far more useful document than Dalrymple's compilation, which Hurd no longer distributed.[42]

Like Francis Beaufort, surveying at the same time on the coast of Karamania, Durban realised the importance of providing information on the conduct of his work.[43] The memoir on his chart revealed the skill and personal investment in astronomical instruments which had secured the results: 'The positions of the dangers here enumerated were determined [. . .] from the mean result of six chronometers; their rates having been carefully examined both previous to, and after the survey was finished'. Dalrymple's verdict on the inadequate provision of chronometers to the fleet was justified. Allocation often depended on firm lobbying by commanding officers. Remarkably, in the hurried preparation for deployment to the Mediterranean, and even with the astute Thomas Atkinson on board, *Victory* had sailed without a chronometer.[44] The number of those instruments carried in the minor warship *Weazle* reflected the same calibre and enthusiasm on Durban's part that Home Popham had demonstrated in his Red Sea surveys. They represented a significant outlay for Durban and his counterpart in eastern seas, Lieutenant Peter Heywood, for purchase of one chronometer would take at least one year of their pay. All in all, the accuracy of the observations and estimations from the traverses from Sicily reflected a distinctly higher level of mathematical competence than the swift compass surveys made in coastal and inshore waters.

Durban was a man of wide interests and accomplishments. His family had ancient links with the Duchy of Milan. He spoke Italian and would be employed in diplomatic missions to the Sicilian court as well as to Tripoli, Tunis and Algiers.[45] At St Vincent's direction he was promoted into *Ambuscade* (32) by Nelson, who had studied information which he had gathered on Pula Roads and described him as a 'very clever good Officer and Man'.[46] His hydrographic and diplomatic activity also commended him to Collingwood and to British and Russian military commanders in the theatre. He was charged with assessing landing places on the east coast of Calabria and in the bays around Naples.[47] His established repute is evident in a remark by St Vincent in 1807 that he understood that Durban had made a survey of 'the most essential parts' of the Adriatic, where he had joined a Russian squadron in operations against the French on the Dalmatian coast.[48] There is also evidence of Admiralty interest in despatching Durban to the Black Sea.[49] He was subject to some criticism in the winter of 1808 for failing to prevent the displacement of the small British garrison which had been established on Capri.[50] By the summer of 1809 *Ambuscade* was assessed as very defective and ordered home. Durban paid her off in September 1809, and his record of active service ends at this point.[51] He was not to be a support to Thomas Hurd as he lobbied for the formation of a permanent hydrographic cadre, but he had demonstrated the skills which Hurd had spotted in the young man whose appointment he had secured as Admiralty Surveyor for the Mediterranean theatre.

William Henry Smyth's heritage and early experience had made him tough and determined. He was born on 21 January 1788 in Westminster, where his loyalist family had settled in exile after forfeiting their property in East (now North) Jersey in the aftermath of the War of American Independence. By 1796 his mother had been twice widowed and thereafter William's guardians set out to counter the attraction of a naval career for a high-spirited boy in that decade of stirring British victories. They placed him on board a West Indiaman for a voyage during the short truce in 1802, hoping that this would dispel the enchantment of a sea career. The ship was commanded, however, by John King, a Royal Naval master in peace-time employment like Alexander Briarly. He happily gave the young man a thorough grounding in seamanship and navigation.[52] They were at Tobago when hostilities resumed, and Smyth observed the operations of Columbine's *Ulysses* and the other ships of Hood's squadron which resulted in the recapture of the island. Surviving a hurricane and a fall overboard during the return voyage to England, Smyth tried in vain to overcome the implacable refusal of his mother's friends to support his entry to the Royal Navy. He set off in search of adventure as a free mariner in the East Indies, where he signed on in the East India Company cruiser *Cornwallis* (50), which was subsequently purchased and commissioned by the government as a frigate. Smyth's ambition of joining the Royal Navy had been realised.

In 1807 his interest in navigation and survey would be thoroughly fuelled during a remarkable voyage. It had been intended that

Admiral Murray's expedition to Chile be reinforced from the East Indies station. Following the diversion of that squadron to the Plate Estuary (as described in Chapter 2), Admiral Pellew, Commander-in-Chief East Indies, deployed *Cornwallis* on a lone foray to the west coast of South America. After ranging from Valparaíso to Acapulco she re-crossed the Pacific by the Sandwich Islands to pick up an East India Company convoy at Canton.[53] Whilst counterparts were detached on raids and to take prizes to Port Jackson, Smyth remained on board helping with observations. Amongst the work which he would show to Thomas Hurd were eight plotting sheets of the track of the ship and the running survey of uncharted islands, one of which would be named after Captain Charles Johnston.[54] Smyth subsequently removed with his captain to a 74-gun ship in which they returned to England. He was soon on the front line in the campaigns on the coast of the Spanish mainland and islands which are described below in Chapter 7, during which he conducted a number of thorough surveys. Recommendations from his commanding officers assisted Hurd to highlight Smyth's ability and his contribution to the improvement of Admiralty charts. Following his commendation to Lord Melville, the First Lord, Smyth was promoted to lieutenant and appointed to the substantial Anglo-Sicilian flotilla of gun-vessels stationed at Messina to assist the land garrison to defend the most vulnerable point in Sicily, against the French forces commanded by Joachim Murat, Napoleon's brother-in-law and puppet ruler of the Kingdom of Naples.[55]

Smyth's mettle and his 'talents of an eminently scientific navigator' were well known to Captain Sir Robert Hall, the commander of the squadron, who was only too ready to comply with the Admiralty's orders to employ him on survey work.[56] Smyth arrived with a memorandum from Hurd which stressed the importance of this task:

Our knowledge of the coasts and neighbourhood of Sicily is extremely deficient; and although there are the three observatories of Palermo, Naples, and Malta, the exact position of any one of them is undetermined. We are also unacquainted with the true place of the important land-fall Maritimo, which, we are assured by experienced officers, is placed in the charts twenty miles too far to the westward; and Cape Bon, on the African shore, six or seven too much to the eastward. [...] All the charts of Sicily that I have examined are at variance with each other; and, from our having no good authority for either, we are at a loss which to select as the best [...] nor have we any particular plans to be depended on.[57]

Hurd had suggested that Smyth's work might be extended into the Adriatic and that he should be furnished with the necessary instruments. He provided him with a theodolite, a micrometrical telescope, a sextant and a station pointer – a basic toolkit for boat surveys.

On arrival, the affable young man took full advantage of British standing in Sicily. In 1813 the British were firmly entrenched in the island, which, with Malta, was an entrepôt through which British industrial goods and colonial produce were smuggled into the Mediterranean ports of Napoleon's 'closed' continent. British exports to the Mediterranean had quadrupled since 1805, and the importance of the island bases increased as restrictions on access were tightened in the German ports in the North Sea and Baltic. Quite apart from this war-time boost, the British factories had a solid pedigree. The wine trade in the western ports of Mazara del Vallo province had been founded in the early 1770s. There was a well-established network of British consuls and vice-consuls throughout the island. Royal Naval hydrographic surveyors in every age have understood the importance of cultivating local allies, and the longer periods in a location which their work demands usually result in closer bonds than warships making a brief call can achieve. Numerous references in the *Memoir of Sicily* which Smyth would later publish indicate that he found fellow spirits amongst the extensive British community:

men such as Mr Woodhouse, the wine merchant of Marsala who had supplied Nelson's ships, and who, like other contemporaries, gathered in their findings of coins and artefacts as they dug the foundations for new farm complexes, known as baglios, and warehouses. Smyth, a polymath with numismatics amongst his enthusiasms, would include illustrations of those coins on his survey sheets.

The Sicilians were reaping the benefits of a British government subsidy and the spending of a garrison which had built up to over 20,000 men. Local builders, shipwrights and craftsmen had never known such steady employment. The farmers, too, were content, for Napoleon's Continental System had cut off competition from the mainland. Meanwhile, if the harvests were poor, incoming American grain cargoes benefited from naval convoy protection. Sicilian coastal shipping was also more secure, for the descents of the North African corsairs had been curtailed. All these benefits outweighed the sometimes arrogant attitude of the incomers.[58] Smyth's memoir shows that he worked hard at maintaining good relationships with local authorities, assisted by his generous nature and his appreciation of sound qualities where he found them.[59] He was rewarded: 'a good vessel and crew were allotted to me, and the stores of the arsenal were at my requisition'.[60] He had been loaned 'one of their finest gunboats, a large paranzello manned with thirty Sicilians; to which was supplied a capital luntra, or boat like a whaler's, but larger, being sharp at both ends, and double-banked for eight oars'. The paranzello was a swift and handy craft which could be hauled up on a beach in the event of threatening weather.[61] In his memoir on Sicily, Smyth would remark that, despite the resources available, the government had never equipped more than small flotilla vessels, and that these were principally employed in the service of the health office. The sailors, whom he described as 'cheerful, hardy and daring', would almost certainly have welcomed their employment on the survey.[62]

Smyth would also benefit from good relationships with the British army garrison. He was a persuasive enthusiast who enlisted the help of

15. Smyth surveying with his army counterparts.

two other officers for his work: Captain John Henryson of the Royal Engineers and Lieutenant Edward Thompson of the Royal Staff Corps.[63] Smyth records that: 'These gentlemen, as my guests, [...] accompanied me round the island [...] and [...] gave me the only personal assistance I received, aiding me greatly in sketching the topography and fortifications during the time occupied by my nautical and astronomical operations, and assisting in the reduction of the various observations.'[64]

Their help is very evident in Smyth's top-priority survey. He had soon ascertained that the Neapolitan chart of the Strait of Messina which Hurd had provided was full of errors. Henryson and Thompson made a detailed topographical survey which is apparent on Smyth's fair sheets. Their hill-shading employs the 'scale of shade', the darker the steeper, which they had been taught at the Military College, and they used the convention of parallel lines to demarcate the arable fields along the coast.[65] Meanwhile, Smyth got afloat with his willing seamen for the sounding work in the strait, in the middle of which they found 'no bottom with two hundred fathoms of line'. The sailors took turns to heave the lead for the thorough examination of the shelf areas on the coastal margins, calling out the nature of the bottom from the sample retained in the tallow, whilst Smyth took the sextant angles to lay down the sounding lines and to fix the position of dangers such as the whirlpool of Charybdis. Smyth judged

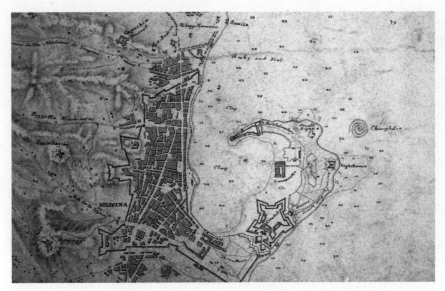

16. *Detail from Smyth's survey of the Strait of Messina,*
showing the whirlpool of Charybdis.

that the real hazards in the strait were the katabatic winds and the
numerous lights of fishing vessels which made it difficult to pick out
the lights at Faro and Messina.[66]

Smyth had no doubt of his most important source of assistance for
his survey of Sicily. Hurd's memorandum had laid great emphasis on
the need to 'obtain accurate observations on the most material
points'.[67] Smyth arrived with a clear geodetic campaign in mind. A
meridian through the island must be defined and a permanent baseline measured for the final determination of Sicily's true position,
extent and form.[68] He had a particularly clear grasp of the importance
of astronomy, of the orders of precise observation and of methodolo-
gies to reduce systematic errors. His competence was considerable
even before he encountered 'the able and amiable Abbaté Piazzi', the
astronomer at the Palermo Observatory. This is situated on the tower
of Santa Ninfa, 'the summit of the pile of building forming the royal
palace' on the edge of the old city. From its terrace a panoramic view
of the cathedral and other great buildings stretching down to the port
can still be enjoyed. In the opposite direction, beyond the Porto

Nuovo, which lies immediately below, the open plain is now covered by an urban sprawl. Today, light pollution precludes useful optical work, but in the eighteenth century the observatory was the southernmost in Europe, and the Sicilian climate was benign for an astronomer. Smyth commented that only the limited horizon in the plain of Palermo, with its surrounding mountains, prevented the observatory from being 'ranked as one of the finest institutions of the kind in Europe'. It was Piazzi who had established its reputation, obtaining the assistance of the most eminent astronomers in Paris and, in London, persuading Ramsden, the leading maker of the day, to manufacture a complete set of astronomical instruments. The most remarkable of these, the famous 5-foot 'Palermo Circle', has been remounted in the original dome in the observatory. This dome had been designed by Piazzi with a massive central pillar to support the circle and an elegant gallery with smaller pillars at each cardinal and half-cardinal point. The connecting rooms in which Smyth and Piazzi met have also been beautifully restored, with the astronomer's writing desk in place and some of Ramsden's portable instruments, including a fine Hadley's quadrant, on display.

Once established in this purpose-built facility, Piazzi had used his state-of-the-art equipment to develop catalogues of stellar positions, which twice earned him the prize of the French Académie des Sciences and also brought election to the Royal Society. His painstaking and meticulous observational techniques became legendary. He had first earned fame in 1801, when, during his plotting of the stars in the constellation of Taurus, he made the first detection of an asteroid, which was named Ceres after the patron goddess of Sicily. Despite the fact that an illness in 1807 had left him blind, Piazzi supervised his staff in the production of an improved star catalogue. Smyth witnessed that his own passion for astronomy 'received its sharpest spur at the close of 1813, when I accidentally assisted Piazzi in reading some of the proof-sheets of the Palermo Catalogue'. He recorded his indebtedness to 'the worthy Piazzi, who I am proud to call my friend'. He had 'always afforded me every assistance; and [...] I got drilled into a more regular system of astronomical observation than I had hitherto been able to learn'.[69] Piazzi is likely to have taken a close interest in all of Smyth's activities, for he himself had made an unsuccessful attempt to execute a trigonometric survey of Sicily. The library of the observatory still holds copies of early Ordnance Survey sheets and the first two volumes of Mudge's account of the Trigonometrical Survey of England, which Piazzi had brought back from London.[70]

Smyth in his turn had to cut his cloth. Despite the precedence given to his survey, he was required to play his part in the high-paced events of the closing stages of the war. He was selected to command the brig *Scylla*, in which Commodore Hall flew his flag, during a confidential mission to Palermo to assess the wavering loyalty of the Neapolitan court as the Napoleonic Empire in Europe began to collapse in the early months of 1814. In March, Lord Bentinck, the British envoy in Sicily, finally achieved his ambition of landing a force on the mainland at Leghorn to encourage an Italian rising to match that in Spain. Smyth was present with him as naval aide-de-camp at the surrender of Genoa.[71] He nonetheless turned these deployments into good account to extend a network of observed positions and 'chronometric arcs' between them. Napoleon's subsequent escape from Elba prompted Murat, King of Naples, to throw his lot in with his brother-in-law's desperate venture and renew the threat to Sicily. Smyth was stationed with an armed boat amongst the Aeolian Islands. Looking out from 'the peaked summit of Panaria', he spotted a large Neapolitan gun-vessel standing in. He descended swiftly to the coast and laid a successful ambush. In his mountain eyrie Smyth had been taking observations to extend the remit given to him by Thomas Hurd.[72] Their Lordship's Surveyor in the Mediterranean had launched the campaign which would add a reliable general chart of the sea to the Admiralty folios. He had done so whilst following his mentor, Thomas Hurd, in applying skills in the combat zone.

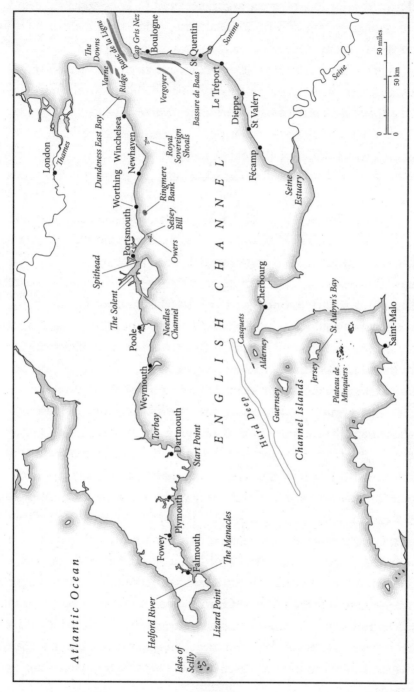

Map 5. English Channel and Strait of Dover.

CHAPTER 4

Holding the Centre
Home Waters and Invasion Coasts

T he field work in Bermuda had taken a toll, and Thomas Hurd
was unfit for a sea appointment during the latter years of the
French Revolutionary War. The veteran of the War of American
Independence was irked that on return to England he had been
turned down by the First Lord for promotion on the grounds that he
had not been actively employed during the current war. He would
lose no opportunity in coming years to tell the Board of Admiralty
that front-line surveying service, facilitating access and the reach of
British sea power, was receiving insufficient recognition and reward.[1]
A change of administration and the advent of St Vincent as First
Lord altered his prospects. Six months after he reported completion
of his charts, he was appointed 'For Rank' to the *Glatton* (56) on
29 April 1802. This was an appointment on paper only to advance
him to post captain. He would never set foot on board. William
Bligh had brought her back from the battle of Copenhagen, and she
was under repair at Chatham. It would not be long, however, before
Hurd, with his health 'in some degree re-established', followed in the
footsteps of Bligh and others in active service on the Channel coasts
of England and France.

With the resumption of hostilities, Napoleon Bonaparte had mustered his great Armée d'Angleterre along the coast near Boulogne. The Ordnance Board's surveyors were dedicated to 'the survey of the sea coast' in the vulnerable counties of Kent and Essex and in the West Country.[2] Dalrymple urged the Board of Admiralty to appoint suitable men to produce hydrography to match this work. Just as Hurd had emerged from the joint surveys on the eastern seaboard of North America, other practitioners had been schooled in the great exploring voyages on the Pacific coasts and into the great ocean beyond. The high profile of these endeavours ensured top-level interest in the career officers of the ships and brought their skills to mind in times of emergency.[3] The astute and influential Joseph Banks was quick to commend them to the Admiralty, where First Secretary Evan Nepean, who had been involved in planning Captain George Vancouver's voyage, would also view them with a favourable eye. Thus, for example, St Vincent was careful to assure Banks: 'Your friend Capt. Johnstone is or will be confirmed'.[4]

James Johnstone was a Scot with a distinguished record in boat survey work gained during the voyages of exploration of Captains Colnett and Vancouver. His front-line service during the War of American Independence and the French Revolutionary War had culminated in command of a sloop on the West Indies station.[5] Lord Keith, now commander-in-chief in a new North Sea station, was delighted when St Vincent placed him under his direction. In the winter of 1803, Johnstone was tasked to report on the suitability of Bridlington and Filey Bays as rendezvous anchorages for ships of Keith's squadrons watching the Dutch coasts and German rivers from bases at Harwich and Leith. Johnstone selected Bridlington as the better anchorage, with good access to water and provisions. He embarked in the *Hunter* revenue cutter in January 1804 and completed a thorough survey which was published as a fleet chart before the close of the year.[6] Keith then redeployed him to the other end of his command to assist the operations of the squadron blockading the French ports in the Dover Strait and the estuary of the Seine.

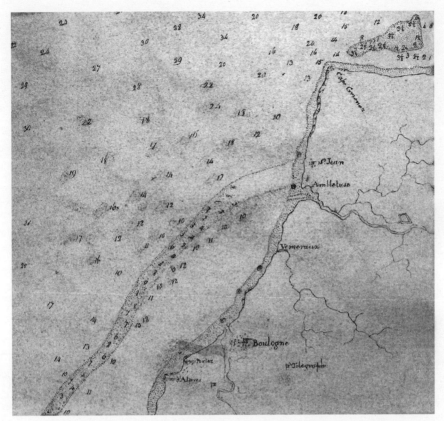

17. *Extract from Johnstone's survey of the French coast showing the offshore banks and some of the prominent marks, churches and telegraph, used to fix the work.*

Johnstone applied his skill to examine the shifting shoals in the approaches to the squadron's base in remote East Bay at Dungeness, to fix and survey the Varne and Ridge banks which lie in mid-Channel and to conduct reconnaissance on the enemy coast. He continued to depend on the loan of craft for his work. The flag officers on station allocated small warships for him to anchor along the mid-Channel banks, enabling him to measure between them for a baseline from which he extended his boat-sounding to fix the extremities and to mark the shallowest part with a buoy.[7] He deployed in vessels of Rear Admiral Louis's squadron as opportunity offered, and he found and alerted them to a 3-fathom patch on the Vergove (Vergoyer) shoal in the south-west approaches to Boulogne.[8] Keith had no hesitation in endorsing Louis's opinion that much greater benefit would arise if Johnstone was given command of a 'good sloop of war', actively employed in the blockade but providing a stable platform and adequate manpower for surveying work.[9] He was allocated the ship-sloop *Alert* (18), a hastily purchased and converted collier, a hull-design which Cook's voyages had proved ideal for survey-tasking.[10] He was soon deploying with the Dungeness squadron to watch Boulogne, Dieppe and Fécamp.[11] He saw plenty of action but still found time to survey in the approaches to the River Somme off St Valéry, St Quentin and Tréport and on the banks off Calais and Boulogne, which he reported to be very little known by the pilots employed in the fleet. The density of sounding which he achieved gave the ships of the squadron a good picture of the Banc de la Ligne between Cap Gris Nez and Calais, and the Bassure de Baas extending from Ambleteuse past Boulogne. In 1807 it was reported that the engravers in the Hydrographical Office had nearly completed work on a chart of his work.[12] By 1809, with the benefit of Johnstone's survey, the blockade had been drawn ever tauter, with ships of the British squadron regularly anchoring overnight on the outer edge of the Bassure de Baas.[13]

In the winter of 1803–4 Alexander Dalrymple was indisposed and William Bligh oversaw the Hydrographical Office. It fell to him to interview another Pacific veteran recently arrived in England, bringing a consignment of charts arising from Matthew Flinders' work for the Admiralty on the coasts of Australia. Twenty-eight-year-old John Murray came from a humble background, for his father was a day labourer at the Tron Church in Edinburgh High Street, but he may well have profited from a good, broad Scottish education. He had taken part in the examination of Bass's Strait and had identified Port Phillip, site of the future settlement of Melbourne. He was a sound practical observer whose journals contain numerous examples of awareness and ingenuity, especially in obtaining baseline measurements.[14] Bligh recommended his employment, and Murray was tasked to extend the sounding work westward of Johnstone's work, examining shoals and suspected features off the Sussex coast which might be found 'dangerous to line of battle ships'.[15] He worked from His Majesty's surveying vessel *Sorlings*. Her grand designation was misleading. She was only 52 feet in length and was continually driven into port in foul weather. Service in her was clearly rigorous, and Murray's assistants were discharged one by one with broken-down health.[16] Her light armament of four swivel guns provided scant reassurance when Murray witnessed an action in the offing and heard gunfire 'towards Boulogne'. His correspondence and records indicate a determination to overcome these difficulties. He also demonstrated competence in establishing control along the coast, measuring baselines by sound and taking angles to lay down the fixing marks for the sounding work. Where conspicuous buildings such as windmills were not present, these stations were marked by flags. He measured horizontal sextant angles between these marks to lay down his soundings. These were reduced to allow for 'the tides [...] which along this part of the coast seem to deserve particular attention'.[17]

Murray successfully located the shoalest point on the Royal Sovereign Shoals, and the priority work east of Beachy Head was completed in 1804. By the end of 1805 he reported that he was nearly as far as Worthing and that, carrying the work out to 7–8 miles offshore, the survey had not revealed 'any spot or part of the least danger to shipping of the largest size'. Such ships 'may in this distance venture in working down Channel to within a mile of the shore', and they would find good holding ground in the coastal anchorages. In his final two seasons he completed the western part of his allocated area, identifying the Ringmere Bank (Kingmere Rocks) as the only significant offshore feature in an area where 'vessels of war are daily anchoring'.[18] His work between Winchelsea and Beachy Head was published in an Admiralty chart in 1807. In May 1809 he reported that completion of final examinations of the shoals was close at hand. But just a few weeks later he was superseded abruptly, and command

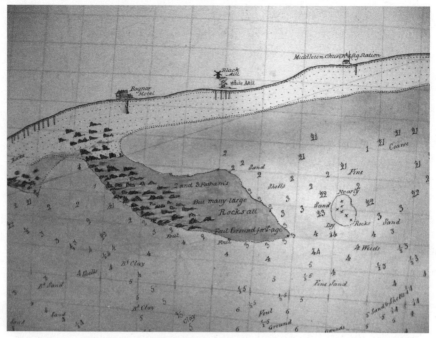

18. Detail from a survey by Lieutenant John Murray showing control points and delineation of dangers.

of *Sorlings* passed to Mr William Chapman, another Pacific veteran who had been selected as an Admiralty Surveyor.[19] The Admiralty had been presented with a damning verdict from their Hydrographer on the time Murray had taken for his work despite 'all the advantages resulting from the constant attendance and entire command of a vessel adapted to the purpose of his employment, which has continued upwards of five years'.[20] All his work would ultimately be published, and Murray retained sufficient standing with the Lord Commissioners to secure two more small ship commands during the last years of the war. His detailed monthly reports had certainly ensured that significant dangers to the ships of the squadrons operating in the eastern part of the Channel had been despatched to the Admiralty in timely fashion.[21] But there is no sign that they were ever passed to the new Hydrographer, Thomas Hurd, who might then have modified the jaundiced tone of his judgement.

✳

Hurd's comments undoubtedly reflected frustration. He had never had command of one of His Majesty's surveying vessels for his own endeavours on the western parts of the vulnerable invasion coasts. He was on half-pay throughout, being paid expenses and an allowance for stationery, and additional pay whilst engaged on the survey which increased from 1 guinea to 30 shillings per day. He rendered his first results in May 1806, a resurvey of Falmouth and approaches which Dalrymple had requested as part of his efforts to improve chart coverage in the English Channel.[22] Hurd identified a suitable anchorage there for vessels of the blockading force off Brest when taking refuge from westerly gales.[23] In August 1807 the Admiralty put into effect a proposal from Hurd to alleviate the difficulties arising from the lack of an allocated survey vessel. He was authorised to employ the revenue cutters stationed in the Channel, splitting his work into segments centred on their home ports of Falmouth, Fowey, Dartmouth, Weymouth and Poole.[24]

During this time he was himself subjected to critical comment within the Admiralty. Graeme Spence, the talented civilian surveyor whom the Board had employed in home waters, still had an office in which he was drawing up his detailed surveys. He alleged that Hurd was not aware of new techniques.[25] But this is not borne out by Hurd's correspondence with the Admiralty, which gives every indication of alertness to beneficial developments. Hurd was selected by Dalrymple because of his competence in control by horizontal sextant angles, a methodology of particular merit now that the Trigonometrical Survey extended a firm network of surveyed positions along the south-west coast.[26] Once shown the station pointer which Spence had invented to facilitate the plotting of the angles, Hurd applied to have one, and the Admiralty Board approved the order for manufacture. Surviving catalogues of the instrument manufacturers suggest limited production of station pointers at this time

19. *A station pointer in use, with the two observed angles set and the arms aligned with the plotted positions of the three shore stations used for the fix. In this modern instrument a pencil is inserted into an aperture in the centre of the instrument to mark the fixed position. The earliest models were fitted with a needle at the centre which was liable to tear the plotting sheet, and this was a further discouragement to carrying out the plotting whilst underway rather than retrospectively once at anchor or, better still, ashore.*

to meet such individual orders.[27] When preparing for the 'survey of the sea coast from Poole to the Lizard', he asked permission to purchase copies of Faden's published sheets of the Trigonometrical Survey and an improved pattern of compass, and he secured issue of a 'Massey's Machine for taking soundings' (see Glossary).[28] His final season in the field, following the presentation of and follow-up to the Chart Committee report, was on the coast between the Needles and Start Point.[29]

The war-time survey for which Hurd is justifiably best remembered was made in the very front line of operations, off Brest, where the ships of the Channel Fleet's Inshore Squadron faced the perils of

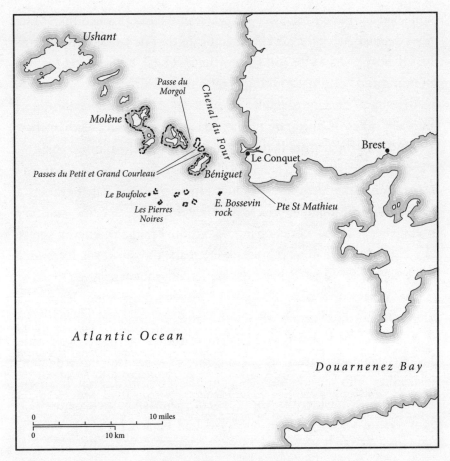

Map 6. Approaches to Brest.

onshore gales and the 'tides and rocks' which had given Rear Admiral Collingwood restless nights. Captains soon discovered that neither the products of the commercial chart publishers in London nor the official atlases of the French government furnished completely reliable navigational guidance. In 1800, Captain John Knight, in command of *Montagu* (74), was assigned by St Vincent to the advanced squadron. Like Hurd, he had worked with the land surveyors in North America, and thereafter he had been assiduous in gathering hydrographic data and having it published. He lost no time in making his own surveys, which resulted in four charts published by Faden together with a set of sailing directions.[30] The more detailed, larger-scale charts indicate that he landed on some of the offshore islets to fix and survey them. The *Montagu*'s log records sounding and bottom-sampling in the ship and all her boats. Memoirs on the charts declare that 'all the adjacent dangers are shown', and there are notes on the state of the tide at which many of them first show. Where the feature had not been fixed, and the plotted position is approximate, this was indicated. These are fine examples of front-line reconnaissance surveys, produced in a tight timescale to satisfy a demanding commander-in-chief. They included specific military intelligence, such as notes of the operational range of enemy shells. The circumstances in which they were made did, however, introduce one error which was to have dramatic consequences at the height of the invasion threat. Knight's directions stipulated leaving a safe distance of a league off all the lesser islands between Pointe St Mathieu and Ushant, and he had run lines of soundings inside this recommended track to delineate the hazards. Unfortunately, misleading information on some of the published French charts led Knight to misidentify the dangerous outlying rock named Le Boufoloc on which *Magnificent* (74) had been wrecked in March 1804 whilst patrolling as part of the Inshore Squadron.[31]

Admiral Graves had no hesitation in nominating a qualified man to investigate the circumstances of this blow to his squadron. His Flag Captain in *Foudroyant* (74) was Peter Puget, another of Vancouver's lieutenants, who had subsequently earned the interest of Admiral St Vincent, reached post rank and spent the closing years of the French Revolutionary War in command of 74-gun ships in these waters. He was busy at this very time, drawing on his knowledge to put the final touches to a plan for a fireship attack on the French fleet in Brest.[32] The Admiralty, however, had made a different choice. Evidence of Hurd's competence was at hand, and it is undoubtedly significant that his main recommendations for a base at Bermuda would be endorsed only a few months later.[33] By the end of

May the Board had approved the issue of the instruments which he required and the hire of a chaise and pair of horses to bear them safely to Plymouth. Hurd embarked in *Terrible* (74) on Sunday 16 June. Given that he would require to work very close to the enemy coast, his task was not cloaked in secrecy, and by the following Wednesday the departure of 'this experienced officer' was being broadcast in papers and journals.[34]

Many yachtsmen today follow in the wake of the chasse-marées and other French coastal craft which threaded the inshore channels of the Breton coast carrying supplies to Napoleon's fleet in Brest. Even though these modern craft can resort to mechanical propulsion, their helmsmen heed the caution in the *Sailing Directions*: 'The area between Île d'Ouessant and the mainland SE is encumbered by islands, reefs, and shoals, which it is imprudent to approach without local knowledge.'

These were the waters where Hurd would work from small, oared boats, waters where the *Directions* warn of being set towards the dangers 'in thick weather' and where exposed bays are subject to swell and 'heavy breaking seas'.[35] His progress would depend on days of calm 'or when the wind is moderate and off the land'.[36] Those of us who have spent long days in sounding boats, exposed to the elements, constantly balancing against the lively motion in a seaway, can enter some way into Hurd's experience – though we had advantages of an engine and a cockpit for occasional shelter, whilst he was in an open boat. We can imagine him wiping the spray from the lens of his sextant and watching for the emergence of his fixing marks from passing rain squalls, all the time alert for the changes in soundings called by the leadsman.

His impressive achievement in this summer of 1804 can be seen in the detailed record, preserved in the Hydrographic Office archive, from which the picture painted in the prologue to this book was drawn. He showed admirable coolness in his prolonged occupation of the un-garrisoned islands and the skerries. Hurd measured two

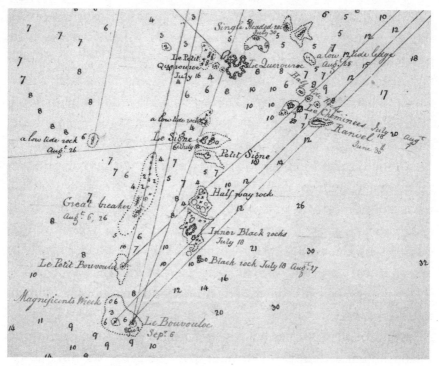

20. *Detail from Hurd's plot showing the dangers around Le Boufoloc and the wreck of the* Magnificent. *The dates of occupying each station, including ship stations over shoal soundings, are shown and agree with the record preserved in Hurd's remark book.*

baselines with his 100-foot chain on Béniguet.[37] It is hard to believe that he went unnoticed as he deployed from *Diamond*'s boats, landing on the East Bossevin rock and twenty-nine other stations. Here he used his theodolite and sextant of 9-inch radius to extend a network of triangulation out to a total of fifty-seven stations on the inner fringes of the archipelago. As well as the Boufoloc and the nearby wreck of the *Magnificent*, they included both major features and small drying rocks, and fleet anchorage positions off Les Pierres Noires, the dreaded Black Rocks. Compass bearings to conspicuous and prominent marks, probably taken with his 'Miner's compass with sights', were recorded alongside the observed angles.

Another remarkable survival, a plot of this first season's work, shows how he built up his survey on this framework of control.[38] He laid it down on six sheets of tracing paper which had been pasted together and to a wooden roller. He then laid this composite sheet over another on which the triangulation and subsequent fixes would have been plotted. The survey detail could then be added from the record in a notebook carried in the sounding boat. The scale of Hurd's plot, 1 nautical mile represented as 1.6 inches, is twice that of the eventual published chart. In the bottom right-hand corner he has recorded the observed bearings of the Pointe du Raz that would be needed to lay down the coastline at smaller scale. There is further evidence of careful selection of the information which would be shown on the chart, particularly the marks for dangers.

At the end of this work season, Hurd knew that much remained to be done, and he had a grasp of the challenges and frustrations of the task, not least because he was operating without a self-sufficient establishment. Admiral Cornwallis had allocated the brig-sloop *Rambler* as 'a proper vessel' to employ in examining the area of the wreck of *Magnificent* and obtaining an exact position, 'while their Lordships endeavour to find a person qualified to make a survey of that part of the coast'.[39] By the time Hurd arrived on scene, she does not seem to have been available. He relied on the cutters of the frigates *Diamond* (38), *Santa Margarita* (36) and *Sirius* (36) to transport him ashore and to take soundings. These ships were familiar with the duties of the Inshore Squadron and the attendant dangers. The following year, the master in *Santa Margarita*, Mr William Lowes, humbly rendered 'the only remarks that could be made'. In fact, these comprised a careful list of soundings and natures of the seabed in the Bay of Brest, with bearings and tidal information, together with marks, bearings and soundings over Le Boufoloc and another shoal about a cable to the north-east by north.[40] Writing from on board *Santa Margarita*, Hurd had explained his difficulties to Admiral Cornwallis. He was happy to pay tribute to the support that the ships had given him, but he noted that because of their other duties on station he often spent half the working day on transit to and from his survey area. Moreover, in westerly winds they kept well to seaward of the areas he needed to examine.

Hurd was based in *Diamond* from 1 July to 29 August. After the initial work to establish control, Captain Thomas Elphinstone mentions the specific deployment of boats to survey on only five days. He had, however, taken his ship into the close proximity of dangers such as the Basse du Lis to enable Hurd to fix them. Hurd spent eight days in *Santa Margarita*. He joined her at anchor off Ushant in thick, hazy weather. On 6 September the fog cleared as the frigate shifted berth to the vicinity of the Black Rocks, and he got away to survey in the large cutter, taking observations on the Boufoloc. At 8 a.m. the following day the captain 'sent the Boats with Captain Hurd on a survey'. Only three and a half hours later they were recalled.[41] He spent 9 September surveying round the Black Rocks with two boats from *Sirius*.[42] These snippets from the logs are consistent with the density of boat-sounding to the south of Béniguet on Hurd's survey sheet and with the lines of soundings and spot depths recorded from the frigates as they carried him to fix the outlying dangers such as La Vandrée and Basse de la Parquette.

These statistics support his representation to Cornwallis that he needed 'a proper boat for my own particular use' and the ability 'occasionally to take one of the cutters or schooners to attend me in my distant work'.[43] He undoubtedly reiterated these views to the Admiral when he called on him two days before return to Plymouth, from where he wrote a letter to the Board of Admiralty laying out his argument: 'amongst very strong tides where it is necessary at all times to have one man constantly at the lead, and frequently two, these [...] six-oared [...] boats do not possess either the requisite strength of men [...] or sufficient room for myself and the different instruments I must necessarily use.'

The shifting between ships had also meant that he could not work up a proper team. He urged that the task would be expedited by 'the

21. This contemporary image of a sounding boat shows the constraints of space which Hurd described.

constant attendance of a suitable vessel of an easy draft of water with proper boats and conveniences'. He emphasised that this was work in a combat zone: 'Could I have free access to the shore, most of these impediments would be of little consequence, but under all these circumstances the task I have to perform is both a difficult and tedious one.'

As the autumn approached and he faced 'contrary winds, much fog and extreme hazy weather', Hurd sought permission to come to the Hydrographical Office to lay down his work and compare it with any records that might be found there, 'as well as to supply myself with such things as are wanting, particularly a few good Boat compasses on a proper construction'.[44]

In London, Hurd prepared a report for the First Lord based on his observations from 'these last four months employed on a nautical survey of the seacoast in the neighbourhood of Brest'. He argued for the occupation of Ushant and Molène, to deprive the French of the line of telegraphs by which they received intelligence of the movements of the British squadrons. He noted that from there it would be possible to send observers to watch the French coast from the smaller islets further inshore where he had been making his observations. He stressed also that Ushant and Molène lay on either hand of the 'fair and open channel' which John Knight had identified 'by which our whole fleet might pass through whenever it was necessary'. He had also discussed with Lord Melville the use of Douarnenez Bay as a refuge in westerly winds. His report was now despatched to Admiral Cornwallis under cover of a 'Private and Secret' letter urging the importance of evaluating these options 'at this crisis'.[45] As the campaign of Trafalgar unfolded, Hurd was confined by the prevailing westerly winds to the English coast. Here he continued the survey of Falmouth and approaches, progressing along the coast past Helford to the great hazard of the Manacles, working up the results during the winter.[46]

As the spring of 1806 slipped past without directions from the Admiralty Board, Hurd wrote to clarify their intentions. On 30 May he was directed to resume work in the Bay of Brest. During the summer, through the influence of Rear Admiral Markham, he had the use of the revenue cutter *Ranger*.[47] Hurd complimented the commander for his 'great zeal and attentive assiduity' but noted that her sharp hull, 13-foot draught and low deck made her a hazardous platform amongst the islands between Ushant and the main. When the cutter returned to Plymouth for refit, Hurd spotted the gun-brig *Conflict*. Some forty years earlier, James Cook had urged the many benefits of the brig configuration, not least the stopping power provided by square sails laid aback when encountering unexpected dangers.[48] Hurd requested the allocation of *Conflict* for his work, and the Board issued the necessary orders.[49] In *Ranger* and *Conflict* Hurd probed the complex area west of Béniguet Island. But each autumn he reported the same shortcoming:

My great and principal want in carrying on the survey of the French coast is well-manned boats, which [...] are only to be procured from the Inshore Ships when stationary in the bay: but as from the appearances and general uncertainty of the weather joined to the increased length of the nights at this season of the year the Squadron are very cautious of trusting themselves at anchor I am left without a possibility of doing anything further than taking a few soundings as the ships occasionally work in and out of the bay.[50]

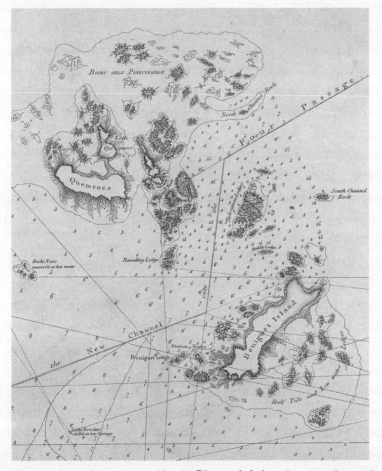

22. *Extract from Chart 43 in Hurd's* Channel Atlas *showing the results of his survey of the 'New Channel' for exploitation by the fleet.*

His painstaking work had, however, now fully surveyed the channels that are called the Passes du Morgol et du Grand et Petit Courleau on today's charts. He reported that these would allow the Royal Navy to penetrate the Chenal du Four, the highway for coastal traffic from Normandy bringing supplies to Brest, without coming in range of the heavy batteries at Le Conquet and Pointe St Mathieu.[51] In a fresh plan for a closer blockade, Peter Puget had already noted the advantage that Hurd's discovery gave to ships close in between St Matthew's and the Black Rocks if the onset of onshore winds made it necessary to put to sea.[52] Hurd paid particular attention to the interests of the squadrons off Brest as he superintended the publication under his name of the charts based on his work. A larger-scale chart which appeared in 1809 depicted his 'New Channel' leading into Le Four. A smaller-scale chart was also included in a printed set of directions entitled *A Nautical Description of the Bay of Brest with indications for its navigation; also for A NEW CHANNEL into the FOUR*.[53] This was illustrated with a series of plates showing profile views of the main dangers, such as the Boufoloc, with least depths and bearings from them to prominent marks ashore. This was a handy methodology for an area where a veteran of the Brest blockade in the Seven Years' War had declared 'this is all Pilotage Navigation, and recourse must be had to the different marks on the Land for avoiding the Rocks and Shoals that lye along the coast'.[54] Wherever possible, Hurd used natural transits – that is, two conspicuous objects which, when brought in line, keep a vessel on a safe track or indicate where a danger lies without recourse to an instrumental observation. In other instances, the navigator could keep his ship in safe waters by observing the bearings of the marks or the angle between them. Pulls have survived from the cancelled plates for the diagrams of dangers, suggesting that Hurd may also have issued them as small 'Fleet Charts' to the vessels in the blockading squadrons.[55]

All in all, the rigour of this survey, conducted within sight of the enemy and without access to the mainland coast, makes it one of the most remarkable products of the period. Hurd's own later verdict, in a letter to Rear Admiral Hallowell in 1815, is worth quoting:

A new chart of the Bay of Brest is now in the hands of the engravers formed from my own surveys thereof, and from the last corrected edition of Cassini's great map of France, in which has been introduced everything this office has been favoured with from Mr Sidley's observations and remarks, as well as from other officers, who have contributed their mite of information. This chart will I flatter myself be both useful and satisfactory [...].[56]

His results off Brest confirm that Hurd was unquestionably a thoroughly experienced practitioner, who could also supplement his chart with a pragmatic seaman's sailing directions based on his careful field notes at each station. He was certainly aware of the limitations of his work. A note to the record of the compass bearings for a 'spot of foul ground in the Bay of Brest' declares: 'As I suspect there are many such spots in this extensive Bay, it would be a proper precaution to sound about every ship to a certain distance whenever an anchor is let go.' There can be little doubt that it was this front-line work which made Hurd the Admiralty's choice both as member of the advisory Chart Committee and then to succeed Alexander Dalrymple as a number of demanding major campaigns in testing waters got underway. Not only was it rigorous, but also, like his contemporary John Knight, he had kept an operational perspective, ensuring a focus on data-gathering of immediate interest to deployed commanders.

He had also demonstrated powers of analysis and confidence in proposing improved organisation for hydrographic support to the fleet. His own experience of working from vessels of convenience sharpened his case for the commissioning of survey vessels for the Royal Navy. A letter written in July 1807 reiterated the difficulties which he had experienced off Brest without permanent allocation of a suitable vessel properly fitted out, 'capable of stowing the necessary boats adapted to it and possessing accommodations of sufficient extent to allow the surveyor and his assistants both room and light enough to lay down their work as it occurs or whenever the opportunity of moderate weather may permit of its being done'.

As Hydrographer, no doubt with his experience in *Conflict* in mind, Hurd would secure the allocation of four gun-brigs as survey ships, and they gave sterling service in home waters, the Mediterranean and Newfoundland, whilst another took part in the search for the North-West Passage. Furthermore, his experience off Brest had underlined the need for 'some regular and fixed assistance'.[57] Once in post as Hydrographer, he was unflagging in his support of requests from his surveyors for suitably skilled assistants.

What is crystal clear in the letter is that his field experiences had already spawned the great objective which he would pursue as Hydrographer:

> I feel it a duty incumbent upon me to make this representation of the insufficiency of the means to the accomplishment of their Lordships wishes and intentions in ordering me on this service and trust it will have the good effect of showing the great necessity there is for an establishment being formed of officers and scientific young men who being early initiated in the practice of this employment may be thereby rendered useful and capable of making nautical surveys in whatever part of the world their future services may happen to place them in.[58]

He would be on the watch for such men, potential Admiralty Surveyors like William Henry Smyth, as major campaigns got underway within months of his assumption of the post of Hydrographer. These campaigns are considered in the next chapters.

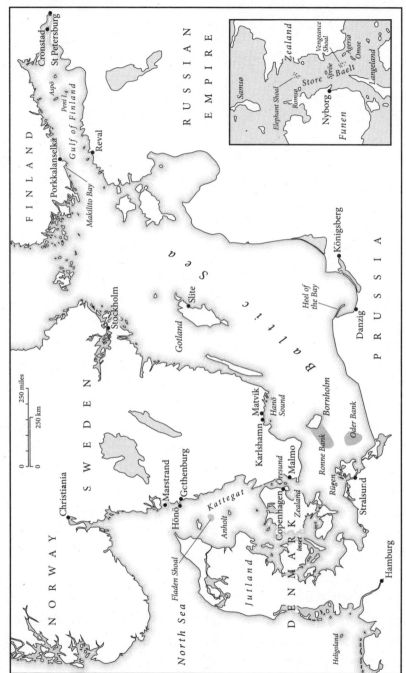

Map 7. *Baltic Sea.*

CHAPTER 5

Sea Power Projection
Northern Europe

The victories secured by British sea power in 1805 were balanced by Napoleon's military domination of the European continent. Now there were threats of pressure to cut off British exports and imports, especially Baltic naval stores, and to build up a new naval threat through alliance or by seizure of fleets. In 1807 false intelligence that the Danish fleet was ready to sail, and the fear that it might fall under French control, led to the implementation in under ten days of a British plan for intervention. Dalrymple played a distinguished part, supplying a significant collection of information, including the best published charts and sailing directions, but supplemented with primary material from Royal Naval sources. These reflected past experience of the challenge of identifying safe tracks for British warships, which were of deeper draught than those of the navies in the shallow Baltic Sea. Admiral Gambier's fleet was supplied with manuscript sailing directions, fifty-six copies of directions printed in the Hydrographical Office and fifty-nine copies of a draft chart based on a survey of the Great Belt made by Thomas Atkinson in 1801.[1] That survey had earned Nelson the Admiralty's approval for 'having attended to that essential part of your duty'.[2] The campaign of Copenhagen in 1801 had indeed brought the traditional practitioners of the fleet to the forefront, for hydrographic intelligence was as critical as it had been in Aboukir Bay.

Dalrymple annotated one set of master's remarks from the Baltic: 'By Mr Briarly Master of the *Bellona* a very clever man known to Lord St Vincent when he was master of the *Audacious*'.[3] Briarly had certainly caught the eye of St Vincent, who had transferred him to *Thalia* (36) as part of the team to back up Nelson's wayward stepson, Captain Josiah Nisbet. With characteristic courtesy, Nelson had told Briarly that, whilst 'a tutor was needed' and he would welcome his presence there, he trusted that he would be content with a move into a ship of lower rate. After a torrid experience, Briarly was discharged in Minorca in September 1800.[4] In England he saw his Mediterranean charts through to publication and was ready to take up a warrant for *Bellona* (74), Captain Sir Thomas Thompson, at the end of January 1801.[5] He was poised to take part in another of Nelson's victories, and, ever the self-publicist, he would have been delighted at the record in some secondary sources and historical fiction. These have dramatised Nelson's famous confrontation with reluctant pilots on the morning of the battle, during which Briarly, undoubtedly eager to safeguard his standing with Nelson, broke the tension by volunteering to lead the fleet round the shoals and into the King's Deep. They go on to state that he piloted *Edgar* (74) at the head of the line.[6] His own logs and the detailed account preserved by Midshipman William Anderson show that this did not happen.[7] His true contribution was acknowledged in a prized testimonial from Nelson:

> These are to certify that I have known the abilities of Mr Alexander Briarly for several years, and on the morning of the second of April Mr Briarly was particularly useful to me in sounding and taking marks which I gave out to the squadron, which gave my mind more ease than any opinions I could get from the Pilots and I venture to recommend Mr Briarly for any preferment Government may think proper to give him.[8]

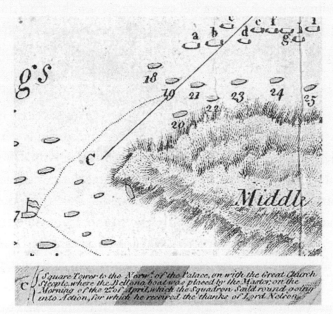

23. *Details from Briarly's plan of the battle of Copenhagen.* Bellona *is number 22.*

The pilots had been particularly concerned about the extent of the southern end of the Middle Ground, and Briarly's log confirms that he took the final soundings and placed a buoy and boat, after which the signal was made for the attack to begin.[9] Hence, it must have been especially galling to him that *Bellona* herself would strike on a spur on the north side of the shoal as she manoeuvred past the disengaged side of consorts which were already in action but which had not closed the enemy as much as Nelson wished. Briarly would show his marks for clearing the tip of the Middle Ground, and emphasise the narrow gap where *Bellona* came to grief, on another battle plan, rather more accomplished than his earlier one of Aboukir Bay, with much more information and embellishment.

Midshipman Anderson, a talented artist who had set about producing some representations of the action, noted that Briarly, who 'likewise draws very well; he and I are on very friendly terms', intended to publish 'a plate of the Grounds of Copenhagen and the small vignettes of the Battle' for which 'the subscribers [...] pay half a guinea each'.[10] It is one of two broadsides of 1802 bearing Briarly's name which were designed to meet the huge public interest in the battle.[11] A prominent legend, with supporting text boxes, defends Nelson's conduct, as well as recording Briarly's previous service at Aboukir Bay. There are comprehensive directions keyed to the marks on the plan, recording depths on the shoals and in the channels. The shoals are clearly delineated with the positions of the small craft which buoyed the Outer Deep. Briarly would receive a letter from Nelson praising the plan as 'correct and leaving nothing to be desired'. He had told the Prime Minister of his indebtedness to Briarly's efforts and that he could never forget the confidence which he gained from the marks, soundings and other observations, which enabled him to attack in full confidence of success. His letter ended with the hope that Briarly would call on him.[12]

Briarly ensured another reference in the history books with the publication in the *Naval Chronicle* of an extract from a letter to his wife Maria describing Nelson's subsequent boat journey into the Baltic and extolling 'the singular and unbounded zeal of this truly great man'.[13] Faced by contrary winds, Nelson had left his deep-draught flagship *St George* (98). She had been lightened and manoeuvred across the shoals at the southern end of the Sound (Öresund) through the 'excellent management' of Briarly, whose 'local experience was very great'.[14] The grounds of this reputation remain to be identified, along with other details of his life before 1795. Back on board *Bellona*, Briarly would contribute to the data-gathering whilst Nelson's fleet lay off Revel. His log records that he went away sounding in the yawl, and one copy of his sailing directions refers to an accompanying survey which has not survived.[15]

There is indeed little evidence that the sounding work of Briarly and others in the front line in the lead-up to the first battle of Copenhagen was recorded and rendered to the Admiralty. One exception is a report from a team of five masters sent by Admiral Hyde Parker in the brig-sloop *Kite* (16) to check the reliability of the published charts of the Great Belt.[16] The team included Thomas Atkinson of *St George* and Alexander Parker of *Polyphemus* (64), who had already reported the shoal north of Romsø Island which still bears his ship's name. The directions prepared by this strong team set out details of leading and thwart marks for dangers, illustrated in three views.[17] Following the battle Atkinson made his detailed survey of the Great Belt and forwarded another set of directions made with Parker and the master of *Amazon* (38), complete with recommendations for positioning small vessels to buoy the passage for a fleet. This was the information which would benefit the 1807 campaign.

It is particularly noteworthy, however, given the pressure under which Dalrymple's team was working, that the proof chart supplied to Gambier's fleet is not a straightforward engraving of Atkinson's survey. It gives clear indication of careful comparison of sources and of compilation. The Hydrographer took account of reports from *Vengeance* (74) of dangers not detected during Atkinson's work and added them to the proof chart in red.[18] A survey by the master, James Squire, of a shoal in the narrows between Langeland and Agersø had found a least depth of 18 feet. Vengeance Shoal (Vengeancegrund) is still so named on the modern-day chart, just one of several dangers commemorating the British capital ships of this period. This was vital hydrographic intelligence for the safe deployment of Gambier's ships to secure a key objective of the campaign, the isolation of Zealand and the prevention of the passage of Danish or French reinforcements from the mainland.[19]

Although Dalrymple would complain later that none of the data which he had supplied for the 1807 expedition had been returned to the Hydrographical Office, it had clearly encouraged the rendering of

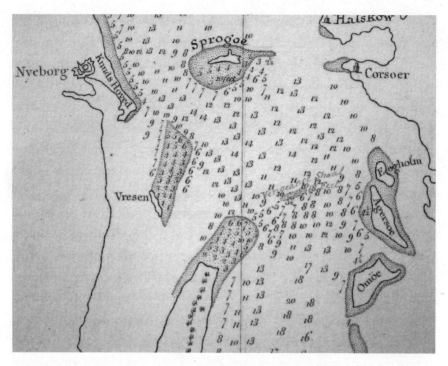

24. *Thomas Atkinson's survey had not detected the 3-fathom shoal on which* Vengeance *(74) struck whilst on passage through the Great Belt, and it was added in red on the proof chart supplied to Gambier's ships in 1807.*

new information.[20] Officers and masters with Gambier off Copenhagen had been employed once again in sounding and laying buoys, as well as in the troop landings and preparation of the captured Danish fleet for sea.[21] A fine 'Chart of the Grounds survey'd and buoy'd by Edward Strode, Master, HMS CENTAUR, August 1807' (Plate 8) was drawn by Lieutenant George Lawrance, a veteran of service with William Bligh. It is complete with a view of the city showing the advanced squadron commanded by Captain Peter Puget exchanging fire with the Trekroner battery and Danish gunboats. The chart gives ample evidence of Strode's competence as a hydrographic practitioner. It shows the bearings that he observed to fix the positions where he placed buoys on the shoals. With Lawrance's assistance he had laid down a thorough and regular pattern of soundings in the channels. He had applied his astronomical skill to observe latitude and longitude. There is, in fact, no evidence that this chart ever reached the Admiralty.[22] However, Strode, veteran of Aboukir Bay and of Columbine's surveys in *Ulysses*, kept a meticulous set of remarks which survive in the Hydrographic Office archive. On return from the operation, Gambier forwarded other remark books and reports to the Hydrographer.[23] Data would continue to flow in when Admiral Saumarez's new Baltic command was formed in the spring of 1808 in response to an appeal for support to Sweden. Mastery of this information and early re-dissemination to ships in theatre was a top priority for Thomas Hurd as he established himself in the rooms of the Hydrographical Office on the attic floor above the Admiralty board room.

A squadron of four ships of the line was maintained in the Sound to protect convoys passing east of Zealand. In 1813 Captain Francis Austen, brother of the novelist, deployed in the theatre. He was tasked with sounding the greatest danger in the Kattegat, the reef extending from the island of Anholt.[24] When the Danes built up a force of gunboats which posed a major threat to the convoys, British attention switched back to the Great Belt. Austen undertook a thorough examination of the route, and the Elefantgrund, named after his ship, remains on the present-day chart. Austen's surveys were published promptly by Thomas Hurd, together with all the earlier Royal Naval work.[25] Austen was another officer whose hydrographic interests and application were well known to the Hydrographer. They had undoubtedly played a part in his promotion to Lieutenant by Commodore Cornwallis and his appointment, albeit briefly, to the survey vessel *Dispatch* in the East Indies.[26] Austen subsequently rendered a list of positions from all the theatres in which he served, based on astronomical and chronometric observations. His papers in the National Maritime Museum contain notes on methodology for surveying coasts and harbours, and a dissertation on chronometric measurements which had been passed to him for informed comment.[27] There are also copies of a number of most competent sketch surveys through to the very end of his career, illustrating techniques such as 'starring' from anchorage positions and delineating shoals by running zigzag lines until the defining contour was crossed.[28] These same techniques were used in the Baltic, and Austen is most careful to note instances where time did not permit full examination of dangers. The standards which he attained when circumstances permitted are indicated in the following comment on the survey work encompassing the Elephant Shoal:

> The chart, which the foregoing remarks are intended to accompany, was constructed on Trigonometrical Principals [sic], the most remarkable points and objects being laid down from bases measured on Spröe and Romsoe, connected together and verified by numerous sets of angles in various situations.
>
> The shape of such parts of the coasts as there was no means of accurately determining was taken from Arrowsmith's large chart of the Belt. The whole of the soundings were taken either on board the *Elephant*, or in her boats, or on board the *Mariner* and *Earnest* gun brigs under my own personal inspection, and the position of a great part of them determined by angles between 3 or more known objects carefully measured with a sextant, the intermediate casts of the lead being placed by estimation of time and distance.[29]

Other units deployed deeper into the Baltic Sea and on into the Gulf of Finland to deter Russian naval intervention and to protect trade passing through this area of shoal water, tortuous coastlines and complex coastal archipelagos and skerries. They had urgent need of good navigational data. One of the active squadrons in the Gulf of Finland was commanded by Captain Thomas Byam Martin, who would later, as Commissioner at the Navy Board, correspond regularly with Hydrographer Hurd. He forwarded remarks for the sea area by Thomas Moore, master of *Implacable* (74), including directions for the important trading port of Danzig.[30] He also sent a survey of Danzig Bay by the future polar explorer John Ross.[31] Ross had made three peace-time voyages to the Baltic in the merchant service, during which he became fluent in Swedish. At the outbreak of the Napoleonic Wars he was appointed to Saumarez's flagship and served as a highly valued liaison officer with the Swedish fleet. From 28 July to 9 October 1809 he was appointed in acting command of the sloop *Ariel* and 'detached on a particular service'.[32] No logs have survived for the period, but he appears to have been tasked to assess the potential of Danzig Bay as an anchorage in which to gather homebound convoys. Ross focused his reconnaissance on the bight within the Heel of Danzig (Zatoka Pucka), which Byam Martin had assessed to be suitable as a summer rendezvous for the Baltic trade. His delineation of the shoals at the head of the bay would confirm the danger of early formation of sea ice, which was one of the major factors which led Saumarez to reject it and other anchorages in the southern part of the sea for use by the convoys. His judgement is supported by today's *Sailing Directions*, where it is noted that in a hard winter ice cover can persist for over 120 days. Martin's advice and Saumarez's conclusion were included in a transcript of information which was drawn up for Admiral Napier in 1853 during war with Russia.[33]

The convoys were gathered instead in an important secret rendezvous, Hanö Sound on the south coast of Sweden, where there were two harbours, Matvik and Karlshamn.[34] A British secret agent commented on the downside of this remote location where, with Swedish connivance, a base was established and shielded from French intelligence gathering. It was, he suggested, 'rather disadvantageous from being in a corner and difficult to get out of' and there was clear need for a chart.[35] The plan which the Hydrographical Office produced for this area was based on the work of Mr James Lash in the 64-gun ship *Ruby*. He was in the Navy Board's list of North Sea

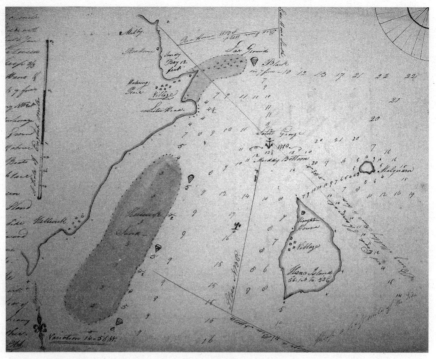

25. Mr Jeremiah Beltt's plan of the anchorage in Hanö Sound.

masters, and his correspondence with them suggests a background in the Baltic trade. Another plan of the vicinity of Hanö Sound origin- ated from Mr Jeremiah Beltt, Rear Admiral Reynolds' master in *St George* (98).[36] He noted: 'All the soundings are laid down in feet as there are a number of sunken rocks and shoals with less than a fathom water on them'. He would have used his survey when bringing the severely disabled *St George* into Matvik Harbour in November 1811 after the homebound convoy it was escorting was hit by a gale. The British commanders were now faced with a dilemma. If the convoy stayed in Swedish waters, it ran the risk of an embargo; if it sailed, experienced Baltic hands doubted that it could be taken safely through the Belt and Kattegat at the advanced season of the year. The feat was achieved with the help of active hydrographic practi- tioners on the station, who buoyed the Malmo passage and conducted

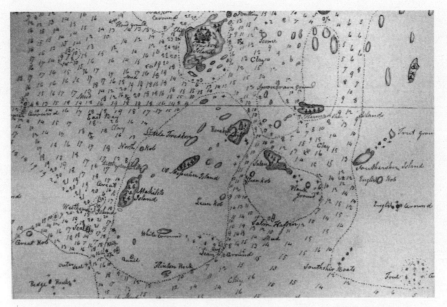

26. *Detail of James Reeves' survey of the approaches to Makilito Bay.*
The dotted boundary indicates areas where passage should not be
attempted amongst the islets and rocks.

the pilotage at the head of the convoy. Tragically, in the meantime, the crippled *St George* and *Defence* had been wrecked on the west coast of Jutland in one of the costliest disasters of the Napoleonic Wars. Beltt was not a survivor. He left a widow, who hailed, like himself, from the parish of Warwick in Bermuda.[37]

Once again, the masters in the fleet played a full part in the efforts to provide hydrographic intelligence in a demanding theatre. In May 1810 Saumarez wrote to the Admiralty, urging the benefit of having a Surveying Master appointed to his command. He proposed to embark this practitioner in one of the small vessels under his orders. He recommended Mr James Reeves of *Bellerophon* (74). To indicate the competence of his nominee, Saumarez forwarded a survey which Reeves had made during operations in complex inshore waters. *Defence* (74) and *Bellerophon* had been stationed on the coast of Finland in 'Makilito Bay', an anchorage north of the island of

Mäkiluoto and on the flank of the route through the archipelagos at the east side of Porkkalanselkä. Their presence forced the Russians to run heavily defended convoys of provisions even closer inshore under their batteries.[38] Reeves had ample experience of inshore operations during earlier service in the frigate *Clyde* with Captain Charles Cunningham, a bold commander with a keen appreciation of hydrography.[39] His survey is an example of earnest rapid environmental assessment.[40] He is particularly careful to indicate the limitations in his examination of areas adjacent to the western and eastern entrances to the bay. His comprehensive key also indicates areas 'where it is improper to attempt a passage between the islands and rocks'. His survey was incorporated in the war-time charts issued for the fleet.

Saumarez's suggestion was now referred to the Hydrographer, and Hurd's response is worth quoting in full:

Great benefit would no doubt arise to the Naval Service were a Surveying Master employed, not only with the Baltic Fleet, but with the Commanders in Chief on every one of the Stations. The Master so appointed should however thoroughly understand the principles of Nautical Surveying and be capable of using the various instruments necessary in making them. I have no further knowledge of the person's abilities who has thus offered his services to Sir James Saumarez than what appears in the specimen of his works accompanying these Remarks. In making this sketch of Makilota [sic] Bay I presume no other instruments were used than a compass, and it is needless to state to the Board that surveys so made are of very little use to science: they may serve as memorandums of existing dangers in particular places and as such materially aid the memory of the person who makes them but cannot otherways be employed for the general benefit of navigation.[41]

This judgement was conveyed to Saumarez, who was authorised to employ a Surveying Master 'if he can find a person fully qualified to perform the duty <u>scientifically</u> but not otherwise'. Later that year Reeves petitioned the Board in vain to be employed on the surveying service in the Baltic.[42] Saumarez did not give up, and in April 1811 he secured agreement that Reeves be put under his orders to take soundings in the Kattegat and Belt.[43] He encouraged the endeavours of other practitioners on station when Reeves was invalided later that year. At the very end of the season in 1814, James Squire, now Master of the Baltic Fleet, embarked in the cutter *Algerine* to sound, delineate dangers and lay down recommended tracks in the leads offering sheltered passage along the Swedish coast from Marstrand to Hönö.[44]

Saumarez's proposal and its reception mark a most significant point in the narrative of this book. The incident also encapsulates a tension that remains today. Champions on the Admiralty Board saw the importance of encouraging those in the fleet who appreciated the value of rapid environmental assessment and who made the best use of the means available to them. The interest and connections of the Naval Lords ensured that the surveys of such motivated individuals were published and reissued for the benefit of the Baltic squadrons in their vital role of influencing the decision-making of the littoral states. But Thomas Hurd was looking for a step change in capability which would benefit the task of compilation and promulgation of sound navigational guidance in official publications – guidance which would be dusted off when access by the fleet to the Baltic became a major issue once more in the mid-century. He convinced the Board to examine critically the qualifications of a practitioner selected for a specialist data-gathering role. He had identified several suitable men, some of them masters. One of them was brought to notice by efforts on another testing war-time station in Northern Europe.

Britain rather than France had acquired the Danish fleet, and her warships had also escorted the Portuguese fleet to Brazil. Napoleon's efforts were now focused on a major ship-building programme and

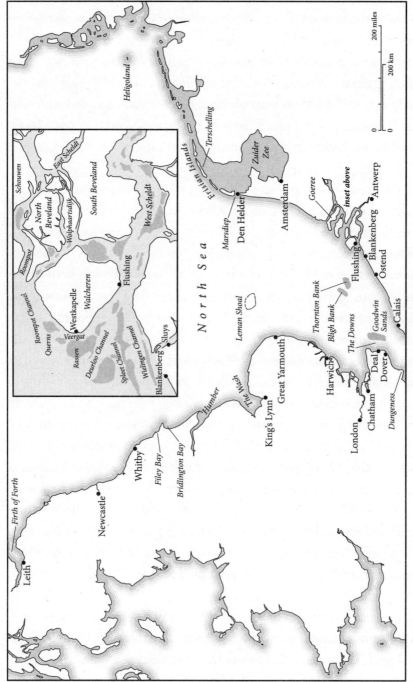

Map 8. Southern North Sea.

North Sea

Leith
Firth of Forth
Newcastle
Whitby
Filey Bay
Bridlington Bay
Humber
The Wash
King's Lynn
Great Yarmouth
Leman Shoal
London
Chatham
Harwich
The Downs
Deal
Dover
Dungeness
Goodwin Sands
Calais
Ostend
Blankenberg
Flushing
Bligh Bank
Thornton Bank
Antwerp
inset above
Goeree
Amsterdam
Zuider Zee
Den Helder
Marsdiep
Terschelling
Frisian Islands
Heligoland

Schouwen
East Scheldt
North Beveland
South Beveland
West Scheldt
Roompot
Wolphaartsdijk
Roompot Channel
Querns
Rassen
Veergat
Westkapelle
Walcheren
Deurloo Channel
Splet Channel
Wielingen Channel
Blankenberg
Sluys
Flushing

200 miles
200 km

– 116 –

the development of Antwerp to turn the Scheldt into the 'pistol pointed at the heart of England'.[45] Data from this quarter was another priority for Thomas Hurd as he took post, for he shared with other practitioners an acute appreciation of the local challenges. As they sought to gather hydrographic data to aid the watching ships of the North Sea fleet, they groped amongst shifting shoals, often in poor visibility that shrouded landmarks on the low-lying land. One young officer, eager for action but instead toiling in a frigate's boats under William Bligh's direction during the autumn of 1803, described it as 'a very tedious piece of work'.[46] Bligh's task was to ascertain whether an inshore squadron could be kept on station near the mouth of the estuary during the winter months. Like Hurd off Brest, he was undoubtedly constrained by operating from vessels of opportunity. He did have a time-keeper, but his efforts to fix the work were hampered by very inclement weather.[47] When his sketch survey of Walcheren Roads and the Wielingen Channel was published for the fleet, it prompted questions.[48] A pilot suggested that Bligh had made some mistakes in his bearings. Other work by him in this theatre is commemorated in the name of one of the long offshore banks which endangered the British warships on transit to the estuary.

This hazard was one topic in a series of compendious reports from the theatre which reached Bligh during his subsequent incumbency in the Hydrographical Office.[49] They came from another veteran of Pacific exploration, Captain William Broughton, now in command of *Penelope* (36), which was based at Yarmouth for long patrols off the Dutch coast. Fresh from an inshore engagement with a large enemy squadron of shallow-draught craft which had emerged from Flushing,[50] Broughton described the efforts of the squadron to fix and survey the banks and to reconcile the conflicting information from previous surveys. He reported his gratitude for the assistance of his sailing master, Jeremiah Beltt, later of *St George* in the Baltic. Beltt was a 'very good observer', and they took great care with their simultaneous observations for the latitude of Westkapelle, the bearing of which had 'always been taken by two azimuth compasses agreeing at the same place and the angles by a quadrant when it could be done, which was seldom'. Control by either compass bearings or horizontal sextant angles depended on the precision of the accepted positions for the fixing points ashore, which were derived from lists in the British *Requisite Tables* or the equivalent French publications. Errors in these sources were soon exposed by misclosure in the fixes and by inconsistencies in the soundings when closing the coast. They had embarked in the cutter *Fox* for some of this inshore work.

Mr Beltt was deployed again in *Fox* with Mr Henry Thornton, a North Sea pilot, this time offshore, to continue the survey of another offshore ridge athwart the approaches to the Scheldt. It had a least depth of 2 fathoms. Thornton had located it, and it retains his name. He had transferred from *Rattler* (16), commanded by Francis Mason, who had been drilled in hydrographic work during Popham's campaign in the Red Sea.[51] Broughton included Mason's reports together with those from other commanders also operating under his direction: John Hancock in *Cruizer* and William Bolton in *Aimable*. Bolton was destined to be a knowledgeable veteran of the squadron watching the Scheldt. In 1808 he would produce a survey based on 'seven years observations' in successive command of *Wolverine* (13), *Arrow* (28), *Aimable* (32) and, finally, *Fisgard* (38).[52]

He was an acknowledged expert to whom the Admiralty Board submitted plans and remarks from the station for his opinion as another major amphibious operation got underway in 1809. As well as striking a blow at what was now the largest concentration of enemy naval strength, Britain was under pressure to assist Austria by drawing French troops from the Danube.[53] The campaign is remembered for the sickness which ravaged the troops and for the parliamentary enquiry which pitted army and navy in a bitter debate over blame for the failure to penetrate to Antwerp. This obscured the strategic importance of what had been achieved. The fortified naval base at

Flushing on the island of Walcheren had been destroyed. It was vital to French plans, for it lay close to the mouth of the estuary, was clear of winter ice and had deep water for larger ships of the line. Bolton was a prominent proponent of occupation of Walcheren, urging that it was a 'key to the Scheldt and anchorage for our own fleet, rendering Antwerp of no effect' and advising that his local knowledge would assure a safe debarkation.[54] In advance of the arrival of the troopships, he had buoyed some of the offshore shoals, and he subsequently assisted to sound the Roompot, where Home Popham led the force to safety after the onset of an onshore gale. *Fisgard* and the brig *Raven* were the two ships designated by Rear Admiral Strachan to mark the dangers as British forces advanced into the Scheldt.[55] Captain Bolton was the ideal man to encourage a newly appointed master, Mr George Thomas, who now completed a remarkably thorough survey of the main Deurloo channel south-west of Walcheren, together with the adjacent waters, as *Fisgard* continued her pathfinding mission.[56]

Thomas, the son of a tailor in Southwark, had been admitted to Christ's Hospital in 1789, at the age of eight. He would boast in later life that he had distinguished himself over his fellows by carrying off a first-class medal in the mathematical class. In fact, no such medals were issued at that time. He had, however, caught the eye of the Mathematical Master, William Wales, who had sailed with Cook and who gave Coleridge his fascination with the records of voyages and travels. Little over a year after Thomas joined the mathematical class under the Stone's Foundation, Wales recommended his transfer to the prestigious King's Foundation, with its path to a seven-year apprenticeship at sea. Thus, on 12 November 1794, Thomas proudly sported the badge of the Royal Mathematical School and took his place at the most senior table in Hall. The high-spirited boy would have further need of the Mathematical Master's interest. The 'incorrigible' Thomas was twice disciplined in 1795 for going out of school without permission and escaped expulsion only because Wales pleaded that he would not be able to keep up the numbers taught and qualified if boys were expelled.[57] Not many months would pass before Wales reported that George Thomas had completed the prescribed course in 'Elements of Navigation'. He was sent to Trinity House for examination and there certified 'fully qualified for sea service'. On 2 June 1796 he was officially discharged and indentured to Captain Welham Clark of the ship *Commerce*, which sailed from Deal within the week for the Southern Whale Fishery, a burgeoning industry which would be encouraged by an Act of Parliament in the following year.[58] As a King's Boy he would have left with a generous allowance of sea clothing, books and instruments.

Thomas had the very highest estimation of his own abilities, which he was never backward in broadcasting. To the end of his days, he would resent his exclusion from the commissioned ranks of the navy, and his bitterness would frequently find vent in prickly relationships with officer contemporaries in the Surveying Service. These sentiments coloured the account of his early seafaring days which he left with William Mogg, who served with him as clerk two decades later.[59] This tale of shipwreck, almost four years marooned on Mas-a-Fuera, rescue by an American ship, a fortune made by selling seal skins in China and passage back to Europe as a first-class passenger culminated in impressment in the chops of the Channel and confinement in irons at the behest of a young midshipman, 'probably a scion of some noble house'. His fortunes were reversed when his mathematical training and experience came to the notice of the captain, himself an old Christ's Hospital boy. Thomas was able to give the name of the headmaster in his time, who 'more strange still, proved the same in the period at which the Captain himself was under, although many years prior to the prisoner'. James Boyer was indeed headmaster of the school from 1778 to 1799. Unfortunately, whilst rich in such apparently circumstantial detail, the recorded story, which was designed to highlight Thomas's achievements in the

Scheldt, is difficult to reconcile with surviving evidence and chronology in official documents.[60]

In October 1796, as the *Commerce* called at Rio de Janeiro for water and provisions, Spain declared war on Great Britain. Captain Clark continued his cruise, oblivious to this development. In May 1797 he entered Pisco in Peru, where the *Commerce* was seized. His crew, including Thomas, would now find themselves prisoners together with the men of eight other English South Sea whalers. Spanish records suggest that they proved to be a troublesome burden. At least one of Thomas's companions would die in captivity.[61] His own tracks are lost for the best part of a decade, and in his account for Mogg he may have wished to hide some murkier episodes. Later, he would claim 'nine years and a half have I spent in the South Pacific Ocean, without even repassing once to the east of Cape Horn during that period'.[62] In addition to the stations on which he had served in the Royal Navy, he would claim experience of 'the coasts of Chili, Peru, California, & New Albion'.[63]

His tale of adventure may have some substance, since at this time US trade with China was building up, with smaller vessels sailing round Cape Horn to pick up silver in Peru and seal skins gathered by gangs on Mas-a-Fuera. English officers and seamen were hired along the coast.[64] When a boarding party brought him on board a British frigate it was as one of the crew of the American brig *Harry and Jane*, which had just sailed from Montevideo Harbour with a cargo of hides and tallow for Boston after the lifting of an embargo prompted by the British descent on the River Plate. The vessel was sent to England as a prize.[65] Thomas meanwhile made his first appearance in Royal Navy records as a twenty-five-year-old volunteer, rated Able Seaman, on 9 November 1806. The captain of *Medusa* (32) who spotted Thomas's ability was not a former 'Bluecoat Boy' but an earl's son, albeit an 'Academy Royal Scholar' with an appreciation of the importance of good charts and a time-keeper.[66] The Honourable Duncombe Pleydell Bouverie was one of the alert captains who would provide information to the Hydrographer on their return to England from the expedition in the River Plate.[67] Bouverie rated Thomas midshipman after barely a week on board and master's mate on 4 January 1807.[68] Such an experienced seaman would soon be employed in the frigate's boats, sounding for anchorages and landing areas, and embarking and landing troops and guns. He found time to compile a meticulous journal, complete with copies of the plans of the area on Faden's version of the Spanish chart of the River Plate.[69] These suggest that he had taken the opportunity to make his own observation of latitude and longitude.

That his hydrographic acumen was encouraged whilst in *Medusa* is confirmed beyond doubt in subsequent products from that ship. She returned to England in November 1807 and, after a short period of Channel service in the following spring, deployed with *Thalia* (36) for the foggy and ice-bound coasts of Newfoundland and Labrador, where it had been reported that French frigates were resuming operations against British whalers.[70] The senior officer, Thomas Manby, had sailed as a midshipman with Vancouver. Both captains encouraged data-gathering as the squadron worked its way north, checking the principal bays.[71] The masters, John Willis of *Thalia* and Robert Fletcher of *Medusa*, were comparatively young men and good examples for Thomas. Both masters produced independent surveys of Croque Harbour, Newfoundland and Port Manvers on the Labrador coast, where the ships spent some time 'wooding and watering'. Thomas assisted in the work and drew up his own plans, one of which, probably because of his official position and reputation by that time, was published almost a decade later.[72] He almost certainly had more time to allocate than the busy masters, and his plan of Port Manvers shows more soundings, indicates coastline which had been surveyed rather than sketched, and includes two views and a more accurate observed position.

On return to England in November, Thomas left *Medusa* 'on promotion'. The papers rendered to the Admiralty include a certificate from Captain Bouverie that he had completed – though barely – the requisite two years' service as midshipman or master's mate, and an affidavit to the effect that he had 'served 5 years as first mate in the Merchant service, 2 years in the Navy and 5 years in other capacities at sea'. Less than a fortnight after leaving *Medusa*, Thomas reported at Trinity House and was found qualified to take charge as master of any of His Majesty's sloops.[73] On 23 November the gunboat *Hardy* delivered him to *La Fleche* (16), which was urgently in need of a master. On 15 January Admiral Montagu ordered his removal to *Fisgard*.[74] There he worked latterly under Captain Francis Mason, who had been promoted from *Rattler*. It was Mason who forwarded 'Charts of the Deurloo Channel taken by Mr Thomas' to the Admiralty on 22 February 1810 and who testified 'how fully competent I think Mr Thomas to construct a chart'. The huge sheet, over 7 feet in length, was accompanied by a letter from Thomas to the Board seeking their approbation, remarking that he had observed numerous errors in published charts: 'neither labour or genius has been spared to make it the most correct chart of that channel now extant, and being on an extensive scale, His Majesty's Vessels cruising off the Island of Walcheren will be enabled, without danger, to enter it and reconnoitre the enemy with greater facility.'

He went on to note that the 'great extent of the chart delayed me from sending it to their Lordships sooner' and to beg the Secretary to 'represent to their Lordships that I have sent the original Survey. I humbly entreat they will order me a copy of the same'.[75] This characteristically robust and confident correspondence led to consultation with Hurd, who reported that 'Mr Thomas's survey of the Deurloo Channel is by far the best nautical survey that has made its appearance since his appointment'.[76] Sir Robert Strachan was requested to signify to Thomas their Lordships' approbation.

There is ample evidence of Thomas's self-opinion, which would cause friction with contemporaries throughout his subsequent career. Two decades later, when attention was again focused on the Scheldt as the Royal Navy established a blockade to deter Dutch intervention following the declaration of independence by Belgium, he claimed that the Scheldt expedition had been detained 'until I offered my services to conduct the Fleet to Flushing in opposition to every Master, and Pilot, in the Fleet'.[77] Here his memory is certainly confusing his experiences in 1809 and those in a later deployment in 1814. Many other practitioners were active in the Scheldt during the Walcheren campaign. Home Popham, who had advocated from the outset that Flushing should be the target, was sent with eleven sloops, brigs and a light flotilla to sound and buoy channels in the West Scheldt. James Whidbey, veteran of Vancouver's voyage, was one of two Master Attendants who surveyed the Wielingen and Deurloo channels and reported unfavourably on the practicability of using block-ships to contain the enemy.[78] Captain John Sykes, another veteran of Vancouver's voyage, whose old 50-gun *Adamant* was part of the huge assembly of ships which Popham had shepherded into the shelter of the Roompot, rendered a sketch of the channel leading on to South Beveland, where troops were landed.[79] Competent work went on during the remainder of the war under the direction of Commodore Owen and other senior officers of the inshore squadron such as Captain John Hancock. In 1820 Admiral Sir William Young would visit the Admiralty with a large and detailed survey sheet made by Captain George Lennock of *Raven* (16) in 1811. This belated submission now gained recognition for the efforts of other masters and pilots in identifying 'Hancock's Gatt', an expedient approach to the Wielingen for the watching ships. It was, Young commented pointedly, a 'valuable and important discovery [which] was afterwards assumed by an Admiralty surveyor'.[80] A decade later the Hydrographer would be fielding complaints from Lennock and rebuttals from Thomas, who was once again embarked in a squadron off the Scheldt.[81]

There is, nonetheless, a marked advance in technique when Thomas's operational survey of the Scheldt is compared to reconnaissance surveys from the theatre. His results, plotted at a scale of 3½ inches to the nautical mile, compare well with the peace-time surveys by McKenzie or Spence in home waters. The soundings are shown in feet throughout, avoiding confusion from mixed values and allowing greater precision in indicating safe water for the major units of the expeditionary force. The sheet is fully annotated with navigational marks, transits and leading lines, and detailed information on tidal streams at springs and neaps. The latter would be especially valuable information for the larger ships in the force. In his letter to the Secretary of the Navy Board, Thomas had emphasised that, whilst laying buoys and placing floating lights at the entrance in preparation for his pilotage of the expedition, he had exerted himself 'to gain the necessary angles etc. [...] and the soundings carefully taken at low water spring tides'. He concluded: 'if attention be paid to the directions on the chart, no ship of whatever size can get onshore in the Deurloo at half tide; neither can any ship less than a <u>seventy four</u> at low water spring tides'.

Thomas left the *Fisgard* in April 1810. Hurd had secured his appointment as their Lordship's Surveyor on the coasts of Great Britain. He was embarked in the ketch *Gleaner*, which the Hydrographer had been asked to inspect and approve as fit for the work.[82] Soon, the skills which had been revealed on the remote coasts of North America and honed in the front line on the enemy coast were being deployed in harbours and anchorages of interest to the Admiralty. He began with check surveys of banks and anchorages off the Thames Estuary and on the East Anglian coast.[83] The purpose-built *Investigator* was commissioned on 1 May 1811, providing the platform for a meticulous survey of Fowey Harbour, at 8 inches to half a nautical mile, followed by the careful delineation of the New Gatway into the anchorage in Yarmouth Roads.[84] When *Investigator* returned to the Thames in November 1813, at the end of a season's work off Liverpool, Thomas barely had time to report to the Hydrographical Office before receiving orders to join Admiral William Young's flagship *Impregnable* (98) in the Downs.[85] Back off the Dutch coast, Thomas was deployed in the armed cutter

Countess of Elgin and the lugger *Defender*, 'sounding and taking marks for the Roompot' and sounding on the banks and laying buoys in the channels leading further up the Scheldt. He reported frequently on board the flagship and acted as pilot during a visit by the Duke of Clarence and subsequently when the fleet moved up the estuary. He would later recall *Investigator* taking the ground in the Wielingen Channel while 'following the French Fleet up to Flushing'.[86]

He drew up the results of this work, often undertaken during severe winter conditions, in an immensely detailed sheet at a scale of ¾ of an inch to a nautical mile entitled 'A survey of part of the Coast of Flanders and Holland performed [...] in the years 1809, 1812, 1813 and 1814'.[87] In earlier years he had had to plot his results starting from an assumed baseline value on the enemy coast, but now he and his assistant, John Frembly, were able to land to measure a baseline on Wolfast Dyke (Wolphaartsdijk) and to extend control by theodolite observations from church towers. He stressed that the boatwork was controlled using two sextants to observe the angles between shore marks. His survey was plotted using a station pointer, and he would recall affectionately that he showed this still-unfamiliar instrument to Commodore Owen, who had 'very kindly offered me his cabin to lay my work down'.[88] Thomas also produced *A Nautical Description of the Banks, Shoals and Channels at the mouths of the River Scheld* [sic], with sailing directions, the manuscript of which survives in the Royal Naval Museum Portsmouth.[89] Extracts from this had been printed and promulgated as Admiralty Orders.[90] It was this high-quality work which had caught Hurd's attention and which would recall Thomas to duty as a pathfinder in 1832.[91]

This opportunity for George Thomas reflects the lessons of the expeditions in the years after Trafalgar, such as those to Copenhagen, Lisbon and the Scheldt. They illustrated that, whilst the blockade of continental naval bases, the interruption of enemy seaborne commerce and the advancement of British trade would remain primary tasks, the fleet would also need to operate close inshore to support the armies which would eventually end Napoleon's military domination. Incursions into less familiar waters had produced an impressive level of rapid environmental assessment and the sharing of hydrographic intelligence. This sharing had been supported by Dalrymple's ability, with help from alert Naval Lords, to produce and distribute copies of plans in quick time. But, as Hurd emphasised whilst building up the new system that the Chart Committee had devised for supply to the fleet, this was not enough. The plans had to be underpinned by smaller-scale planning charts, which in turn needed a network of precise positions for their construction. This was work for practitioners with higher skills, skills which were recognised on land in the corps of the army and the Ordnance Board which would play such a prominent part in the final campaigns of the war in Spain and the south of France, which will be considered in the next chapter. The operations off the Low Countries had identified at least one man with such talent. But were there yet enough of them to form a cadre for the Royal Navy's needs?

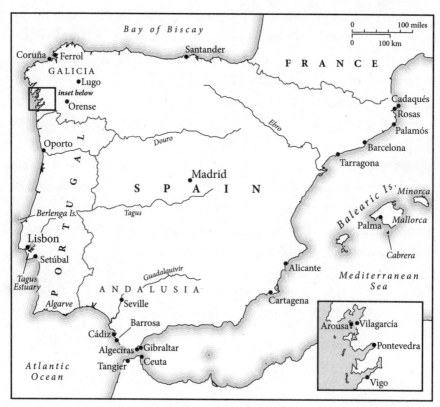

Map 9. Iberian Peninsula.

CHAPTER 6

Sea Power Projection
Iberian Peninsula

Thomas Hurd's first weeks in office as Hydrographer were high paced. Hard on the heels of supply to the squadrons in the Baltic came new demands. What is known in Britain as the 'Peninsular War' was underway. Exploiting arrangements to march forces to Lisbon in the failed attempt to capture the Portuguese fleet, Napoleon had stationed a large army in Spain. In 1808 he imprisoned the Spanish royal family and declared his brother Joseph as king. On 2 May an uprising in Madrid was brutally suppressed, but a powder trail had been lit, and rebellion spread through the Iberian Peninsula from Oporto and the Algarve. Amphibious capability would enable Britain to land, re-embark and re-land an army elsewhere to exploit the insurgency, and ultimately to build up an impregnable base in Portugal for a campaign which would wear down the French.

Astute land commanders had learned lessons in the operations in the Low Countries. They placed high value on reconnaissance survey and mapping. They had an acute appreciation of logistics, the identification of routes and the marshalling and maximisation of sea and river transport.[1] They looked for similar awareness on the part of the Royal Navy. The Admiralty would be extremely sensitive to criticism from Arthur Wellesley, now Lord Wellington, directing Rear

Admiral Byam Martin to travel to the army headquarters and discuss naval cooperation. He would record 'a very remarkable observation' of the great general: 'If anyone wishes to know the history of this war, I will tell them that it is our maritime superiority gives me the power of maintaining my army while the enemy are unable to do so.'[2]

That maritime superiority needed a foundation of geographic intelligence. On 12 July 1808, Hurd wrote to the Board, suggesting that, 'as the communication with Spain is now open', the flag officer off Cádiz be asked to arrange purchase of Spanish maps and 'the Mediterranean Charts of the latest editions'.[3] The residence in England of the respected expert on navigation José Mendoza y Rios had made naval men and publishers aware of the high quality of Spanish hydrography. In the report which the Chart Committee had made at the very time that the Spanish revolt got underway, they had recommended that every ship of the line and frigate in the Channel Fleet should be supplied with copies of plates from an atlas which had been republished by the commercial sellers in London.[4] These were based on the fine surveys conducted during the 1780s by the great hydrographer Vicente Tofiño de San Miguel with his team of students from the Naval Academy in Cádiz. The charts had been hard to come by in England. Mr Richard Turner, Master and Commander of the *Woolwich* transport, tasked on the Iberian coast, had made no fewer than fourteen rough tracings of Tofiño's charts on the back of printed Admiralty stationery.[5] When Admiral Pickmore, in command off Cádiz in 1810, asked for copies, Hurd would explain that he had only one copy of the atlas in the office. The admiral would continue to be supplied with copies being engraved in the office and by the commercial publishers, who were facing repeated requests from 'distinguished officers of the Royal Navy'.[6] Pickmore's predecessor, Rear Admiral Purvis, had in fact received a complete set of the latest editions of Tofiño's charts and views from the Captain General of the Department.[7] These were clearly not passed on, and this was not the only failure which would have irritated the

Hydrographer had he been aware of it. Out in Cádiz a significant opportunity to share data went unexploited.

✳

On 1 May 1809 Capitán de Fragata Felipe Bauzá, Assistant Director of La Dirección de Trabajos Hidrográficos (DTH), slipped a bribe to his guard and escaped from the Retiro prison in Madrid. During the turbulent days since the French occupation of the city in December, he had been involved in a contest of wits to deny the documents of the DTH to the senior officers of Napoleon's Topographic Bureau. Within twenty-four hours of the arrival of the emperor's entourage, a visitor had presented himself at Bauzá's house. Alexandre de Laborde, author of a major work on Spain, was keen to ingratiate himself with Napoleon, who had brought him along as a specialist adviser. Now he sought to tempt Bauzá to make his fortune by offering the emperor the maps, plans and papers under his control. Bauzá had only thwarted him by falsifying an order and a receipt note indicating that they had already been sent to the Supreme Junta, which was coordinating Spanish resistance from Seville. Generous backhanders had enabled him to get six crates of material from the DTH out of the city and on the road across Andalusia. In early June he followed them, with the prize in his briefcase which the French had wanted more than anything else – the map of the Pyrenean border territory, on which he had been working since the previous autumn.[8]

Bauzá was bound for Cádiz, where he established a depot in an abandoned public building in the old city. As the French closed in and began a long siege, he kept his materials ready for further flight to the Canaries should it prove necessary. In February 1810 he described the threat in a letter to Lord Holland, whom he had befriended during the latter's travels and studies in Spain. In the following month the First Lord of the Admiralty informed Admiral Purvis that he had no objection to this 'very scientific geographer [...] receiving a safe conveyance to this country in any ship of war in

which you may think it proper to provide for him a passage'.[9] Bauzá
had been authorised to assist his British army counterparts and,
during later exile in England, claimed to have supplied maps to
Lieutenant-General Thomas Graham at Cádiz and to Sir Arthur
Wellesley.[10] The latter would have shown an acute interest in the
mapping of the frontier of Spain and France, which remained the
top priority for Bauzá and his staff.

Whilst Bauzá might later find it expedient to highlight help to
the British forces, cooler relationships appear to have prevailed on
the ground in Cádiz. The British minister had offered him equivalent rank in the Royal Navy to facilitate direction of operations by
the allied engineers. Bauzá declined and affirmed that he answered
only to the Junta.[11] He may have found it difficult to forget that
several of his fellow veterans of the great Pacific expedition of
Alejandro Malaspina had fought at Trafalgar, and Alcala Galiano
had been killed. Bauzá had been ready to share navigational data for
the wider Atlantic region through his counterpart José Espinoza
Tello, who had now set up another outpost of the DTH in London,
and in 1812 the *Naval Chronicle* had included such information
promulgated by 'The Hydrographical Depository of Cádiz'.[12] But it
seems that the Royal Navy was not offered new charts of Iberian
waters which were being compiled there.

Teniente de Navío Francisco Catalá had worked alongside Bauzá
as senior pilot during Tofiño's surveys and under Malaspina in 1789–
94. He had been selected to conduct detached boat surveys because of
his competence in astronomy.[13] In 1807 he was tasked to work from
the felucca *Escorpion* and make large-scale plans of Mediterranean
ports which had not been included in Tofiño's atlas. In the spring of
1810 Bauzá obtained the results, together with additional information from the Captain General of Cartagena. In 1813 he published a
Portolano de las Costas de la Península de España, an atlas of plans
encompassing the coast from the border with France in the
Mediterranean right round to the northern border of Portugal with

Spain.[14] There is no evidence in the surviving papers or journals of Purvis and his successors of liaison with Bauzá during this period.[15] Thus, invaluable information was denied to officers, who would rely on front-line sketch surveys in a number of harbours which Catalá had examined thoroughly.

Raw memories of 1805 undoubtedly complicated liaison at Cádiz. The diplomatic skills of the successive flag officers were tested during the French siege of the city, which was now the seat of the Supreme Junta, and later of the Regency of Spain and the Indies. Cádiz lies at the northern tip of Isla de León, essentially an isthmus separated by the natural canals of Carracas and Sancti Petri from a coastal hinterland of marsh and salt-pans. The isthmus lies parallel to the mainland, from which the Trocadero Peninsula extends westward, creating an inner roadstead at the head of Cádiz Bay. The end of Trocadero lay just three-quarters of a mile from Isla de León, and fortresses had been established to deny the point to an enemy. The French would find great difficulty in traversing the hinterland, but eventually they took the fortresses and established other batteries from which shells could reach the city of Cádiz itself. This was to be a theatre of gunboat battles backed up by bomb-vessels which pounded the French positions. Skills in boatwork and pioneering were at a premium.

In 1810 Rear Admiral Sir Richard Goodwin Keats worked closely with General Graham and Spanish commanders and helped to encourage cooperation between British and Spanish 'engineers of navy and army' in assessing and improving the defences of the fortified isthmus. David Bartholomew, with recent, renewed experience of combined operations on the Scheldt, was now amongst the gunboat commanders. Keats selected him to operate under Graham's direction and probe far into the inner waters of the bay, having ascertained that 'he is a pretty good surveyor and has a reputation of being a very gallant officer'. Remarks which the forthright Scot subsequently submitted on the defence of Cádiz would be rebuffed by Keats as 'indelicate and presuming', but Bartholomew's successful observations of French movements during a six-month detachment in the channels and gutters extending from the Canal Sancti Petri brought him generous praise from his fellow countryman, Thomas Graham. Bartholomew was careful to include these in his entry in Marshall's biography.[16]

A year earlier Admiral Purvis had hosted a grand ball on board his flagship to cement relationships with Spanish counterparts and to reciprocate hospitality ashore. Amongst the long list of invitees is a familiar name: Alexander Briarly.[17] By the spring of 1809, and only a few months after his rejection by the naval authorities in London, he was established in Cádiz as a wool merchant, acting as agent for the freighting of 1,000 Spanish merino sheep, a gift from the Supreme Junta to King George III.[18] Like Bartholomew, he seems to have made easier relationships with army counterparts. As the French siege got underway in the following February, Major-General Stewart reported a proposal by Briarly to facilitate his plan for the garrisoning of Fort Matagorda, an island redoubt off the tip of Trocadero.[19] On 20 March, at the invitation of the Spanish Regency and the request of the British Minister Plenipotentiary, Briarly entered into Spanish service with the rank of capitán de fragata and acted as adjutant to Admiral Cayetano Valdés, assisting in liaison between the allied inshore squadrons which were bearing the brunt of the gunboat battle.[20]

The admirals off Cádiz may not have made contact with the Deposito Hidrográfico, but a young practitioner in the British inshore squadron did use his initiative. Admiral Keats sent the ships of the line to cruise outside the bay whilst personnel were deployed in gunboats to work alongside the squadron that Admiral Valdés had built up once craft were released from running supplies into the beleaguered city.[21] One of the midshipmen from the flagship was William Henry Smyth, commanding a gunboat in the thick of attacks on the French batteries. He made himself known to Valdés, a fellow spirit who had conducted survey work in north-west America, where he had cooperated with Vancouver. The admiral gave the young man a copy of Tofiño's *Atlas Marítimo*. The professional enthusiasm that would earn Hurd's support was evident when, perhaps through an introduction from Valdés, Smyth also met with Felipe Bauzá, whom he described as 'the hydrographer of the Spanish navy', and sought his advice on the tidal regime along the coast.[22] In the course of operations, Smyth in turn gathered intelligence on the coast and channels, which was invaluable as the allied forces took the initiative in the following spring, transporting a combined force to advance along the coast from the south and take the French from the rear whilst diversionary assaults were made on the batteries around Cádiz Bay. On the strength of these efforts, Smyth was sent by Keats to carry despatches to General Graham during the flanking operation from Tarifa which culminated in the battle of Barrosa.[23] The chart of the whole theatre which Smyth would draw up extended from the Wood of Barrosa right along the coast to cover the reefs in the approaches to Cádiz Bay. Comprehensive soundings extended into the shallows and creeks from which the gunboats engaged the forts and batteries, all of which were laid down on the plan. His subsequent career would illustrate the important elements of Hurd's

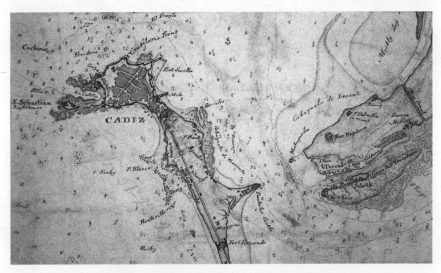

27. *Extract from Smyth's survey of Cádiz and environs.*

philosophy which are clear during the Peninsular campaign: close liaison with foreign hydrographic departments and with British army counterparts, and the identification and employment of talent and enthusiasm in the fleet.

These lessons were also apparent on another Iberian station of the Royal Navy. On 28 July 1809, following the savage battle of Talavera which earned him his viscountcy, Wellington began his withdrawal towards his logistic base at Lisbon. He was moving into a promontory bounded to the west by the steep-to Atlantic coast, and to the east and south by the River Tagus and its estuary. In London, government ministers feared that their only field army would need to be evacuated once again from the peninsula, and they had ordered the assessment of the best place to achieve this between Setubal and Peniche. The direction of this task had been given to Mr Joseph Seymour, master in Vice Admiral George Berkeley's flagship *Barfleur* (98), working in the tender *Mary*, a handy schooner. Berkeley ordered 'all officers to render every assistance in their power'.[24] The resultant survey, which had been carried as far as the estuary of the Tagus up to Lisbon, was laid down on a massive sheet, nearly 7 feet long, labelled 'Admiral Berkeley's Chart of the Coast of Portugal'. Seymour had plotted a network of triangles observed by compass bearings, with length of the sides expressed in 'English fathoms'.[25] It was another rapid environmental assessment using slender resources and showing a limited number of sounding profiles. When the sheet reached London in August, Hurd noted that there was no evidence of measurement of a baseline, or of the taking of any angle by sextant or theodolite. There was no graticule of latitude or longitude, or any indication of whether the scale used nautical or statute miles. Only a few soundings were 'very acceptable' for the new chart from the Straits of Gibraltar to Oporto which was under preparation.[26] These were along the coast south of the Tagus, where I would visit one of my ships, *Roebuck*, as she took observations to support a twenty-first-century NATO exercise landing on the long fringing beach.

Meanwhile, planning and preparation had been underway in Portugal for a very different outcome to evacuation, one which may have led to Seymour's survey effort being redirected. On 21 July 1809, whilst Seymour was absent, overseeing work in the tidal estuary and approaches, Major Joseph Thérèse Michelotti of the Portuguese Royal Corps of Engineers boarded *Barfleur* to consult with him and pass memoirs and plans. He also had information specifically requested by the admiral. Following a meeting with Wellington at Abrantes, Berkeley had returned to Lisbon down the Tagus, proving it as a route along which reinforcements for Wellington were now being transported. Michelotti was an expert in hydraulic engineering who had worked with British officers to examine the upper reaches of the Tagus and now brought recommendations for the improvement of the navigational channel.[27] He also advised that fords could be deepened to reduce the number of crossing places which would need to be guarded if the French reached the left bank, especially between Valada and Abrantes. He was preparing a chart of the whole course of the Tagus from Vila Velha de Ródão to Sacavém, into which soundings could be inserted and married up with the results which Seymour was coordinating in the estuary.[28]

Wellington had made provision for evacuation from a defensive position at São Julião at the mouth of the Tagus, but there was a much more ambitious scheme underway. He had directed his engineers to provide a northern boundary to the area into which he was withdrawing with a line of defences from the Foz do Sizandro on the Atlantic coast to Alhandra on the Tagus. Between Alhandra and Lisbon, Michelotti's and Seymour's efforts paid dividends, as Berkeley deployed a flotilla of armed launches and flatboats to harry the approaching French army.[29] William Walker, another master employed by Berkeley for hydrographic work, sounded and buoyed the river as the gun-brig *Growler* (14) towed and warped up to ply her 12-pounder shot and grape against the French outposts below Vila Franca.[30] Walker would be proud to list 'Torres Vedras' in his statement of service.[31]

*

As Wellington returned to the offensive and moved back out of Portugal in 1811, one important task for the Royal Navy was to support and encourage the Spanish armies engaging the French on other fronts, including Catalonia. Captain Charles Adam of *Invincible* (74) was in the forefront of operations around Tarragona, inserting supplies, disrupting coastal communications and capturing and destroying Fort St Philippe, which commanded the strategic Coll de Balaguer.[32] Adam had served as a young man with Keith at the Cape of Good Hope, gaining early appreciation of the importance of hydrographic intelligence. In remarks rendered to the Admiralty in 1812, he commented that he had derived 'perfect confidence' in navigating with Tofiño's charts and directions and 'only in the few instances which will be mentioned has the slightest error been discovered'.[33] He used Tofiño's coastline for a chart of his own that included soundings, notes of watering places and other matters of interest such as a 'canal not finished'.[34] This was essentially an intelligence compilation built up from field reconnaissance. He added fresh remarks on the inshore anchorages occupied by *Invincible* and smaller consorts, with particular comment on the shoals formed by the outflow from the rivers. This information does not appear to have reached the Hydrographical Office in time for it to be reflected in the coastal sheet which Hurd compiled from Tofiño and French authorities and published in December 1813. Four transports and a gunboat were lost on the shoals off the mouths of the Ebro in that year.[35]

The chart did include as an inset a competent survey at 2 inches to half a nautical mile made by another active captain on the coast, Richard Thomas of *Undaunted* (38).[36] He led a landing party of marines from his ship and *Blake* (74) at Cadaqués on 3 May 1811.

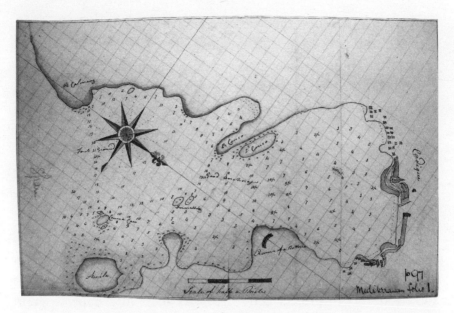

28. Survey of Cadaqués Bay by the boats of the Undaunted. *The battery on the N shore was 'effaced' by a party from the ship during the operations in the area.*

They occupied the heights above Rosas for twenty-four hours, used their broadsides to drive off French troops which subsequently approached the town, and remained in the vicinity for a month.[37] On 6 May two boats were sent away and achieved the systematic sounding in the harbour that is shown on Thomas's plan.

This front-line survey work on the coast of Catalonia was addressing the gap which Bauzá's *Portolano* would have filled. Lieutenant Benjamin Baynton of *Cambrian* (40), Captain Francis Fane, had begun his naval career in the Mediterranean in Nelson's *Victory* and would provide input to the Hydrographer throughout his career. He distinguished himself in dangerous operations in the bay off the strategic citadel of Palamos but found time to produce a workmanlike compass sketch survey to position a dangerous sunken rock in the offing – a rock that was shown clearly in Catalá's plan in Bauzá's atlas.[38] Palamos was the landing place recommended by Rear Admiral Hallowell in 1812 for the insertion of a large expeditionary force designed to assist the Spanish commander, General Ballesteros, and to take some pressure off Wellington's army during the advance to Madrid. This force consisted of troops which the British government had insisted be spared from the garrison in Sicily, supplemented by a Spanish detachment which had been formed in Mallorca. Two prominent characters in this book, Alexander Briarly and William Henry Smyth, were involved in the operation.

After the lifting of the siege of Cádiz, Alexander Briarly had been given command of the naval station at Mallorca, where he soon found himself in a situation as volatile as Trinidad. He applied himself with energy and initiative, setting up a telegraph between the top of Palma Cathedral and the summit of Puig de Randa, with its commanding vista of most of the coast. He struggled, however, to form a flotilla to protect commerce and assist in convoying grain from Barbary. With his own resources, he fitted out a vessel and undertook a challenging mission for the British commander on the island, General Whittingham, to inform the Regency in Cádiz of suspicion of plots between French officers confined on Cabrera and supporters in Palma. He returned with recruits and supplies for the force which Whittingham was forming.[39] When the captain of the port refused help, it was Briarly who impressed twenty ships from their unhappy owners and captains and fitted them out in four days to carry the cavalry and artillery mules of the Anglo-Sicilian force under General Maitland.[40]

But already a story very reminiscent of Port of Spain was emerging. As he struggled to secure funding for his flotilla, Briarly was accused of heavy-handed and insulting communications with the local authorities. He resented criticism which they published in the liberal journal La Aurora Patriótica and turned to the more conservative Diario de Mallorca to promote himself, even reprinting early praise from Governor Hislop in Trinidad. Relationships reached their nadir when in April 1813 Briarly sent his Memorias on the causes of the parlous state of the Spanish navy to Ferdinand VII, who had just returned to Spain.[41] Briarly would throw in his lot with the reactionary camp and, conscious of opposition to the employment of '*un Inglès*', write plaintively that he was 'Irish, Catholic, and in his present situation had no homeland but Spain and no King or patron' but Ferdinand. Not for the first time, he may have been economical with the truth, for he had been married in the Church of Ireland and his son would later be baptised as an Anglican in London.[42] Furthermore, his career in the Royal Navy, his half-pay and his place in the British Admiralty list had all been lost before, rather than as a consequence of, 'agreeing to enter the service of Spain'. But now, he claimed, without interest he faced 'total ruin'.[43]

William Henry Smyth's adventures had continued during the campaign on the Mediterranean coast of Spain. He was now serving in *Rodney* (74), which had supported amphibious operations in the vicinity of Algeciras to draw French forces away from the main theatre on the Portuguese border. French fears for Andalusia and Valencia were stoked by the transport of a British force to Cartagena. Here, Smyth made what he described as 'sketchy re-examinations' to compare with Tofiño's charts.[44] He did the same at Alicante, a port of particular importance both as a watering place and as a safe anchorage. When General Maitland turned down the option of Palamos, it was selected as the landing place and chosen base for his force in August 1812.[45] His survey of Alicante was amongst the work which would be discussed when Smyth made his call on Thomas Hurd, who would be well aware that the port was not included in Tofiño's atlas. Smyth's fine plan in the Hydrographic Office archive compares favourably with the chart which Bauzá would publish from the work of Catalá. It was compiled after the war, as indicated by the depiction of hill-shading and fortification which he had learned from his army counterparts in Sicily, but it includes observations from his time in *Rodney*.[46]

✻

On the Atlantic coast, Lisbon remained the key logistical base as Wellington took the offensive. Whilst Hurd laboured to improve the supply of navigational data for the theatre, the flag officers on station welcomed any initiative on the part of their few cruisers. The loudest complaints from the fleet related to the inadequate coverage of the Portuguese coast. In response, Hurd had pointed out the secrecy which had always surrounded official charts produced in that country: 'Their men of war as well as all other requisite services for national purpose are, I understand, supplied with manuscript instead of published charts. Tofiño complains of this and offers it as an apology for any incorrectness that may appear in his chart of their coast.'[47]

Although most of the contents of the Portuguese map archives had been taken to Brazil during the evacuation of the government, there is evidence that a small number of coastal sheets were passed to the British. Then, in 1810, after his appointment as High Admiral of the Portuguese Navy, Admiral Berkeley employed Major Marino Miguel Franzini of the Portuguese Royal Corps of Engineers to address the lack of hydrographic information. Franzini, who had previously served in the navy, drew together existing high-quality surveys, especially of the bar of Lisbon, took supplementary soundings and produced a chart of the entire Portuguese coast, a sheet of harbour plans and a volume of sailing directions.[48] Franzini was a stern critic of the surveys which Royal Naval practitioners had made to aid their operations. He did commend the plans emerging from *Lively* (38), commanded by Captain George McKinley, who had been operating in Portuguese waters since 1806, had evacuated the British merchants from Lisbon during the first French invasion and conducted reconnaissance in the Tagus. These included a sketch survey of the 'tall and ship-like' Burlings (Berlengas), a traditional watering place for British warships blockading the Tagus, where the main island was subsequently occupied and fortified to cover communications with Northern Portugal.[49] This survey had been conducted by the frigate's master, Mr James Crawford, who had served with

Home Popham and Bartholomew as master in *Romney* and with Francis Mason in *Rattler*.[50] His successor, Mr Peter Gawthrop, was a Yorkshireman who would be described by a colleague as 'a man of blunt manners' but 'sterling' honesty, 'distinguished as a good seaman and correct navigator; his career in the navy had also been marked by his abilities as a surveyor of coasts and harbours'.[51] He rendered a survey of the entrance to the Tagus at 2½ inches to the nautical mile, with a careful record of the leading marks across the notoriously mobile bar between the North and South Catchup Sands. He was to produce further work which was prized by the Hydrographer.

With his experience in North America and Bermuda, Thomas Hurd was well aware of the capability of the engineer surveyors to whom Wellington might be expected to look in the first instance for cartographic expertise. Few land maps had been available at the outset of British operations in Iberia, and they were stylised small-scale commercial products giving little indication of the rugged terrain which the army would face, especially as Wellington advanced into the northern provinces. Arrangements for 'campaign mapping' had been improved under the political direction of Lord Castlereagh and the leadership of the Duke of York.[52] The engineer surveyors, trained in the field in England by the Royal Military Surveyors and draughtsmen of the Interior Survey, could bring to bear the principles of baseline measurement and triangulation from their general surveys, pacing baselines and measuring horizontal and vertical angles with a box sextant. The scale of the task in the Iberian Peninsula, however, and the pace of events, demanded swift reconnaissance survey. For this, the officers of the new Royal Staff Corps, mostly on temporary transfer from infantry or cavalry regiments, had been given training which did not include the sciences of triangulation and traversing. Armed with a field kit of compass, rectangular protractor, and some-times a pocket sextant or clinometer for taking vertical angles, they applied a technique for relief-sketching and hill-shading which became known as the 'British National Standard' and gave impressive

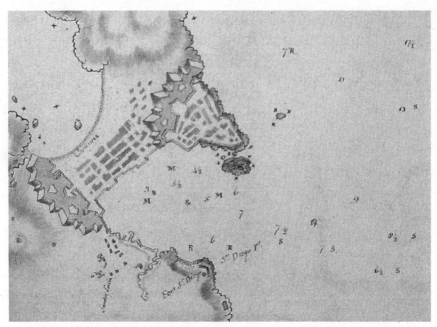

29. *Detail from Anthony Lockwood's survey of the roadsteads of Corunna, Betanzos and Ares, showing part of the anchorage off Corunna in which the survivors of General Sir John Moore's army would be embarked in January 1809. The port subsequently became an important supply base as Wellington's army moved further away from the Tagus and Douro.*

unity to their work.[53] Sir George Murray, Wellington's Quartermaster General, a man with an acute interest in history and geography, formed these men into an effective organisation for gathering topographic intelligence.[54] Their sketch surveys were matched by 'memoranda', very much akin to the navy's 'remarks', describing the rivers, roads and bridges.[55] Despite copious scale errors and inconsistencies, the rapid results enabled the commander-in-chief to outflank his opponents again and again with river-crossing operations and to outmanoeuvre them in the complex Pyrenean foothills.[56]

Similar reconnaissance and survey work was now needed by the Royal Navy, to find new logistic bases as Wellington moved out of Portugal, and for amphibious operations in support of Spanish forces

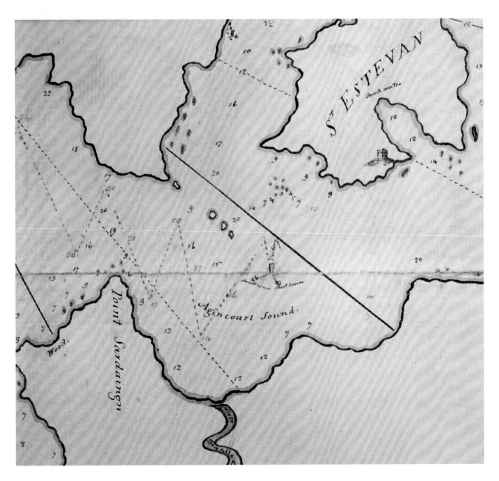

1. The track of HMS *Victory* on first entry to the famous anchorage of Agincourt Sound in the Maddalena archipelago, plotted on the manuscript chart made by the pathfinders.

2. Thomas Hurd, whose vision for a RN Surveying Service was forged when pathfinding on the enemy coast.

3. John Knight, assiduous collector of hydrographic information in all his ship commands.

4. Francis Beaufort, whose superior skills as a hydrographic surveyor were spotted by Alexander Dalrymple and Peter Heywood.

5. William Henry Smyth, the eager volunteer snapped up by Hurd and deployed as the Admiralty Surveyor in the Mediterranean.

6. Cutters were the workhorses for many surveys. The leadsman is at work in Edward Columbine's *Resolution*.

7. HMS *Griper*, one of the gun-brigs that Hurd identified as ideal survey ships.

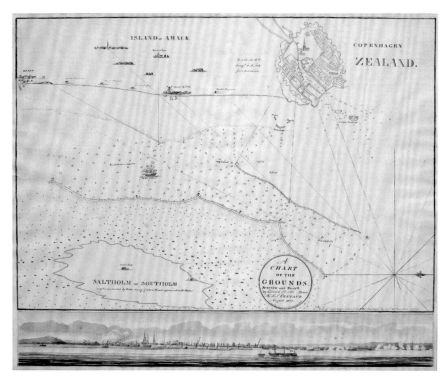

8. A survey and view made during the operation at Copenhagen in 1807.

9. Pathfinding in HMS *Ranger* in the channels leading to a secret convoy rendezvous off the harbour of Matvik.

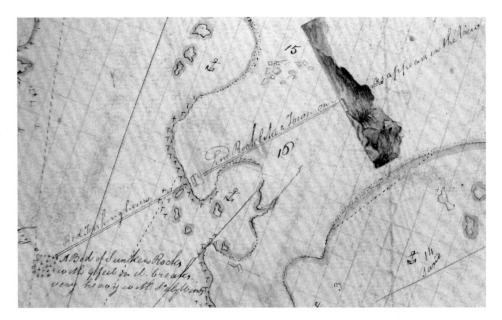

10. Reconnaissance survey in the rias of Galicia enabled support to Spanish forces and to Wellington's army as he advanced north.

11. George Thomas's detailed front-line survey during the 1809 Walcheren operation earned him employment as an Admiralty Surveyor.

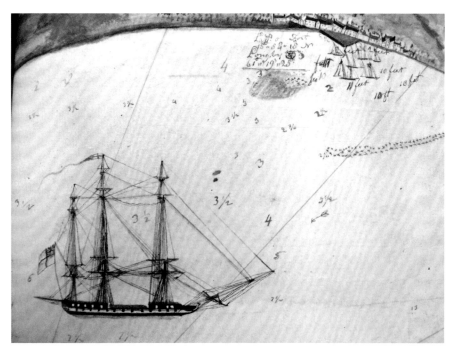

12. A sketch in Mr John Noble's remark book from HMS *Cerberus* (32) shows the rapid reconnaissance survey that enabled capture of Vieux Fort, Marie Galante, in 1808.

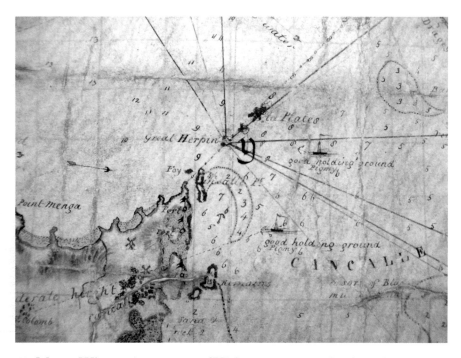

13. Martin White uses vignettes of HM cutter *Pigmy* on his front-line surveys to indicate good anchorages for ships of the Royal Navy's inshore squadrons.

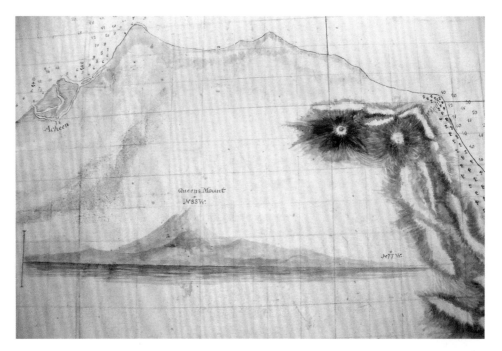

14. Peter Heywood's fine depiction of the coast of Sumatra showing 'Queen's Mount', the volcano Seulawah Agam, in a 'view' designed to assist safe landfall.

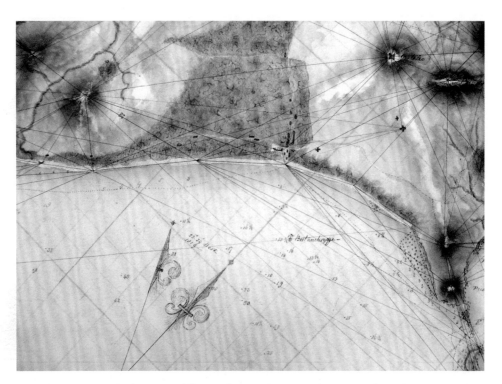

15. William Mudge's plan of Porto Santo showing the control work, topographic survey and thorough sounding achieved by David Bartholomew and his officers.

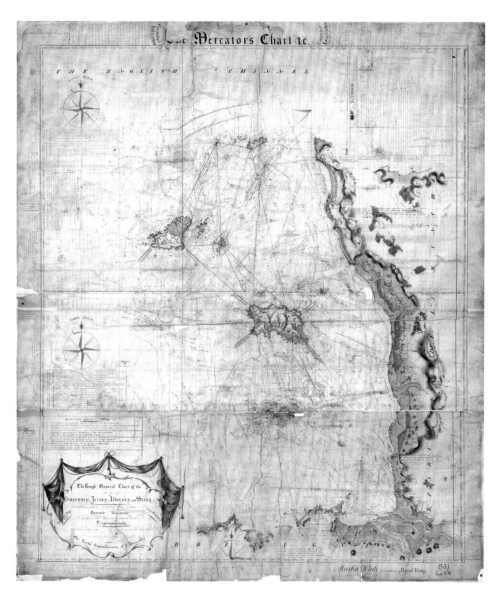

16. One of Commander Martin White's huge fair sheets recorded his pathfinding work on the enemy coast.

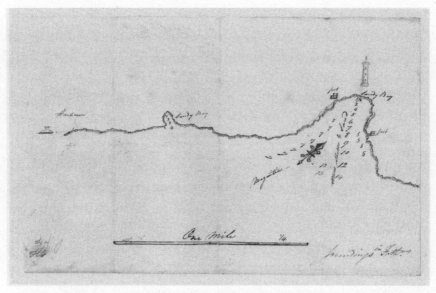

*30. Simple scale, indication of magnetic north, and specification that sound-
ings are in fathoms characterise this swift reconnaissance survey of a bay near
Corunna. The light script of the sketch of the leading mark of the ancient Torre
de Hércules signals that this is a 'view', for the lighthouse lies on an eminence
further west, beyond the bounds of the plan.*

in the north-western provinces. For Hurd's efforts to publish improved
chart coverage were still hampered by the backlog resulting from
inadequate resources and guidance for the clerks who had hitherto
been responsible for archiving hydrographic records. The remarks
which had trickled in from the fleet included much useful information.[57] Good surveys made by Mr Anthony Lockwood during Admiral
Cochrane's watch on the coast in 1804 lay neglected amidst the piles
of manuscripts in the Admiralty attics, including one of the harbour
of Corunna and the approaches.[58] The Quartermaster General staff
preparing for evacuation of the British Army at the end of its first
campaign in Iberia in 1808 noted that the port was commanded by
shore batteries, liable to be closed for long periods by adverse weather,
and had no quays for the embarkation of horses.[59] The need for

detailed charting was acute, and front-line capability invaluable. Amongst the papers of George Murray in the National Library of Scotland is a simple but effective sketch survey of the Ensenada de San Amaro, a sandy bay on the peninsula north of the port and out of range of French artillery.[60] Here, boats collected the rearguard until the onset of an onshore gale.[61]

In February 1809, Captain McKinley in *Lively* oversaw the evacuation of the British community from Oporto and then began to patrol the deep inlets and rias of the Galician coast, monitoring French activity and forging contact with the Spanish patriots. This would lead to the expulsion of the French from Vigo, an operation in which *Lively* played a vital part.[62] In April, Mr Gawthrop made a sketch survey of the Ria de Pontevedra and Ria de Arousa, plotted at 1¼ inches to the nautical mile, which was used by the Hydrographer for an update of Tofiño's chart. The Marqués de Maceda, commander of Spanish forces in the vicinity, had come on board *Lively* in her anchorage off the island of Ons and requested that McKinley bring the frigate up to Vilagarcia to support his operations against the French. Working from an observation for the latitude and longitude of Ons, laying down the ship's tracks, Mr Gawthrop produced a pragmatic and thorough intelligence document (Plate 10). All the towns and villages in the inlets, such as Marin, where they obtained information from the patriots and released vessels detained by the enemy, are marked with numbers and named in a table.[63] The primary purpose of supporting safe navigation and ease of access was not forgotten, and additional pilotage information was submitted in a comprehensive set of remarks.[64] The memoir on the chart enables some deduction of his survey methodology. He specifies that bearings are magnetic and gives a value for variation, suggesting that some shore control was established with a network of compass observations. The locations where observations were made for position, variation and tidal height and range are identified. Boats had been sent away to sound in the fairways and over the dangers. The visible

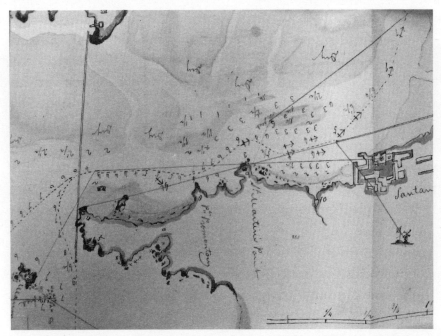

31. Detail from a sketch survey at Santander by Mr Peter Ney, master of the Insolent *(14), one of the vessels that sounded ahead as Popham's squadron attacked the port.*

rocks are labelled with letters and tabulated in the memoir. In the inlet of Marin, soundings were run in lines between the headlands. As in the mouth of the Tagus, Gawthrop cautioned that in the rainy season, which lasted here from Christmas to the end of March, run-off from the many small rivers could be more significant than the tidal stream. As will be seen, Gawthrop's competence as a hydrographic practitioner did not go unnoticed in London.[65]

Hurd's old colleague Home Popham was senior officer on the coast as Wellington's army moved closer to the French border. The expectation that the Royal Navy would maintain conduits for logistic support gave ample opportunity for the exercise of the skills which the Hydrographer sought. The captains and masters of the squadron were deployed in rapid environmental assessment of a key base at

Santander and of other captured ports.[66] Amongst them was Joseph Needham Tayler, a scientifically minded officer and close associate of both men, who made a sketch survey of St Jean de Luz.[67] Subsequently, the squadron on the Biscay coast came under the command of a man who would play a significant part in advancing Smyth's career. This was Charles Penrose, the captain who had noted and reported Hurd's work in Bermuda, now a rear admiral. As Wellington's army crossed into France and invested Toulouse, Penrose oversaw the crossing of the notorious bar of the River Adour to complete the investment of Bayonne. He then encouraged the master of his flagship, Mr William Hamilton, as he conducted surveys of the Garonne and Gironde so that close support could be given to the two divisions advancing on Bordeaux, whose mayor was ready to declare against Napoleon. With the resultant manuscript chart in his hand, Penrose took his flagship *Egmont* into the Gironde, to the astonishment of the embarked French pilot. Never before had a 74-gun ship entered the river fully armed and stored. The *Egmont* led the attack, which caused the abandonment and burning of the French squadron on the river. In their sounding boats, the masters of his ships opened the way for the assault on the shore batteries. By 6 May 1814, Penrose had sufficient knowledge of the rivers to reach Bordeaux and fly his flag in the sloop *Podargus* (14) off the very centre of the city. These exploits brought him to note, and he was appointed to command in the Mediterranean, where he would soon observe the skill of William Henry Smyth, Hurd's Admiralty Surveyor. Meanwhile, as hostilities drew to an end in Europe, Mr Hamilton would use his survey to pilot transports into the Gironde to embark troops bound for an ongoing war in an unwelcome new theatre on the far side of the Atlantic. Here, whilst Smyth was honing his skills, other recruits for Hurd's cadre were active on the front line.

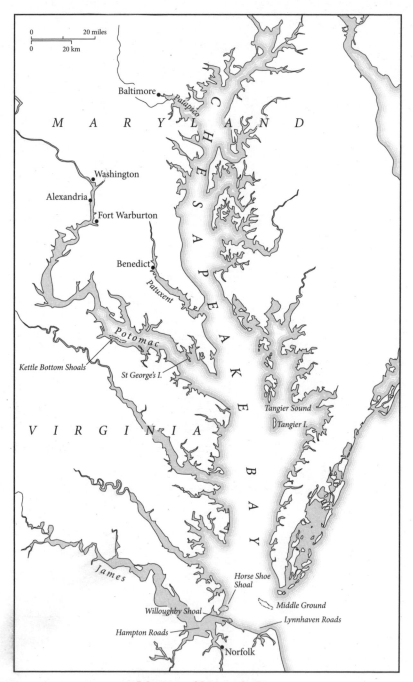

Map 10. Chesapeake Bay.

CHAPTER 7

World War
The Americas and the Pacific

The summer of 1812 was wet and cool, which brought some relief on the often stifling attic floor of the Admiralty Building, where all hands were called to the pump when it was time to load the chart boxes which clogged the rooms and passageways. Thomas Hurd's task of chart supply had been ratcheted up. War with the US was a highly undesirable outcome for the British government, which was keen to ensure the supply of American food to the army in Spain. This view was shared by the New England states whose ships would carry it. In an effort at appeasement, the British government's Orders in Council, restricting neutral trade with Europe in response to Napoleon's Continental System, were repealed on 23 June. One month later, news arrived in London that this concession had been in vain. President Madison's government had declared war on 17 June. The conflict would intensify the global war confronting the Royal Navy, but it would also bring opportunity. Hurd would benefit from the support of commanders who prized hydrographic intelligence and who would encourage the activities of a significant number of men who would be prominent figures in his new cadre.[1] Once again, scope would be given to expound the clear military focus for his vision: 'Captain Hurd has ever been of opinion that the

Commanding Admiral on each of the Stations should be furnished with (at least) two Surveyors for the purposes of making Nautical Surveys where necessary and still hopes to see such a measure adopted in the Naval Service for the great benefit of Navigation.'[2]

He was delighted, and he did not hesitate to declare his support when, in January 1814, Vice Admiral Alexander Cochrane, another officer who had been familiar with his work in Bermuda, asked for the attachment of two surveyors to his squadron which was bound for North America. Their Lordships approved the measure, together with the provision of chronometers and surveying instruments and drawing paper, and eventually also the portable printing press and copying machine which Cochrane had requested. However, Hurd was little more impressed by Cochrane's nomination of a protégé for the work than he had been with Admiral Saumarez's choice in the Baltic. Anthony Lockwood had produced his survey of Corunna under Cochrane's command. As acting Master Attendant at Barbados, he had produced a plan of Carlisle Bay. He had come under Cochrane's command once again and been employed on surveys in the Caribbean, most notably in the Virgin Islands. Lockwood was technically competent but a touchy and difficult character who had offended senior naval officers during employment in 1805–6 among the Channel Islands, leading to termination of his survey and the end of his aspirations to succeed Graeme Spence.[3] Hurd did not entertain a high opinion of him, and his post-war tenure as 'their Lordships' Maritime Surveyor' in Canada would be short-lived.[4] Now Hurd was content that he be tasked by Cochrane to correct the errors in Des Barres' charts of Nova Scotia.[5] Hurd made sure of securing the appointment of his preferred candidate to the second position with a remit to survey the coast from Rhode Island southwards.

This was Mr Anthony De Mayne. He had first come to Hurd's attention when serving as master in *Leveret*, one of the sloops tasked by Admiral Keats to survey the entrance to the Great Belt in 1807. He had identified the dangerous shoal which retains the sloop's name to this day. He had subsequently achieved some fame when, as master in *Amelia* (38), he took command when all the commissioned officers were killed or wounded during a drawn battle with a French frigate.[6] Hurd's approbation had been earned by hydrographic work during the same commission on the west coast of Africa in 1811–13, when Captain Irby commanded a reinforced anti-slavery squadron. De Mayne rendered three coastal sheets and copious remarks on positions, variation, currents, coastal soundings and views. He was careful to explain how he had used chronometers and Massey's patent log in the course of the running coastal survey, and he reported that variation had been taken as the mean of observations with three azimuth compasses.[7] Hurd cited this work in his recommendation of De Mayne: 'we are indebted for many valuable surveys and remarks acquired during his service in the *Amelia* on the coast of Africa with which he has enriched this office'.[8]

De Mayne was soon at work on the front line in a sea area which had presented the British squadron with major challenges to the imposition of control. Lieutenant James Scott, a veteran of the defence of Cádiz, now back under the command of his patron Rear Admiral Sir George Cockburn in the rivers of Virginia, bemoaned 'the utter absence of all knowledge of the localities'. There were no commercial charts of this region for Hurd to purchase in London, and he waited eagerly for incoming data, such as a sketch survey which arrived in 1812 showing soundings at the entrance to Chesapeake Bay and athwart the recommended track to Hampton Roads which compares well with modern charts. It included views to illustrate the clearing and leading lines to round the long arc of Willoughby Shoal, a real hazard to any vessel hugging the shore too close.[9] By the end of the campaign, such reconnaissance work enabled Scott to assert: 'We soon obtained a better knowledge of the navigation of the Chesapeake than the American pilots themselves; indeed the Americans were fully persuaded that some of their own countrymen had turned traitor and guided us through its intricacies.'

Both Cockburn and Scott held their fellow countryman Mr George Thoms, the 'excellent and deserving master' in *Marlborough* (74), in the highest esteem.[10] This experienced mariner from Aberdeen would accompany Cockburn to all his flagships during the remainder of the war. On the Chesapeake he played a prominent part in sounding the Middle Ground and Horse Shoe Sand and buoying the channel into Hampton Roads.[11] Other masters in the smaller units submitted sketch surveys to the Admiralty as they probed into the narrower sounds in the bay. Both Mr James Cudlip in *Rattler* (16) and Mr Charles Morris in *Pandora* (18) penetrated Tangier Sound, where a British depot was established on the island of the same name. Morris took thorough soundings in the mouth of the Sound and placed marks on Tangier Island and fringing shoal to fix his chosen anchorage (Figure 33).[12]

Commendable as these reconnaissance surveys were, Hurd needed the involvement of men with higher skills if he was to compile campaign charts. In the summer of 1814, Admiral Cochrane and Major-General Sir Robert Ross planned a major offensive which would lead to the attacks on Washington and Baltimore.[13] It was De Mayne who supervised the sounding of the River Patuxent as Cochrane entered to land Ross and his troops at Benedict for the advance on Washington.[14] The boats and men were furnished from *Royal Oak* (74) by Rear Admiral Pulteney Malcolm, a commander who had encouraged the early efforts of Peter Heywood and always shown an appreciation of hydrography. De Mayne had more time to produce plans of the area of the British base at Tangier Island. These were a substantial advance on the earlier reconnaissance surveys. The soundings in this area are noticeably more complete on the chart of Chesapeake Bay which he compiled in 1814 and which Hurd described as showing 'an entire new arrangement of the eastern side of that bay particularly about the Tangier islands and banks'.[15]

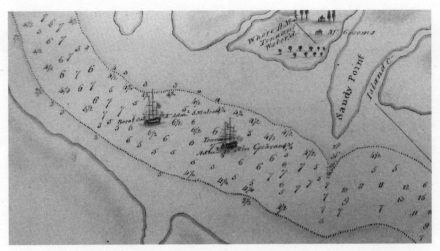

*32. Detail from De Mayne's survey of the Patuxent showing
two of the flagships at anchor.*

Lynnhaven Roads and the approaches to Hampton Roads, the
Potomac as far as St George's Island, and Chesapeake Bay itself as
far as the Patapsco River are also well sounded. De Mayne may have
included information from the squadrons under the direction of
Admirals Warren and Cockburn as they felt their way up the rivers.[16]
He certainly used some material published in America, including
Edmund Blunt's *Coast Pilot* and an enlargement of a map of part of
Maryland. In addition to soundings and natures of the seabed, his
chart includes indications of tidal streams, recommended anchorages
and lighthouses and prominent marks. It would be the best available
depiction of the areas which had been surveyed until the work of the
US Coast Survey got underway later in the nineteenth century. De
Mayne would be one of Hurd's first post-war recruits, spending a
decade as Admiralty Surveyor in the West Indies.

Another future Admiralty Surveyor was also on the front line on the
Chesapeake. Amongst the commanders feeling their way up the rivers
was David Bartholomew, now in command of *Erebus* (18), which had
been specially fitted out with a battery of the devastating Congreve
rockets. She was part of the diversionary force which, without benefit of

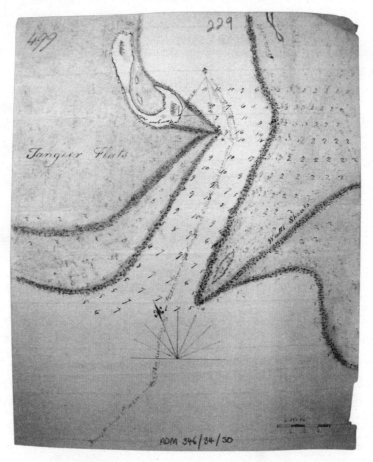

33. Mr Charles Morris's survey of Tangier Sound.

pilots, sounded and warped themselves up the Potomac against contrary winds past the Kettle Bottom Shoals, grounding frequently, to attack Fort Warburton and descend on Alexandria. They spent twenty-three days on the river under enemy fire. Similar endeavours enabled a squadron to penetrate to Baltimore, where *Erebus* fired the rockets at Fort McHenry which inspired the writing of 'The Star-Spangled Banner', which would become the national anthem of the US.[17] She also took part in operations on the St Mary's river in Georgia, where Bartholomew was wounded in the head and, when he put his hand up

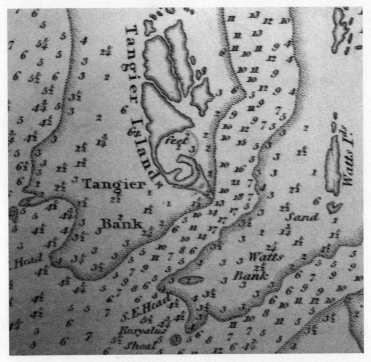

*34. The Admiralty chart showing De Mayne's
coverage of the same area.*

to feel the wound, was struck by another ball on middle finger and
thumb. After demonstrating conspicuous gallantry, the man who had
started in the wars under the shadow of Admiralty disapproval would
emerge as a Companion of the Bath.

A number of the men who would assist Bartholomew in his post-war
surveys around the islands of the north-east Atlantic had been schooled
on another front in the war with the US. President Madison's

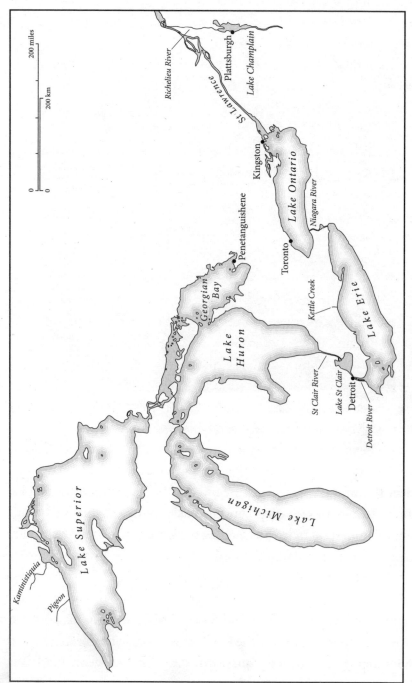

Map 11. Great Lakes.

government launched an early offensive along the Great Lakes frontier. 'Canada, Canada, Canada' had been the war cry of elements with expansionist ambitions. Indeed, Madison had declared war with the confident expectation that Britain, so heavily committed to war in Europe, could be driven out of North America. In 1815, at the end of three seasons of combat afloat and ashore, the British remained on the Canadian shores from the River St Lawrence all the way to the Upper Lakes. The direction of British naval operations in this theatre was now entrusted to two commodores who had commanded squadrons operating aggressively on the fringes of the Napoleonic Empire and who had been eager to acquire hydrographic intelligence. Edward Owen had facilitated the efforts of George Thomas on the Scheldt, and Robert Hall had encouraged William Henry Smyth in the Straits of Messina. Owen was appointed as Commander-in-Chief, Hall as Naval Commissioner. Both had a keen appreciation of the challenge of defending the frontier line, especially with reduced forces after the signing of a peace treaty between Britain and the US at Ghent in December 1814.

The naval personnel who had sustained that defence against the Americans had quickly become aware of the want of information on the tortuous waters. When the bitter contest allowed, they sought to address it. Mr Robert Bryden, acting master of *Confiance* (36), was made prisoner when she was destroyed at the battle of Plattsburgh, Lake Champlain, on 11 September 1814, only sixteen days after commissioning. He was commended for his efforts during the action. After exchange, he remained on this sector of the frontier and made a most competent survey of the River Richelieu.[18] In July 1814, American forces had been deployed far up Lake Huron to displace British forces and threaten the routes of the western fur trade. A naval base was needed, and Lieutenant Newdigate Poyntz, who had served twice with Home Popham, had been despatched in the *Netley* schooner to investigate the head of Georgian Bay. He submitted a glowing report and a sketch survey of the inlet of Penetanguishene and its approaches.[19]

Commodore Owen lost no time in building on their efforts and addressing the lack of hydrographic information, employing masters on the station to undertake sketch surveys of critical areas. They had a limited outfit of instruments. Five accomplished surveys of the north shore of Lake Ontario made by Mr Thomas Chillingsworth appear to be largely controlled by compass bearings. His field book for the work at Kingston Harbour, Navy Bay and Hamilton Cove, which was plotted on a military plan, suggests that casts of the lead were made at regular intervals along a line between two conspicuous objects but that the only positional checks were a record in the sequence of soundings of when the boat crossed another natural transit or alignment.[20] Compass control was used at the western end of the lake, where he was allocated *Montreal* (20) to sound a shoal in the vicinity of modern Toronto. His survey of the Canadian entrance to the River Niagara does show control derived from measured baselines, and horizontal sextant angles may have been employed.[21]

By the last years of war, Thomas Hurd established firm control over the allocation of instruments, ensuring that designated survey parties received what they needed. Thus, a better outfit of instruments arrived in Canada in May 1815, when the Commodore was joined by his brother, William Fitz William Owen. For higher-level survey control, the allocation included a reflecting circle, assorted sextants, a telescope for observing Jupiter's satellites, two artificial horizons, a pocket chronometer and a Gunter's chain. A pocket sextant, two pocket compasses with sights and a perambulator would prove their worth in reconnaissance work.[22] William Owen had distinguished himself in pathfinding in the East Indies, playing a prominent part in leading the amphibious force which had captured Java. He had hoped to be despatched back to the East Indies but had instead been appointed 'For Particular Service' to conduct a military survey of the Lakes Frontier. He was a tough taskmaster. One of his officers would recall a regime of 'incessant application [...] working after the Owen style [...] all day and nearly all night'.[23] His survey team included two former students of the Royal Naval College, Lieutenant Alexander Vidal and Midshipman Alexander Becher, both of whom would go on to serve with David Bartholomew on post-war tasks identified by Thomas Hurd. Vidal was entrusted from an early stage with control observations requiring higher skill, being detached inshore in a canoe to undertake the painstaking work on 'shores and measures', whilst the other assistants undertook the sounding.[24] Along the most vulnerable sector of the border with the US, comprising the Detroit River, Lake St Clair and the St Clair River, this activity was almost bound to prompt adverse attention from the Americans, and Owen's prickly personality guaranteed a robust response to any provocation. This was to cost Vidal five weeks' detention in Detroit when Owen despatched him in pursuit of some deserters and thieves.[25]

Owen did not allow winter to impede work and took his team onto the frozen St Lawrence River to measure baselines. Becher took part and clearly won Owen's trust at an early stage, for later he was despatched to accompany the Earl of Selkirk on a tour of inspection of the further reaches of the Canadian frontier.[26] A survey of the River Kaministiquia, including the baselines and traverse rays which he observed, dates from this time. When triangulation work resumed on the ice in the following year, he was judged to be competent to take charge of a detached party which returned and produced a survey of the coast of Lake Superior, including an inset 'Survey of Pidgeon River on the Ice'. Thus, even before his famous African survey of the following decade, Owen was identifying and schooling young veterans of the Napoleonic Wars who would find peace-time employment in a hydrographic specialisation. Others would emerge from further theatres of the world war of 1812.

The Royal Navy's blockade of American ports would prove to be a vital factor in ending the conflict, not least by intensifying discontent in the merchant communities of the eastern seaboard. The US Navy did, however, succeed in slipping out raiding squadrons. In 1814 several fast sloops deployed into the Caribbean and its approaches. Captain Charles Malcolm, who had served alongside Peter Heywood in his brother Pulteney Malcolm's *Fox* in eastern seas, was senior officer of a squadron sent out in search of American units said to be operating on the Brazilian coast. Two of his officers in the *Rhin* (38), the master, James Douglas, and Lieutenant George Crichton, had been involved in hydrographic data-gathering earlier in their careers. Crichton had conducted seven sketch surveys during operations in the Red Sea. When rendering them to the Admiralty, Crichton declared that he had sought to exercise his skills 'to enable me to fulfil that important duty assigned to the Commanders of His Majesty's ships, should I ever be fortunate enough to obtain that rank'. With Malcolm's encouragement, he now surveyed the harbour of São Luís de Maranhào and took numerous soundings and astronomical observations whilst the ship patrolled the approaches. His work was attributed to him in three new Admiralty charts. Crichton was invalided from the West Indies in June 1814, terminating his career in the navy without his having achieved his ambition of command. He became the manager of the Edinburgh, Glasgow and Leith Shipping Company, holding that appointment until his death in 1844.[27] Hurd used his example, however, to encourage another very competent young officer who submitted similar surveys from the theatre.

Lieutenant William Hewett, a product of the Royal Mathematical School at Christ's Hospital, wrote from *Inconstant* (36), Captain Sir Edward Tucker, on the Brazilian coast. Hurd noted with approval the young man's eagerness to improve chart coverage and his efforts to lay down his boat surveys with reference to principal points on the coast whose longitude he had established 'by the combined products of two excellent chronometers, and various lunar observations'. Hewett concluded by stressing his willingness to undertake further hydrographic work, with his charts affording 'the strongest proof of my abilities'.[28] Hurd assured the young man that 'whenever called

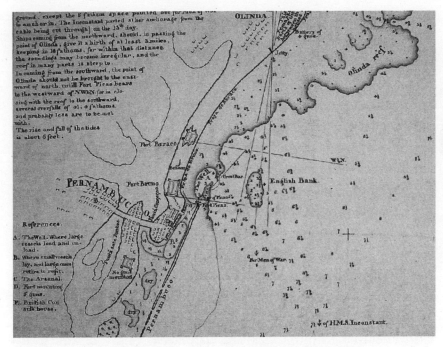

35. *Detail from William Hewett's survey of Pernambuco. His astronomical observations were made at Olinda Point and Fort Picao.*

upon by the Board [...] I shall have great pleasure in putting forward your name as a candidate'.[29] In 1818 he would nominate Hewett to the Board as commander of the surveying ship *Protector*, declaring him to be 'perfectly qualified both as a Draftsman and Mathematician'.[30] Hewett would spend the rest of his career surveying in the North Sea until the tragic loss of his second ship, *Fairy*, with all hands, in a great gale in 1840. In that same year, Rear Admiral Charles Malcolm retired as Superintendent of the Bombay Marine, having encouraged the work of its renowned surveyors, especially in the Red Sea, where they opened the way for steam navigation.[31]

The commerce-raiding strategy of the US spread Royal Naval effort further into remote waters. In 1814 Peter Heywood was serving again on the River Plate station. Here he monitored the reaction to events in the Iberian Peninsula amongst the authorities in Buenos

Aires and across the Andes in Chile.[32] He reported the efforts of the US consuls general to spread the view that Britain was unlikely to support any moves towards independence. He urged the deployment of more Royal Naval ships to the region, and in early 1813 he passed on intelligence of enemy activity culminating in the appearance of USS *Essex* (46) on the Pacific coast.[33] The destructive foray of Captain David Porter into the grounds of the British Southern Whale Fishery, and subsequent reports that another large frigate had been sent to reinforce him, led to the diversion of several Royal Naval cruisers to track them down.[34]

Porter had found no difficulty in picking up intelligence of British shipping in the ports of Chile and Peru, where there were many inhabitants who were rather more sympathetic to the US than to a power now allied to Spain. He had confirmed that he was most likely to find the whalers in the Galapagos group and had made his way there after looking into Callao and watering at Paita.[35] Learning that British units were on his trail, Porter was well aware that they could pick up intelligence on the South American mainland just as readily as he had done. He therefore sailed out to westward with his prizes, heading for the northern group of the Marquesas Islands (Îles Marquises). Both in the Galapagos and here, he was able to exploit hydrographic information from published accounts of British voyages, especially the one commanded by George Vancouver. Vancouver's atlas, published in 1798, contained a bare outline of the westernmost shores of the Galapagos archipelago, derived from a track chart made by James Johnstone, later the front-line practitioner whose contributions in the southern North Sea and Dover Strait were described in Chapter 4.[36] In 1792 the Marquesas were visited by the store-ship *Daedalus*, on its voyage to join Vancouver. Her commander, Lieutenant Richard Hergest, a veteran of Cook's second and third Pacific voyages, would not survive to serve in the wars of 1793–1815. He and the embarked astronomer, William Gooch, were killed when they made a landing in the Hawaiian Islands. The two men had identified and made a sketch survey of a sheltered anchorage in the Marquesas, which Hergest named 'Port Anna Maria, Nooahuvah, or Sir Henry Martin's Island' (Baie de Taiohae, Nuku-Hiva). His report had been reproduced at some length in Vancouver's *Voyage of Discovery*.[37] Porter took his prizes there and set up a base, which he named Madisonville. When Captain Sir Thomas Staines of *Briton* (38) and Captain Philip Pipon of *Tagus* (36) reached the bay, they found the base abandoned, with the burnt wreck of one of the whalers lying in the shallows. They made a survey and rendered fair sheets to the Admiralty.[38] One of the draughtsmen was Lieutenant John Shillibeer, in command of the contingent of marines in the *Briton*. He also published a narrative of the voyage, which sadly says nothing of any survey work. It is best known for its account of what has become the most famous incident of the voyage: the chance landfall at Pitcairn Island and the encounter with the community established by the *Bounty* mutineers.[39] The experiences under Staines' command will undoubtedly have inspired two of his young gentlemen. In due course, Midshipman Francis Crozier would distinguish himself as a polar explorer, whilst William Skyring would develop his skills under the tutelage of Hurd's Admiralty Surveyor in the Mediterranean and earn respect as an outstanding surveyor of his generation in *Beagle*, working once again in Pacific waters.[40]

The practitioners in the frigates deployed into the Pacific could not be classed amongst those later criticised by a successor in the theatre, Captain Basil Hall: 'Officers are too apt to undervalue the nautical knowledge which they acquire in the ordinary course of service; and to forget, that every piece of correct information which they obtain, especially on distant stations, is essentially valuable. If it be new, it is a clear gain to the stock already accumulated; if not, it is still useful as a corroboration.'[41]

Captain James Hillyar of *Phoebe* (36), who was first to deploy in pursuit of Porter, had rendered to the Hydrographer manuscript charts and views made at Callao, Juan Fernández and Valparaíso in

*36. Detail of Mr Brady's atmospheric view from the anchorage
at Callao which complemented his 'trigonometrical survey'.*

the course of the hunt for the *Essex*.[42] His personal log from the
deployment is preserved in the National Maritime Museum, and the
views and surveys pasted into it confirm his interest in gathering
navigational data. One of his midshipmen, Allen Gardiner, the future
missionary to the indigenous peoples of the southern regions of
South America, was a product of the Royal Naval College, and his
journal includes a careful record of directions for the ports and
anchorages which they visited.[43]

The bulk of the data-gathering and rendering was performed by
the Schoolmaster, Patrick Brady, who hailed from Cavan. He had
joined *Montagu* (74) with fifteen other Irish volunteers in 1806, aged
twenty-two, and been rated landsman. During the intervening years
in flagships in the Mediterranean, he had risen to midshipman,
suggesting that above average mathematical skill had been noted and

that he was enabled to acquire competency in astronomy. These attributes would earn him his warrant to serve with Hillyar, who would recommend him for similar employment in the lean post-war navy. His duties would give him the time for the draughtsmanship of his charts of Valparaíso and Juan Fernández. They may be based on Spanish originals, but his distinctive hand is evident in the fine view on the latter sheet, which is annotated 'A Chart [...] with several improvements by P Brady'.[44] He described his survey of Callao as a 'trigonometrical survey'. He would use this same term when employed as schoolmaster and acting master in ships on the south-west coast of Africa after the war. He applied in vain to the Admiralty to be allowed to pass for master, but his worth was appreciated by Thomas Hurd, who published one of his African surveys as an Admiralty chart.[45]

After his own deployment in *Conway* (20) in 1820–21, Hall acknowledged the 'practical skill in hydrography' of his first lieutenant, Alexander Becher: skill honed under Owen and Bartholomew. Becher had drawn up fair sheets including a track plot liberally annotated with observations of prevailing winds and currents and compass variation, from which the chart in Hall's published journal would be derived.[46] Hall's deployment illustrated the opportunity which Hurd had urged the Admiralty Board to exploit in the early spring of 1814:

The return of peace to this country makes me consider it as an official duty to represent to the Lords Commissioners of the Admiralty the great deficiency of our nautical knowledge in almost every part of the world, but more particularly on the coastline of our own Dominions, and also with the hopes that the present favourable moment for remedying these evils will be made use of, by calling into employment those of our naval officers, whose scientific merits point them out as qualified for undertakings of this nature – of which description of officers there are I am happy to say many who stand eminently conspicuous.[47]

The context for Hurd's argument for the vital importance of hydrography, namely a 'great Maritime Empire, whose flag flies triumphant in every part of the world', had been epitomised in these far-flung episodes of the war with the US in 1812–14.

His case would be bolstered during the transition to an uneasy peace. In the latter years of the war, Wellington's exploits had aroused pride and interest in the army. Hurd's son Samuel had been swept up in the enthusiasm, choosing not to follow in his father's footsteps. As a newly appointed Ensign in the 1st Foot Guards, he would gain a campaign medal as Napoleon's dramatic bid to recover power was defeated at Waterloo in 1815. But victory was still underpinned by sea power. Admiral Cockburn carried Napoleon into exile at St Helena, where Mr Thoms made a survey.[48] Other surveys arrived from ships landing garrisons on Ascension and Tristan da Cunha to prevent their use in any attempt to rescue Napoleon. As Hurd extended the folios of Admiralty charts, he would suggest that the best way to address the survey of oceanic islands and reported dangers was for 'the admirals on the several stations, and in the proper seasons, to send their cruisers to search'.[49] Fresh tensions would also enable him to sustain his case for the deployment of survey parties, such as those on the Great Lakes and on the coasts of Newfoundland. Intelligence that the French were planning a return to the Pacific and resumption of the exploration of the coast of Australia accelerated the despatch of Lieutenant Philip Parker King with two carefully selected assistants to pick up the work of Matthew Flinders. The next chapter will examine how the turbulent post-war years assisted Hurd to select and champion a corps drawn from the war-time practitioners and those to whom they were now passing the baton.

CHAPTER 8
Securing an Uneasy Peace

In 1816 Thomas Hurd, a canny pragmatist, drew on a decade of experience in the Admiralty and restated his case in a carefully worded argument: 'The Captain [...] submits the expediency of selecting a certain number of officers well acquainted with the science of maritime surveying and forming them into a distinct and separate corps something similar to that of the Engineers of the Army and transmits a list of officers entitled to consideration for such employment.'[1]

Hurd was conscious that he was making this pitch at a time of rigorous post-war retrenchment. The pace and scope of the reduction in the numbers of ships in commission would be unparalleled until the close of the Second World War in 1945. He was not, however, without support. John Wilson Croker, the First Secretary to the Board of Admiralty, has been depicted as a bête noire whose hostility cast a 'cold shade' over the young Hydrographic Department.[2] Amongst those who are said to have resented his imperious direction was William Henry Smyth, who was not permitted prolonged use of a chart table in the Hydrographical Office such as Hurd had enjoyed a quarter of a century before. Edward Parry, Hurd's successor, indicated that interference by the First Secretary was a factor in his dissatisfaction with the post. Yet Admiralty correspondence reveals interest and support for the Hydrographer consistent with Croker's pursuit of staff efficiency and care and management of records.[3]

Furthermore, Croker and his colleagues in government were confronted throughout this period by challenges to the peace in Europe and the Near East, the enforcement of British policy for the suppression of the slave trades around the coasts of Africa and the protection of British mercantile interests in the evolving polities of the Americas. Indeed, John Barrow, powerful Second Secretary, the renowned promoter of exploration, was wide of the mark in his assertion that: 'During all this period of tranquillity there was but little demand on the services of the Royal Navy. It had since the year 1817 afforded a fitting opportunity of employing a few small ships in voyages of discovery for the advancement of geography, navigation and commerce.'[4]

This was no 'period of tranquillity', and Lord Melville, the First Lord, fought hard to retain sufficient assets for deployment to trouble spots and to protect British citizens and their trade. Thus, hydrographic practitioners in the naval squadrons and units would continue to produce the fruits which Hurd had highlighted during the Napoleonic conflict. The front-line pathfinding did more than confer tactical advantage. It provided vital intelligence for planning in Whitehall as the British government faced up to the challenges of coordinating a global imperial system. Rear Admiral Sir Thomas Byam Martin, who had demonstrated strategic grasp as a flag officer in the Baltic and Peninsular campaigns and in supervising the destruction of the French naval facilities at Antwerp in 1814, was now Comptroller of the Navy. He appreciated the significance of the surveying service which Thomas Hurd was launching and worked closely with him to select masters for the new survey ships.[5] In campaigns which took place between 1816 and 1823, more surveys would be rendered than during the French Revolutionary War, with 109 naval personnel making their first contributions alongside those proven during the wars.

*

Mr Alexander John Russel was one of the masters whose qualifications were closely scrutinised by Thomas Hurd before the Navy Board issued his warrant for one of the newly commissioned survey ships. He would not be alone in finding service uncomfortable with the commanding officer of *Shamroc*, whom we will meet later in this chapter. Russel lasted less than a year in post. His career as a pathfinder was not over, however, and he would soon be demonstrating his skills in the front line. With a fresh warrant, he deployed with Captain John Lumley in *Topaze* (38) for the East Indies station. The East India Company continued to look for the support of the Royal Navy in its contest with the 'pirates' of the Persian Gulf and Red Sea. Captain Lumley commanded a combined squadron of Royal Naval and Company ships that appeared off Mocha in December 1820 to demand that the Imam of Sanaa sign a treaty bringing an end to 'injuries to British subjects'.[6] Russel was in the fore from the outset, laying buoys and sounding the harbour before anchoring ships and boats in position for bombardment. He would be responsible for positioning the bomb-vessel *Thames* and assisting the officer of artillery in directing the fire to destroy the substantial north and south forts. When his artillery counterpart was wounded by return fire as they shifted berth to fire on the town, Russel superintended operations through the following night. Lumley recorded that the shells were 'thrown with great precision', reflecting 'the highest credit on Mr Russel'.[7] Russel survived this action in which eight men died and twenty were wounded. He did not survive the voyage. When *Topaze* was homeward bound, he went aloft to repair damage in a gale off the Agulhas Bank, 'fell out of ye Main top and was drowned'.[8] His place as a pathfinder would be preserved, however, in the Admiralty catalogues, which until the early 1880s included charts from his sketch surveys in the Amirante Islands, made during another ongoing campaign, that against the Indian Ocean slave trade.

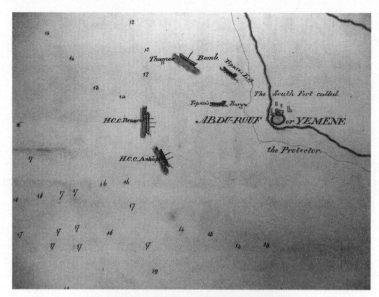

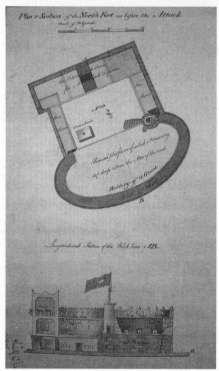

37. *Extracts from Mr Alexander Russel's survey showing the positions of the bombarding units at Mocha.*

Russel's career was typical of those post-war years in which the British government had no appetite for additional burdens of overseas possessions but faced pressure to provide presence for assertion of trading interests and protection of those engaged in commerce. The South American station was maintained, and surveys from that theatre formed a significant component of the incoming data in the Hydrographical Office, with other officers matching the work of William Hewett, though they might not follow him into the surveying service. Lieutenant Matthew Lys had served on the station with Captain Heywood and subsequently demonstrated superior skills in a survey of the reef-fringed approaches to Recife whilst *Doris* (36) was deployed to protect British nationals and property during a Brazilian civil war. He was competent to measure a baseline and to compute distances between the ship and conspicuous buildings and points of land. These would have enabled bombardment of the fortifications on his sheet, had hostilities broken out.[9] Sadly, he was invalided home before the end of the commission and would see no further naval service.

Similar skills were also evident in the regular flow of information arriving on Hurd's desk from the Mediterranean. Piracy and slavery were the drivers for naval intervention in the western basin of the sea. During the Congress of Vienna at the end of the Napoleonic Wars, Sir Sidney Smith had urged action to aid the European slaves held by the North African states. In 1816 William Henry Smyth took his gunboat to join an allied fleet off Algiers. Also present, as master in the bomb-vessel *Beelzebub*, was William Walker, who had been employed in war-time surveys on the coast of Portugal and on the River Tagus. He had served with his fellow Scotsman David Bartholomew and, whilst commanding one of the store-ships despatched around the globe in search of ship timber, supplied the Hydrographer with a fine plan of Knysna Harbour and a running survey of the adjacent coasts, where his name is preserved in the fine bay near Hermanus.[10] In 1824 Walker was back on blockade off

Algiers as master of the flagship *Revenge* (74) following a dispute and the withdrawal of the British consul. Dispositions for bombardment were aided not just by Walker's previous experience in *Beelzebub* but by his plan showing the position of all the Algerine batteries, complete with a handy table to compute range from the shore by measuring an angle to the top of the lighthouse on the Admiralty building. Like Hurd and others before him, Walker had shown how a practitioner proven in more formal survey in favourable peace-time conditions could produce superior results in the testing circumstances surrounding inshore warfare. He had measured two baselines between anchored boats by patent log, by vertical angles to the flagship's main truck and by velocity of sound. From these he had laid down the control network from which angles could be taken to the enemy positions.[11]

Thomas Hurd took office as Hydrographer little more than a year after the British parliament had finally voted for the ending of the British trade in enslaved Africans. The campaign to achieve this had been set back by the impact of the French Revolution and the coming of war. In the intervening years, however, some naval and military officers joined in abhorring the iniquities of the slave economies of the Caribbean and South America. Among them was Hurd's colleague on the Admiralty's Chart Committee, Edward Columbine, who was haunted by scenes from Trinidad.[12] In June 1808 he was Commodore for the trial of a two-ship West Africa squadron and led a hazardous amphibious operation which deprived French privateers of their last stronghold on the coast at Saint-Louis.[13] In 1809 he accepted an Admiralty nomination to join a commission for the examination of the African littoral from the Gambia to the Gold Coast. This commission had been urged on the government by the African Institute, and the other members had been nominated by William Wilberforce. Dissension in the administration of the new

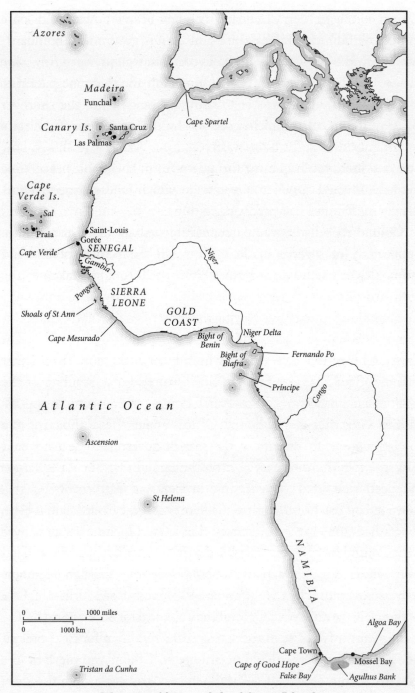

Azores

Madeira
Funchal

Canary Is. Santa Cruz
Las Palmas

Cape Spartel

Cape
Verde Is.

Sal
Praia
Cape Verde

Saint-Louis
Gorée
SENEGAL

Gambia

Niger

Pongas

SIERRA
LEONE

Shoals of St Ann

GOLD
COAST

Cape Mesurado

Bight of
Benin

Niger Delta

Fernando Po

Bight of
Biafra

Príncipe

Congo

Atlantic Ocean

Ascension

St Helena

N
A
M
I
B
I
A

0   1000 miles

0   1000 km

Algoa Bay

Cape Town
Cape of Good Hope
False Bay

Mossel Bay

Agulhus Bank

Tristan da Cunha

Map 12. Africa and the Atlantic Islands.

Crown colony of Sierra Leone, which had been established in 1807, led to Columbine's additional appointment as governor, on a temporary basis. His tenure was short-lived. His second wife, Ann, and his two children had accompanied him. Ann and their daughter died of fever, and Columbine's son Edward was sent home to recover. By May 1811, Columbine himself was too ill to continue. He died of yellow fever during the homeward passage of *Crocodile* (22), when she was 'one hundred leagues to the westward of the Azores'. Fulfilling the fears in the last will and testament which he drew up on board, the young Edward had predeceased him.

Columbine's hydrographic reputation led to some clamour for publication of surveys made by him on the African coast. The Admiralty had approved the expenditure of 200 guineas to equip him with two fine Earnshaw timepieces in his capacity as 'member of a Commission formed for surveying the coast of Africa', and Columbine had applied for a master 'of sufficient talent to assist me in the prosecution of the survey with which I am charged'.[14] Wilberforce acknowledged that Columbine had instructions for a 'survey of the coast in a nautical way'.[15] However, following the decision to appoint him as Governor, the Colonial Office issued a firm directive that Columbine should remain at the seat of government and not take part in 'exploring the coast'.[16] Hurd remarked that his old colleague had been 'well fitted out with time-keepers and instruments' but that nothing had reached the office.[17] There was some evidence that eight sheets had gone astray and that other material had been destroyed with Columbine's papers after his death. At least five sounding sheets were rendered by Lieutenant Robert Bones, who took over temporarily as governor when Columbine was forced to sail for home. One of these gives evidence of Columbine's old zeal for observation during a cruise towards Gorée in the spring of 1810, and of further observations in January 1811.[18] A fine tribute to Columbine survives in a minute on the corner of a letter, where Barrow recalled 'the great many very beautiful' surveys which Columbine had rendered in his career, 'so that he was thought of as a proper person to succeed Mr Dalrymple'.[19]

The career of another captain would draw towards a tragic close as further squadrons were deployed in this theatre after the wars. George Collier was appointed as the first Commodore with a clear remit to operate against the slave trade. He corresponded with the Hydrographer and produced a survey of North West Bay, Fernando Po (Bioco), one of the anchorages on the offshore islands where the squadron found respite from the fever coasts. The title declares that it was 'Taken from Memoranda of the Officers of HMS TARTAR', an interesting reflection of the military terminology and practice which Collier had witnessed during close cooperation with army counterparts in Spain.[20] Similar effort was encouraged throughout the squadron. One of Collier's pupils in *Tartar* (36) was William Finlaison, whom he placed in command of the *Morgiana* sloop. He produced two surveys in the Bight of Biafra, one delineating dangers in the approaches to the Fish Town River, Sengana Branch and Nun River on the Niger Delta. He found time to emulate Collier with ornate titles and accomplished views. Lieutenant Robert Hagan, who had served with Collier on the coast of Spain, distinguished himself in command of the gun-brig *Thistle*. He submitted a very competent survey of the Shoals of St Ann and the adjacent area. Captain Benedictus Marwood Kelly of *Pheasant* (18) rendered two graduated sheets recording his observations during inshore patrols around the Bights of Benin and Biafra.[21] He also made sketch surveys at Prince's Island (Ilha do Príncipe) and Fernando Po.[22] At George's Bay (Bahía de Luba) his starred sounding lines appear to be controlled by observations from a short baseline to the ship at anchor and the two headlands. Kelly had corresponded with the Hydrographer before the deployment, and Hurd had provided him with the latest charts for the African coast.[23] Captain Henry Leeke of *Myrmidon* (20) prepared a collector sheet of soundings and observations of magnetic variation taken in the ships of the squadron off the

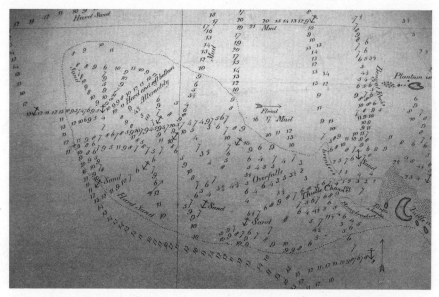

38. *Lieutenant Hagan's survey of the Shoals of St Ann including 'Thistle Channel'.*

39. *Commander William Finlaison's view of Fish Town.*

notorious coast between Capes Verd and Mesurado. The detail is intensified in the entrances to the slaving rivers, including the Pongas (Pongo), where he commanded a major operation to counter a threat to the colony of Sierra Leone.[24] Collier was unaware that whilst this effort was underway William James was studying the naval war of 1812. Collier had been given a squadron command on the strength of his performance in Spanish waters. James's *Naval History* would include a scathing condemnation of his failure to bring the USS

Constitution to action. Denied a court martial to clear his name, Collier took his own life on 24 March 1824.

This new war on the shores of Africa required significant front-line hydrographic effort. It would, however, be exploration which would produce a recruit for the Surveying Service. Mr Lewis Fitzmaurice won much admiration for taking charge of an expedition to the River Congo after the death of Commander James Hingston Tuckey and his officers.[25] He produced the survey from which a chart of the navigable reaches was published.[26] There was much general interest in the expedition, but it was the influence of John Barrow which helped Hurd to retain master and vessel, the schooner *Congo*, for survey work on return to home waters.

Barrow is especially remembered as the promoter of polar voyages. They certainly had profile and pull. In 1817 and subsequent years, the record of letters from volunteers to take part in them exceeds all other entries in the Admiralty digests of correspondence.[27] Hurd's lists of the purchase and allocation of instruments shows that the greatest expenditure was the equipping of the Arctic parties, though his formal responsibility for issue of chronometers did enable him to ensure an equitable distribution to the Admiralty's surveyors and to commanding officers with a scientific bent, such as Collier and Popham.[28] The Arctic expeditions were well prepared, and assertions that the scientific instructions were token gestures, and that the commanders and officers lacked appropriate experience and owed their appointments to networking and interest, do not stand up to examination.[29] The leaders, David Buchan and John Ross, were Scotsmen with benefit of a broad-based education and appropriate field experience. Buchan had been employed in exploration and survey of the interior and coasts of Newfoundland in the schooner *Adonis*.[30] Navigation and surveying were taught at Ross's school, Ayr Academy. He had testimonies from William Wales and Admiral Saumarez to his competence as an astronomer. He justly enjoyed the interest of George Hope on the Admiralty Board, who was not only aware of Ross's survey activity during the Baltic campaign but had passed further work to the Hydrographer in 1815. Two large fair sheets, dedicated to Hope, were replete with observations in the White Sea made whilst Ross was escorting a convoy to and from Archangel.[31] The two junior commanders also had appropriate backgrounds. John Franklin had worked with Matthew Flinders and served subsequently with William Durban. Edward Parry had rendered surveys to the Admiralty from the Baltic and Scottish waters and was fresh from service on the Nova Scotia station. His report of icebergs in low latitudes reinforced Barrow's conviction that icefields were breaking up and affording the opening for exploration of a North-West Passage.[32]

After the return of the expedition, Parry voiced doubts about the mountain range which Ross had discerned closing off Lancaster Sound, and aspersions were soon being aired in London over the conduct of the voyage. Ross attracted some sympathy from his contemporary Peter Heywood.[33] He lost the support of Barrow, with whom he engaged in a volley of published criticisms and refutations. His relationship with Hurd was on a different footing, and he preserved a charming and telling vignette:

> On my return to the Admiralty, in 1818, my Chart of Baffin's Bay, and those of other officers in the Expedition, were spread out beside each other on the floor of the Admiralty, before their Lordships; and a discrepancy being manifest, the Hydrographer and his assistant were sent for, and asked their opinions, when they immediately said, pointing to my chart, 'This one may be right, because it is on true Mercator's principles [...]'.[34]

Ross was particularly aggrieved that Barrow gave him no credit for the significant scientific output from his voyage, and he complained that Barrow's published account of the preparations for the expedition mentioned none of the 'nautical and scientific draughtsmen'.[35] With officers and young gentlemen clamouring to take part, Hurd would have to persevere to secure a place for men of his choice in the parties for subsequent polar voyages.

The allure of the Arctic is shown in William Mogg's record of his chance encounter with Commander George Lyon of *Hecla* on the coach from Greenwich to Charing Cross:

[He asked] 'What are you doing with yourself?' I told him. I was clerk in charge of the Survey Brig *Investigator* under the command of Mr George Thomas, Master and Surveyor in the Hydrographer's department at the Admiralty, engaged in conjunction with the Trigonometrical Survey of Great Britain, under the direction of Colonel Mudge of the Royal Artillery in the Ordnance Department. To which, in derision, he was pleased to designate as ('Gro-ping along shore') although a service of considerable science.[36]

Mogg was duly recruited as clerk to Lyon on the second round of Arctic voyages, but his grasp of the importance of the work in *Investigator* is telling. In the peak year of 1820, by contrast to the 6 per cent from the polar voyagers, 30 per cent of the incoming surveys came from Hurd's Admiralty Surveyors at home and abroad, engaged in another demanding campaign, to improve the safety of navigation.

The Hydrographer may have had limited say in selecting the Arctic parties, but his decisive influence on appointments as Admiralty Surveyors had been established before the war years were over. Just as Mr William Chapman displaced Lieutenant John Murray, so Mr George Holbrook was appointed Master and Commander in the *Sydney*, after just one season's tenure of Captain John Foulerton, Elder Brother of Trinity House, as the Admiralty's 'Superintendent of Surveys and Works on the Coasts and in the Harbours of Great

Britain'.[37] Lieutenant Thomas Evans was appointed to the 'Liverpool Survey' in 1812 on the basis of observations on the shifting sands in the approaches to Liverpool and the evidence of survey work in eastern seas, none of which had commended him to the demanding Hydrographer. Hurd and George Thomas cast doubt on his work, and his official employment ceased, though he retained favour locally and continued to make surveys for another decade.[38] The Hydrographer's verdict on competence carried weight with the Secretary and Lords Commissioners of the Admiralty, and the record of Admiralty correspondence shows routine consultation with him before appointments to the surveying ships.

Almost as soon as he took office, Hurd had been urging the Board to adapt a gun-brig for survey work in the English Channel 'under the direction of a qualified person'.[39] He had his nominee firmly in mind. Commander Martin White came from a prominent family of wine merchants in Portsmouth, and the interest of the Member of Parliament, John Markham, during the latter's service in the Admiralty, had ensured him a place afloat from the outbreak of war in 1793.[40] During White's extensive front-line service he had gathered hydrographic intelligence during commands in the blockading squadron off the Low Countries, and in the cutter *Pigmy* whilst watching the French ports on the coasts of Normandy and Brittany during the invasion scare in the autumn of 1803 (Plate 13).[41] He had conducted boat surveys around Jersey during three years in command of the sloop *Vulture* (16), which had been fitted out as a floating battery and guardship. In June 1812 a remarkable survey of St Aubyn's Bay reached the Hydrographer. It is described as a 'Compass Survey', and a careful note records that this copy had been corrected to remove errors in the polarity of the survey compass caused by the 'magnetic qualities' identified in several of the rocks. An expansive key reflects the detailed depiction of drying areas, tidal stream regime, recommended tracks and marks which characterises all White's work.[42] It was followed by a letter in which White volunteered to progress surveys in the complex waters around the Channel Islands. Hurd now had the opening to suggest that the employment of an officer already on active service would be an economical way of proceeding, and the survey enabled him to report that White was 'very well qualified'.[43]

In August 1812 the cutter *Fox* was hired for White's survey. He would encounter difficulties which earned Hurd's sympathy. The cutter was manned from the Portsmouth flagship and was always short-handed, since seamen had to be sent back in threes to receive their pay and collect slops. The senior officer on station lacked guidance on the status of the survey operation as White begged stores such as lead-lines and a hawser and grapnel for a deep water mooring for tidal stream observations. In November 1813 White reported that he needed one more year to complete his examination of the islands to the standard of his work in St Aubyn's Bay. With benefit of his own experience in Bermuda, Hurd gave White constant and unhesitating support as the examination of the area around Jersey and the extensive shoals such as the Minquiers prolonged the work. In December 1814, conscious of the retrenchment which was underway, White offered to continue on half-pay and suggested paying off *Fox* and substituting a 'fitted 6 oared cutter' which would be more suitable for the examination of the shoals at low water.[44] This adjustment was put into effect in the following spring, but Hurd's intervention remained essential to secure manpower. Hurd held White in the highest esteem, declaring his 'great anxiety to have the survey of so intricate a part of our Channel navigation on the copper' so that 'the abilities you have manifested in its execution' should be widely acknowledged. Not least among these was White's clear appreciation of the military significance of his work: 'You may rely, Sir, on my most earnest endeavours to prosecute through every difficulty, this important service, that in the event of any future war, this part of our Channel navigation may be resorted to by the block-ading frigates with confidence and security.'[45]

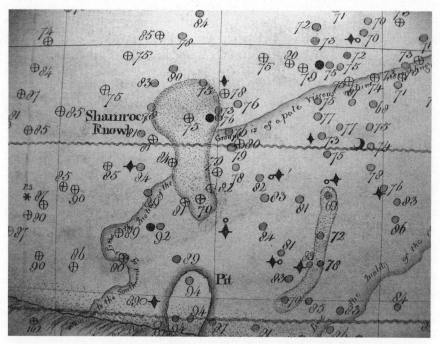

40. *Detail from Martin White's survey of the English Channel, showing a newly discovered feature which he named after his ship.*

In 1817 Hurd persuaded the Admiralty to commission the gun-brig *Shamroc*, in which White was to extend his survey into the English Channel and out into the South Western Approaches. He was tasked to delineate the Nymphe and Sole Banks and to confirm the existence of other features which would enable ships to make a safe landfall if they paid attention to soundings.[46] He would identify a number of new features, the most important of which he named after the Hydrographer. Hurd's Dyke, now known as Hurd Deep, is a trench running west and north of Alderney which would give an alert mariner a warning to alter course away from the notorious danger of the Casquets. The control which he extended from the British and French geodetic stations, and his calculation of *Shamroc*'s track between astronomical fixes when out of sight of land, were recorded in meticulous workbooks. The surveys were rendered on magnificent fair sheets (Plate 16). White trained up a protégé, Henry Mangles Denham, who drew up most of the later work. Denham would follow in White's footsteps as an Admiralty Surveyor on the coast of England, earning fame for finding a new channel through the mobile sand-banks that threatened to choke the commerce of Liverpool, Britain's second port.

Another proven practitioner was involved in similar work further afield. This was David Bartholomew, who had been advanced to post captain at the end of the war but who had despaired of peace-time employment. His survey expertise had not, however, been forgotten. After the expedition to the Plate, he had given further proof as first lieutenant in *Sapphire* (18) during the transportation of a diplomatic mission to Persia. Subsequently, he drew up his own compilation chart of the Gulf, clearly modelled on Popham's Red Sea chart, and submitted it to the Admiralty in 1813 with a dedication to the son of their old patron, the second Lord Melville, now First Lord.[47] Bartholomew's wife Ann, who had barely seen him during the nine years since their marriage, died in 1814 whilst he was in action in *Erebus* on the rivers of the US. They had no children. He was more than ready when, in the summer of 1818, he was selected for a now-rare sea command as the Admiralty Board's accredited surveyor on the west coast of Africa.

He sailed early in 1819 in *Leven* (20) with most comprehensive instructions from the Admiralty. He was to fix the longitude of Funchal, Madeira and Santa Cruz, Tenerife, and the latitude and longitude of the Cape Verde Islands and capes and headlands on the adjacent coast of Africa. The intervening sea area was to be surveyed, and a number of notorious *vigias* – dangers reported by mariners – were to be confirmed or disproved. These included Whale Rock, which was said to lie north-east of the Azores.[48] This task had been the first outside home waters in Hurd's list for the Board in 1814 of 'parts of the world [...] where [...] information is most wanted'. With his customary canniness in stating his case, he had suggested that the work might be undertaken by 'a Lieutenant or Master in a gun-brig or schooner [...] spared from [the West African] squadron'.[49] He will have been delighted with the generous provision which the Admiralty made. For he would soon read a first report from Bartholomew, describing how, with characteristically meticulous care, he set up his instruments, calibrated his chronometers and began his calculations at the Observatory of Lisbon, where he also obtained recommendations to the governors of the islands which he would be visiting.[50]

In mid-June, Bartholomew was reporting the completion of work around the Cape Verde Islands and the adjacent coast of Africa. The large fair sheet of this work, which is annotated 'Made by Order of the Lords Commissioners of the Admiralty', is similar in style to his Persian Gulf chart. It shows how he laid down the position of the islands in the group, examined the main channels between them, searched for reported shoals in the vicinity and completed sketch surveys of the principal roadsteads. A table gives details of measurements of tidal heights and compass variation.[51] A separate list of latitudes and longitudes had been forwarded.[52] His reports of proceedings and his meticulous 'Angle Book' and 'Field and Station Book', with details and diagrams of the observations on which his depiction of the coastline of the Cape Verde Islands depended, have all survived.[53] In these documents, he included comment on phenomena affecting his results, such as the magnetic attraction of the rocks and sand. Astronomical and geodetic observations were hampered by persistent low cloud, rain and haze. There are little windows into his daily efforts: 'I could proceed no further, the high rocks [...] being washed by the sea. Returned back and rejoined Mudge at the foot of Tope de Curtio'.

Bartholomew was an ideal model, and like his own mentor, Popham, he involved all his officers throughout. The titles of the many sheets arising from this deployment record the two mainstays whom he frequently despatched on adventurous independent work.

Owen's former assistant, Alexander Vidal, would recall how, whilst surveying on the heights of Sal in the Cape Verde Islands, he stumbled upon the nest of a large bird of prey, probably an osprey, and was attacked by the parent bird and saved from injury by his 'strong beaver hat [...] which was hardened by exposure to salt water and the sun'.[54] Perhaps that hat was a treasured companion from Canadian days. His counterpart was William Mudge, third son of Colonel Mudge of the Ordnance Survey, who had not prospered under White as assistant surveyor and second in command of *Shamroc* but who now flourished in the team on board *Leven* (Plate 15).

In the course of the deployment, smallpox carried off a young relative, and Bartholomew interred him in the New Burial Ground of the English community beneath the lowering Peak Castle on the outskirts of Funchal, Madeira.[55] He himself would succumb to typhoid before the second season was complete, and he was buried by the walls of the fort at Porto Praia in the Cape Verde Islands. He had, however, passed on the baton. Vidal and Mudge would be selected as the first lieutenants and assistant surveyors in *Leven* and *Baracouta* as the major survey of the coasts of Africa resumed under captains Owen and Cutfield. When Cutfield fell victim to the fevers which decimated the companies of the ships, Vidal was promoted to command *Baracouta*. He and Mudge were destined to stand amongst the most renowned practitioners of the Beaufort period. Alexander Becher had also served with Bartholomew, who made him responsible for training the young gentlemen who had been hand-picked for the deployment. Edward Durnford had shown particular competence and would often accompany Vidal and Mudge. His death from dysentery during Owen's surveys cut off a career of brilliant promise. George Frazer, who had been rated Acting Second Master by Bartholomew, would survive the African surveys and go on to serve with his old shipmate William Mudge on the Irish coast, taking charge of the survey on the death of the latter and continuing it with high distinction in the rank of post captain.

A similar pattern of encouragement emerged on the other side of the Atlantic. When Home Popham, now a rear admiral, was appointed flag officer on the West Indies station in December 1817, Hurd's suggestion that his old colleague on the Chart Committee, 'one of our best observers', should be asked to determine the position of Port Royal, Jamaica, was readily taken up by the Board.[56] Popham had lost no time in proposing a call on Hurd, writing: 'It will be absolutely necessary to have two refracting Telescopes with Astronomical Powers to observe the Eclipses of Jupiter's Satillites [sic]. I hope I shall also be allowed two Timekeepers.'[57] Hurd had advised that Popham should seek assistance from 'the Admiralty surveyor Mr. De Mayne, who also has the reputation of being an excellent observer and calculator'. Thus, the network of influence took effect once again, with a sympathetic flag officer in place.

Since the coming of peace, De Mayne had been working around the Bahama Islands in command of 'His Majesty's Surveying Vessel the *Landrail*', and in 1819 the *Kangaroo* was sent out to replace her.[58] Hurd had listed the Great Bahama Bank and islands thereon and the 'Florida or Gulf Stream' as priorities. However, De Mayne's base for provisions and repair was Kingston, Jamaica. Whilst there, with Popham's firm and enthusiastic support, he would complete thorough surveys of the approaches to Port Royal and Kingston, of other parts of Jamaica and of the great Pedro Bank.[59] There is some evidence that Popham was keen to keep De Mayne in his domain, and whilst writing to acknowledge receipt of the Pedro Bank survey and the consequent update of Admiralty charts with the danger, Hurd urged the importance of resuming the work in the Bahamas, where a potential naval base had been identified and the work of delineating the most dangerous shoals was incomplete.[60] On 24 May 1821 De Mayne was at last able to report to the Hydrographer that, although constrained by employment on 'other services', he had completed the survey of the channels into Port Royal and Kingston harbours, working to 'trigonometrical principles and every pains taken with protracting of the situations of the shoals and dangers'. With the letter and the fair sheets came a fine printed volume of sailing directions.[61] He was now in a position to return to New Providence, where Popham seems to have visited him.[62] The subsequent work resulted in four great sheets, which are preserved in the Hydrographic Office archive.[63] The present-day charts of the 'New Anchorage', now known as the Douglas Road or Cochrane Anchorage, and the Douglas Passage leading to it, are still largely based on his work. They merit Hurd's praise of De Mayne as 'so perfect a master of your business'. The Hydrographer had secured approval to provide De Mayne with assistance and sent out two highly recommended 'scientific young men', writing: 'I trust that you will give both my young men in the course of their services under you an opportunity of shewing their talents and abilities in the line they are placed in and I have to assure them that your express approbation of their conduct and exertions will be necessary to their future views in the service.'[64]

Both Richard Owen, a Christ's Hospital boy, and Edward Barnett were destined for distinguished careers in the surveying service. The latter earned particular approbation from De Mayne, and he would succeed him, spending two decades in command of survey vessels in the West Indies.[65]

A similar chain of succession was being launched in the Mediterranean, where Smyth had gained the unswerving support of the commander-in-chief, none other than Sir Charles Penrose. He spotted young men of talent in his flagship and sent them to work with the Admiralty Surveyor in his theatre. One of them was Lieutenant Charles Malden, who assisted in the most rigorous of Smyth's geodetic work, reflecting ability which would subsequently earn him an appointment as Surveyor for a Pacific deployment in *Blonde* (42). His surveys in the Hawaiian Islands would include the vicinity of the Pearl Lochs near Honolulu Harbour, site of the future US naval base.

Smyth retained Hurd's advocacy and had been furnished with a surveying ship in 1817, the *Aid*, later renamed *Adventure*.[66] By the

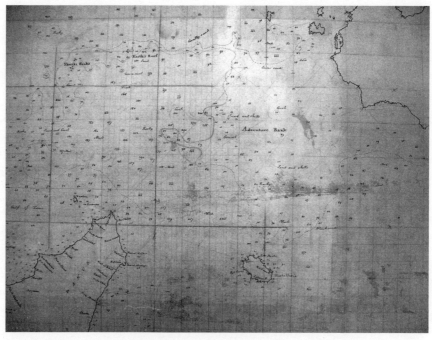

41. Smyth's sounding collector sheet showing how he established the existence of the deep channel joining the two basins of the Mediterranean Sea.

close of her first commission, she was highly acclaimed in the region. In the Adriatic, Smyth conducted a joint survey, and his Austrian and Italian collaborators spoke of '*son observatoire flottant*' and listed her equipment with approbation mingled with awe.[67] As Smyth addressed the core task which Hurd had emphasised in their first meeting, making astronomical measurements at key landfalls and ports and connecting them with careful chronometric observations, he trained up assistants to whom he could pass the torch. Lieutenant Michael Atwell Slater would complete the Mediterranean work allocated to *Adventure* and go on to serve with distinction as an Admiralty Surveyor on the coast of Scotland. Midshipman Thomas Graves would earn fame as a later Admiralty Surveyor in the waters of the Aegean. It was their mentor, however, who earned the sobriquet 'Mediterranean Smyth', whilst his ship gave its name to one of his major discoveries, Adventure Bank in the Strait of Sicily, which hydrographic offices now designate as demarcating the western and eastern basins of the sea.

In 1819 Hurd presented the first Hydrographer's Annual Report on surveys in progress, a practice which would continue until the last decade of the twentieth century. Two years later he prepared the first catalogue of Admiralty Charts, in which the efforts of all his Admiralty Surveyors, in many of the areas which he had enumerated in his minute of 1814, were conspicuous. His war-time vision had been realised in the uneasy peace – 'a mass of valuable information' had been gathered 'that could not fail of being highly advantageous to us in any future war, and would otherwise redound to the credit and glory of the great Maritime Empire'.[68]

Postscript
A 'Great Maritime Nation'

Thomas Hurd had less than a decade in which to realise his vision. His correspondence with the Board of Admiralty suggests that he was in poor health from 1820. He died on 29 April 1823, aged seventy-four, whilst still in harness. The demise of this archetypal public servant, methodical and indefatigable in discharging his duties, attracted no obituary. Over a century later, a legend was still current that this rather shadowy figure had 'walked out one evening from the house in which he was staying and was never seen again'.[1] No private correspondence or memoirs have survived to bring his personality to life. Though very aware of the importance of networking, he appears to have been too busy to cultivate the circles of the learned societies. His persistent representation in memorials to the Admiralty Board of the mismatch between his responsibilities and his rewards, compared to other naval postholders and to the senior clerks, was driven by a passionate belief that his office was of 'high and extreme importance to this Maritime Country'. His desire was 'that men of talents and great scientific knowledge may hereafter look up to it as an object worthy of their attainment'. In 1818 he had written: 'Your Lordships cannot but be aware that it is upon the talents and attention of the Head of this Office and those employed under him, that the success of the enterprizes, and the safety of the Navy most materially depends, as well as of the immense saving which an able and faithful discharge of its duties must cause to the public both in ships and Seamen'.[2] This advocacy was acknowledged in the tribute eventually published, some six years after his death, to a 'zealous friend and supporter' of 'the cause of Hydrography', who had 'employed all the serviceable part of his life in the advancement of a science which was at once honourable to himself, valuable to his profession and to the world at large'.[3]

Hurd's old colleagues Columbine and Popham had predeceased him. So too had David Bartholomew. William Henry Smyth had withdrawn with his records to his home in Bedford, where he welcomed 'the hydrographer of the Spanish navy', whom he had met during his service as midshipman at Cádiz. In 1823 Felipe Bauzá had once again fled to the coast city from Madrid, taking charts and plans. As a liberal member of the Cortes, the Spanish parliament that the reactionary Ferdinand VII had dismissed, he was under sentence of death. With the help of the Royal Navy, he and his precious hydrographic collection were rescued and carried to England. Here he was destined to spend the remainder of his life, forging a strong relationship with the personnel of the Hydrographic Office, commenting on its small size and slender resources in the early 1820s. He noted favourably the surveying vessels that Hurd had obtained and which were 'steadily in service', manned by 'a well educated work force'.[4]

In October of the same year that Bauzá fled from Spain, another player in the story in this book was appointed Second Director of the 'deposito hidrográfico en la Corte'. Alexander Briarly would later describe himself as 'Director of the Hydrographical Department under the Spanish Government in Madrid', though he does not feature in the history of that organisation.[5] In the reactionary regime of Spain, Briarly had found outlets for his energy as a commissioner for the improvement of the River Guadalquivir and, seemingly without losing royal favour, as adviser to the Cortes in the period 1820–23.[6] In 1837 an anonymous writer in the *United Services Journal* discussed Briarly: 'He went, we believe, into the Spanish service, and not having been lately heard of, has probably clued up for a full due.' Sadly, no response was forthcoming to the writer's prompt that 'His adventures would form a capital volume, and we hope that this hint may draw some anecdotes from surviving messmates.'[7] After a turbulent appointment as Consul General in Tangier, fruitlessly pursuing the surrender of exiled liberals to Spanish authorities, he had returned to active naval service in 1832. In 1833 he was back in Mallorca as Naval Commander, where he earned favourable notice and settled down to reap the benefits of his oversight of harbour and other dues.[8] By 1835 he was on the list of Brigadiers los Señores, laden with honours and a martial coat of arms as Knight of the Royal Military Order of Charles III.[9] His motto, by now perhaps appropriate, was *Mesis ab alto*, 'Our harvest is from the deep'. He died on 19 November at San Roque, just five miles from Gibraltar, the first port of call at the outset of his career as master in the Royal Navy forty years earlier.

Whilst William Henry Smith had taken retirement in 1825, focusing on work in his private observatory and forging his reputation as a leading astronomer of the day, others of Hurd's recruits, such as Martin White in the English Channel and Anthony De Mayne in the West Indies, remained on their survey grounds until the end of the decade. William Hewett continued his labours in the North Sea through the 1830s, earning fame for his part in proving William Whewell's deductions on the tidal regime. In the earlier years he rubbed along with George Thomas. The touchy old master would outlast his officer contemporaries but would never be rewarded with the commissioned status which he felt to be his due. In a memorial, he asked plaintively at least for 'some distinguishing mark in his uniform' from the newly entered second master serving under him.[10] He continued to render work of outstanding quality, latterly in the complex and challenging waters of the Shetland and Orkney Islands. At the end of the 1846 season, he was no longer fit for sea service. He died in Fulham in 1850.[11]

Hurd's true achievement between 1817 and 1823 is clear from the following table,[12] which indicates the bearing of the specialisation in 1823, as Beaufort took the helm in 1829, and a decade later in 1839:

	Captains	Commanders	Lieutenants	Masters	Others
1823	2	4	11	3	6
1829	2	9	11	3	8
1839	5	5	15	1	15

By identifying suitable young officers and keeping them employed with his survey parties, Hurd ensured the steady bearing of commissioned specialists in the critical first decade after his death. In addition to those borne as assistants in 1823, at least seven other gifted young officers were serving with the ships and parties, and four of them would survive to join the surveying service. Indeed, nearly all the lieutenants, masters, master's mates and midshipmen serving in 1823 were still active in the field in 1829. Furthermore, the five captains serving in 1839 – Bayfield, Beechey, Bullock, Hewett and Vidal, with Commanders Boteler, Denham, Robinson and Slater – and Mr George Thomas had all been recruited during Hurd's tenure. Of these men, all but Boteler and Robinson had seen front-line service in the Napoleonic Wars.

Hurd had made the case for exploiting the skills of those practitioners in the years of so-called peace. He and his successors used their influence to prevent distraction from the survey task but retained with their war-time experience a conviction that a vital military component of the fleet was being honed. A study of the survey of British waters concluded that 'Knowledge gained in the shoal-beset waters [...] did more to advance the science of hydrography than the exploratory survey of thousands of miles of coastline in other parts of the world.'[13] Many practitioners would witness that some of their most testing experiences have been in UK waters. But one nineteenth-century practitioner held the view that 'no service on home surveys will, I am convinced, give the practice necessary to make officers what is required for survey duties during war on an enemy's coast'.[14]

This was the judgement of Bartholomew James Sulivan, one of the surveyors whom Beaufort sent out to Russian waters in 1854, fulfilling Hurd's vision of Fleet Surveyors in the main theatres. Sulivan had applied his expertise, built up in survey of the Falkland Islands, in combat on the River Paraná in 1840, and he was described by one of his officers as having no equal as a 'pioneer on the enemy coast'. He would tell a Commission on the Surveying Service in 1863 that young officers in home waters were not on 'unexplored and dangerous coasts' and 'only learn a little sounding [...] carrying out details in connection with the ordnance surveys'. He might have received a firm riposte from his old counterpart, Henry Otter, who retired that year after over two decades of work on the intricate coasts of Scotland, interrupted only by his part in the Baltic, where he too had shown ability to lead into 'creeks and corners never intended for ships of the line'.[15] Thomas Spratt, Sulivan's counterpart in the Black Sea, might also have testified that the skills of his front-line path-finders in *Spitfire* had been forged during two decades of painstaking examination of the Aegean. These commanders had fulfilled the expectation of the Hydrographer as 'the Admiral's eyes'.[16] By the end of the conflict they would be pre-eminent advisers to the admirals, forming expert war plans for landings and bombardments. Back in London they would be interviewed by ministers and taken to discussions with allied heads of state.[17]

The continued delivery of combat support was the vital element which preserved the hydrographic specialisation within the Royal Navy's officer corps, unlike in other European countries such as France. A reference by an economy-seeking First Lord in 1872 to the 'non-fighting part of the Navy' prompted a riposte from the Hydrographer that: 'I would venture to point out [. . .] that in all conflicts which have occurred during the last 25 years the surveying vessels have been the Pioneers of the Fighting Fleet'. A Naval Lord added: 'The Hydrographer's remarks as to the distinguished part taken by the surveying officers in all our late wars, I gladly endorse and every officer engaged in China, Baltic and Black seas will gladly do likewise.'[18]

The importance of hydrographic intelligence for strategic and operational planning and the subsequent deployment of offensive naval power is a lesson which has had to be relearned in subsequent centuries. Before the First World War the Committee of Imperial Defence concluded that survey ships would be of no use on the outbreak of war, and in 1914, and again in 1939, the majority were allocated to other tasks. The surveying specialists distinguished themselves in navigational, amphibious warfare and mine counter-measures appointments, but by halfway through both conflicts surveying ships were being reconfigured and manned for urgent front-line operational survey tasks. Surveyors would work alongside the navigational pioneers, especially where more rigorous investigation was required, as on the Normandy coast before the invasion of 1944 to select the sites for the vital Mulberry harbours.[19]

In 1956 the survey ship *Dalrymple*, designated for auxiliary duties in the British task force during the Suez Crisis, provided the crucial survey expertise which reopened Port Said. At the end of the operation, the Flag Officer declared that no future force should be without a survey ship as a unit. The Hydrographer commented: 'the survey ship rather enjoyed itself, and, when all is said and done, the work they were asked to do was so exactly what their training is designed to achieve. If it showed nothing else, I hope that it will persuade the Board that in time of emergency surveying ships should be used as such and not taken away on other duties.'[20]

Yet, in 1982, to my dismay, three surveying ships, with officers and ratings on board who shared my experience of inshore survey in the

Falkland Islands and South Georgia, were designated as non-combatant casualty ferries. On secondment to Fleet Headquarters, I used the historical record in arguing successfully for the preparation of *Hecate*, in which I was serving, for ice patrol ship and front-line survey duties. We did not arrive in theatre until after the conflict had ended, but we worked up threat to ensure safe navigation for the radar picket ships of the follow-up force. A decade later, in the aftermath of the Cold War, there was much pressure to disband the Royal Navy's Surveying Service and to rely on a burgeoning commercial sector – a return to the practice of the eighteenth century. In the new millennium, academic studies of power projection and amphibious warfare debated the impact of general intelligence and improved materiel, with barely a nod to hydrographic support for navigation.[21] In the real world, the challenges of access and power projection in expeditionary warfare campaigns in the Middle East and West Africa reminded planners and commanders that the fleet needs its pathfinders, and pathfinders with a high level of scientific skill. The commander of the amphibious task force for Operation Palliser in 2000 rejected my allocation of a survey ship. It would be 'too slow'. Once in the little-surveyed waters of Sierra Leone, his force struggled to find landing places and was soon running low on fuel for busy helicopters. *Beagle* was deployed and surveyed approaches for landing craft and access routes for frigates to provide naval gunfire support. In 2003 there was no debate about deployment of surveyors to identify safe operating areas for amphibious assault operations against Iraq. However, it was only the Royal Navy which had the specialist warship hulls that could be deployed up threat. In conducting this work and subsequently identifying the path for ships carrying humanitarian aid past the shoals in the straits leading to Umm Qasr, *Roebuck* and her survey motorboats were truly following in the footsteps of the pathfinders of the Napoleonic Wars. The First Sea Lord noted: 'To one of the smallest ships in the Royal Navy befell one of the largest tasks of the operation'.[22]

POSTSCRIPT

The vision of Thomas Hurd, burnished by his own front-line experience, launched by his persistent advocacy and fulfilled by the specialisation which he established on a firm foundation, remains sound and continues to need advocacy. Recent decisions to resort to embarkation of modular specialist equipment in ships of opportunity risks Hurd's successors facing the frustration with which he struggled without a dedicated vessel for his front-line survey. The embarkation of survey teams in ships that are not operated by the Royal Navy betrays a poor grasp of the law of the sea and the importance of warship status. The standing and influence for good of this 'great Maritime Nation' still demand 'competent knowledge' of coasts and seas, and the active employment of qualified and experienced pathfinders of the Royal Navy to gather it.

Appendix of Statistics

The following statistics are based on an exhaustive examination of records in the archive of the United Kingdom Hydrographic Office, supplemented by searches in other repositories, principally the National Maritime Museum, with additional information gleaned in research in primary and secondary sources. From the period 1793–1823, 369 practitioners have been identified. Of these, 84 were active in the French Revolutionary Wars. A further 176 made surveys in the Napoleonic Wars. During the remainder of Hurd's tenure as Hydrographer, 109 new practitioners submitted work. Table 1 is designed to show the total of practitioners in action in each period.

Table 1: Numbers making hydrographic surveys

Period	1793–1802	1803–15	1815–23
Captains	35	74	45
Masters	32	109	56
Others	17	23	38

Table 2: Number of surveys

Period	1793–1802	1803–15	1815–23
Captains	114	216	175
Masters	99	233	134
Others	52	63	97

Notes:
1. The surveys made by captains (i.e. all commanding officers) in 1803–15 include the thirty sheets of Beaufort's survey of Karamania but do not include Flinders' surveys around Australia, from which over eighty manuscript sheets have survived. Those for the period 1815–23 include the substantial input from the Admiralty Surveys being undertaken by Philip Parker King, William Henry Smyth and Martin White.
2. The designation 'others' comprises officers not in command, master's mates and midshipmen, two schoolmasters, a Royal Marine officer and a chaplain.

Surveys 1793–1823

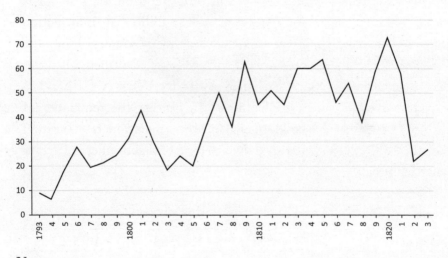

Notes:
1. The distribution of the survey effort illustrates the war-time stimulus and the impact of the advent of Hurd as a proactive champion of hydrographic effort. The post-war output far exceeded that in the French Revolutionary Wars. Between 1816 and 1823 the campaigns of the Admiralty Surveyors, accounting for 41 per cent of the total, were supplemented by output from the anti-slave

trade patrols, the voyages of discovery, deployments in search of ship timber and ongoing fleet operations.

2. The peak associated with the survey effort around the time of the Peace of Amiens (1801–3) in the Mediterranean theatre is clear in the graph. That sea would receive the most sustained hydrographic effort by the Royal Navy across the whole period, with more than 200 surveys being made.

3. The peak year of effort during the Napoleonic Wars was 1809, when sixty-three surveys were rendered. This reflects the operational situation, with six campaigns underway in testing waters such as the Baltic. Surveys made during these campaigns represent 75 per cent of the output. The distribution is shown in the pie chart below.

Surveys 1809

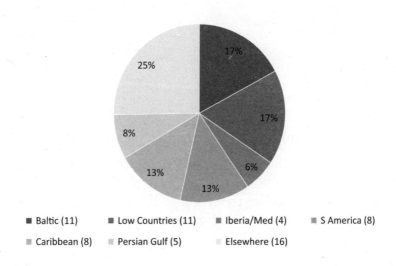

Glossary

Absolute position: In the period covered by this book, an absolute position, expressed in latitude and longitude, would be derived from an astronomical observation. Thus, the precise positions obtained in the observatories at Paris and Greenwich provided the end points for the triangulation work to connect the two countries. Astronomical observations in the field, hence 'field astronomy', would be used to establish a starting point from which a control system could be extended through unsurveyed territory. Field astronomy could also be used to provide a position for important landfalls on a coast. By this period, French astronomers had done this for the main headlands on their Atlantic coast.

Azimuth compass: Unlike a simple steering or boat's compass, this compass was fitted with a sight to enable an observation for variation to be made by observation of a heavenly body. It was a relatively expensive instrument, but it was taken into the field for surveys controlled by compass.

Baseline: When commencing a system of triangulation (q.v.), one side of the first triangle must be measured as precisely as possible to provide natural scale for subsequent survey work. If an area of flat ground is available, this can be done by laying down and marking a line using a chain made of material which is as little susceptible as possible to expansion or contraction with changes of temperature. Such equipment would rarely be available in a ship of the fleet, unless equipped by the Admiralty or by the captain himself. A lead-line might be used. A measurement could also be made by measuring the time elapsed between the observation of the firing of a gun and hearing the report.

Bathymetric survey: The process of determining the shape and composition of the seabed, which in the period of this book was done by deploying a lead, armed with tallow, at the end of a lead-line (q.v.). Some sounding machines were introduced during this period, cf. **Massey's sounding machine**.

Cadastre: A French term for a record book listing estate information. A survey designed to establish property boundaries is called a cadastral survey, and the resultant map is known as a cadastral plan.

Celestial sphere: Because the distances between the Earth and the stars are vastly greater than the diameter of the Earth's orbit around the sun, we may imagine that they lie on the inner surface of a sphere of infinite radius, co-axial with the Earth and rotating from the east to the west. This is the celestial sphere. If the Earth is taken to be at its centre, then a system of coordinates can be established on its surface analogous to latitude and longitude. These are called declination and hour angle, although astronomers use the term 'right ascension' in lieu of hour angle. We can also perform calculations by spherical trigonometry on its surface. This is done by calculating sides and angles of the PZX triangle (q.v.), in which P is the elevated pole, Z the observer's zenith (cf. **meridian passage**) and X the position of a heavenly body.

Collector sheet: A sheet or tracing onto which all the work conducted during a survey is collected. It enables the officer in charge to keep track of the progress of the survey. It is also used to check the fair sheet (q.v.) before it is rendered to the Hydrographic Office.

Equation of time: This is the difference between mean solar time and apparent solar time, or between the clock and the sundial, at any instant.

Errors: See under **systematic error**. See also **precision**.

Fair sheet: The final manuscript drawing of a survey which is rendered to the Hydrographic Office, and from which the engraving for the published chart will be derived. Where an un-faired sheet was received, draughtsmen in the office would prepare a final drawing for the guidance of the engravers.

Figure of the Earth: 'The form of our globe, which is that of an oblate spheroid' (Smyth, *The Sailor's Word-Book*). The Earth is of course not a perfect shape, and nor can its shape be measured directly, but only a section of its surface. Such measurements enable the surface of the Earth at mean sea level, known as the geoid, to be defined at a location, from which a theoretical, regular spheroid of best fit to the geoid can be selected. This chosen spheroid then gives a means of expressing position in terms of coordinates, such as latitude and longitude.

Geodesy: The scientific investigation of the shape and dimensions of the Earth, leading to the definition of a figure of the Earth (q.v.). The higher-level measurements involved are called geodetic survey.

Geodetic station: Strictly speaking, a geodetic station is a point in the principal triangulation network of a country, where survey observations will have been made with the utmost care and precision. It tends to be applied loosely to include triangulation stations in secondary or tertiary networks.

Great circle: Any circle of a sphere whose plane contains the centre of the sphere, e.g. a circle defining a meridian or line of longitude.

High Water Full and Change: A value used to derive a time of high water at a location, also known as the vulgar establishment of a port. It expressed the lunitidal interval, i.e. the time elapsed between the passage of the moon over the meridian of the location and the next high water at the time of the full moon or the change of the moon (i.e. new moon). The method gives good results at the time of spring and neap tides but less accurate results at other times.

Horizontal sextant angle position fixing: If an angle is observed between two marks ashore, then the observer will lie on the position circle subtended by that angle. If three stations are used and the two angles on either side of the centre mark are observed, then the observer's position will be at the point where the two position circles intersect. When controlling a survey by resection using horizontal sextant angles (HSA), it is important to choose the marks to ensure that the two position circles cut at a good angle. The observer must also be particularly alert for a 'circular fix', where their position and the marks all lie on the circumference of the same circle, giving no solution for position.

Intersection: A prominent object or mark in a triangulation scheme is said to have been intersected if angular observations have been made to it, but not from it. Its position can be computed provided it has been intersected from at least two points whose positions are known.

Jupiter's satellites, deduction of longitude by observation of: The planet Jupiter has four bright moons, two of which are eclipsed every two days as they pass into the planet's shadow. The moment of disappearance was referred to as their immersion and that of their reappearance as their emersion. The Greenwich Mean Time (GMT) at which these events occurred was tabulated in *The Nautical Almanac* and similar publications. Observation of the eclipse required a large telescope of c.6 feet in length and was therefore a measurement made ashore and in a chosen strategic location. By the 1830s the method was classed in the advice in *The Nautical Almanac* as one 'where extreme accuracy is not required'.

Lead-line: Lines made up from sisal, a hard cordage with little stretch, used to deploy the sounding lead with its hollow base 'armed' with tallow to provide information on the 'nature of the bottom'. The 200-fathom deep-sea lead-line, used to give warning of arrival 'in soundings', was marked with knots at every 10 fathoms and small knots every 5 fathoms. The associated lead generally weighed 28lbs. The hand lead-line, marked to 13 or 20 fathoms, with a 7lb or 14lb lead depending on whether it was used in boat or ship, was the instrument for the laborious task of building up a picture of the bottom topography of a harbour or roadstead.

Levelling: The measurement of difference of height between two points on the Earth's surface using a portable scale and an instrument with a telescopic sight which has been made 'level' by centring the bubble in a spirit-level. In hydrographic surveying, this practice is principally employed to measure the difference of height between a bench mark and the zero mark on a scale for observing tidal height. The observation is made in a sequence of measurements in which portable scale and instrument are leapfrogged.

Longitude by chronometer: The chronometer is a precision timekeeper which can be set to GMT. Its 'going rate' will be liable to change, both steadily by reason of small imperfections or frictions which the manufacturer seeks to minimise, or irregularly because of changes in environment (e.g. temperature) which the mariner must minimise by good management. The rate would be checked where possible during the course of a voyage by precise astronomical observations for longitude ashore (cf. **Jupiter's satellites**), repeated after a period of seven days. At sea, the time given by the watch, corrected for rate and for the equation of time (q.v.), could be compared with the local time computed from an observation of the altitude of the sun or a star (cf. **PZX triangle**) to give the value of longitude.

Longitude by lunar distances: From 1763, tables were published giving the Greenwich time at which certain bright stars were at a given angular distance from the centre of the moon. The method required teamwork in observation of the distance, the height of the two bodies and local time. The mathematical computation was challenging. The method was also subject to errors in the tables and in observation.

Massey's sounding machine: This was designed to measure depths by means of a rotating cylinder and a counting mechanism attached to a long lead weight. It permitted soundings to be taken whilst the ship was making way, provided that the line was paid out at sufficient rate to maintain the instrument's vertical descent. Hurd made early experiments with the machine in 1807 off the south coast of England.

Mercator projection: In this projection all meridians are made parallel, and the latitude scale is increased in the same ratio as the longitude scale in a particular latitude, usually the mid-latitude of the area depicted. The result is a distortion of area which has become unpopular with some users of atlas maps of the world. However, the projection has the virtue of showing angles as they are observed on the Earth's surface and representing rhumb lines as straight lines. A rhumb line, or loxodrome, is a line on the Earth's surface which cuts all the meridians at the same angle. The course steered in a ship is normally a rhumb line. Therefore, the Mercator projection is favoured for nautical charts used to plot a ship's track.

Meridian passage: The **meridian** is an imaginary great circle (q.v.) passing through the poles and an observer's position and cutting the equator at right angles. It has an equivalent on the celestial sphere (q.v.), on which it passes through the observer's zenith, i.e. the point in the heavens directly overhead. A heavenly body is said to make a meridian passage or transit when it crosses the plane of these imaginary great circles. Thus, when the sun is due south of an observer in the northern hemisphere, at noon, it makes a meridian passage.

Miner's compass: Also known as a circumferentor; a magnetic compass with two fixed sights on brass arms extending on opposite sides, enabling a bearing to be observed to an object.

Pendulum observations: The frequency of the beat of a freely swinging pendulum of known length is modified by the local force of gravity. Observation of this variation in different localities during a voyage, such as that of Captain Basil Hall in the *Conway*, enabled deductions to be made about the true form of the Earth.

Precision: In surveying, precision is the measure of repeatability of an observation, i.e. the degree of agreement between individual measurements in a set. Precision improves with the number of measurements made.

PZX triangle: During the period covered by this book, oceanic navigation was revolutionised by the availability of the chronometer and *The Nautical Almanac*. Now, in addition to measuring his latitude by observation of a heavenly body at meridian passage (q.v.), the navigator could look up a value for the declination of a body in the almanac for the instant at which he observed its altitude. He could thus derive the three sides of the triangle formed on the celestial sphere by the elevated pole (P), his zenith (Z) and the heavenly body (X): co-latitude, co-declination and zenith distance. Then solutions could be obtained by spherical trigonometry, e.g. the hour angle (t), and hence local time, from the spherical cosine formula (cos zenith distance = cos co-lat.cos co-dec + sin co-lat.sin co-dec.cos t).

Resection: A prominent object or mark in a triangulation scheme is said to have been resected if angular observations have been made from it to stations whose positions are known. Each observed angle defines a position circle upon which the observer lies. The observer's position can be obtained by plotting the cut of the position circles, or, more precisely, by calculating the intersection mathematically. A horizontal sextant angle fix is an example of resection. The strength of a resection depends on careful choice of the marks which are observed to, so as to ensure that the position circles cut at a good angle (ideally between 30° and 90°).

Satellite navigation system: A system by means of which position is determined by trilateration (q.v.), a measuring unit receiving data from orbiting satellites giving their location and the time on their integral atomic clocks, enabling computation of the distances to the satellites. The more satellites that can be seen, the greater is the accuracy of the derived position.

Sextant: An instrument for measuring angles. When orientated with its axis vertical, it is used to measure between the horizon and a heavenly body; with its axis horizontal, it is used to measure between two terrestrial objects (a horizontal sextant angle). It can also be used to measure the angle between two heavenly bodies. It comprises a brass frame on which is mounted a graduated arc containing a sixth part of a circle (hence its name) and a rotating arm which carries a vernier or other interpolation device across the arc. The objects between which the angle is measured are brought into alignment using a telescopic sight and reflecting mirrors. The instrument allows the measurement of angles up to 120°. It was first developed in the 1750s, quickly displacing the earlier quadrant, which had an arc of only 45° and measured angles up to 90°.

Station: See **geodetic station**.

Systematic error: Systematic errors are amongst the most dangerous in survey work; they vary in magnitude but are constant in sign. Such an error would arise when a theodolite has not been properly levelled, and it would be eliminated by rotating the telescope through 180° and reversing the direction in which the measurements are made in successive rounds of observed angles. Some systematic errors cannot be completely eliminated. The same applies to **constant errors**, i.e. of constant magnitude and size, which can sometimes be eliminated by observational techniques. **Periodic errors**, of varying magnitude and sign but obeying some systematic law, tend to be reduced or eliminated by repetition of observations under different conditions. Good procedures will also expose **blunders** in observing, recording or calculation. When all the preceding errors have been removed, there will always be **random errors**, which are usually small and arise from imperfections in an instrument, in the observer's technique or from conditions at the time of observation.

Theodolite: A precision instrument for measuring angles, both horizontal and vertical. It consists of graduated circles which can be read against an interpolation device which rotates with a sighting telescope. It is fitted with alignment screws and a bubble to enable it to be levelled (q.v.). The precision attainable with this instrument, as indeed with a sextant, was improved during the later decades of the eighteenth century by new technology for engraving the divisions on the circles.

Tidal reduction: A chart is designed to indicate for the mariner the least depth of water that he will encounter in normal conditions. To achieve this, the height of tide must be deducted from soundings taken during the survey. This could be done, if manpower was available and circumstances permitted, by observing rise and fall against a vertical, graduated 'tide-pole'. Where this could not be done, provided that lowest low water and range of tide at springs and neaps had been observed, approximate corrections could be deduced by the rule of twelfths: e.g. on the spring tide, one hour before and after high water deduct $^{11}/_{12}$ of the range, at two hours ¾, three hours ½, four hours ⅓ and five hours ⅛.

Topographical survey: The process of accurately determining and recording the relative positions of features of the landscape and delineating them on a map or chart.

Triangulation: A process whereby a baseline (q.v.) is measured as accurately as possible from the extremities of which angles are measured to a chosen point, which becomes the third trigonometrical station of a triangle. The remaining sides of the triangle are computed by trigonometry. Then, by similar measurement from the three stations, a chain or network of triangles can be built up and the position of each station computed on a grid (e.g. latitude and longitude or the Ordnance Survey National Grid of Great Britain), thus providing a framework for a survey and the resultant map or chart. From the stations of such a national survey, the hydrographic surveyor can extend their own network at a scale to cover the survey area. In a remote location where no land survey has been conducted, the surveyor must start from scratch, measuring a baseline. The accuracy of a triangulation scheme will depend on the quality of the instruments employed and the time available for the measurements. A first order triangulation, measured with the highest precision between geodetic stations (q.v.), will have an error in the angles of the triangle not exceeding 1 inch. The work conducted by a hydrographic surveyor will generally be of the third or fourth order.

Trigonometrical survey: A survey in which the observed angles, and hence the deduced lengths of the sides, in a triangulation scheme have been checked by calculation using the principles of trigonometry.

Trilateration: The calculation of the positions of stations in a control scheme relative to one another by measuring the distances between them rather than the angles within the scheme. Instruments for this technique were not available in the period covered in this book, and the lengths of sides of triangles shown in some contemporary control diagrams are computed not measured values.

Variation of the compass: The horizontal angle between the magnetic and true meridians, i.e. the meridians running through the magnetic north and south poles and through the geographic north and south poles. This angle differs from place to place and the amount varies from year to year. It can be measured by using an azimuth compass (q.v.) to take a bearing of the Pole Star.

Vigia: A term derived from the Spanish 'look out' and denoting a hydrographical warning on a chart that a dangerous shoal or rock has been reported in the vicinity.

Zenith: If a vertical line is extended from the centre of the Earth through an observer's position until it touches the celestial sphere (q.v.) at the point directly above them, the point so defined is the observer's zenith.

Notes

Prologue

1. Thomas Hurd kept a detailed record of these observations, which is preserved in the archive of the UKHO in Miscellaneous Papers (Remark Books) (hereafter MP) Vol. 103 (De1) fos. 464–86. The operational background and the survey are described in more detail in Chapter 4 of this book. The log of *Diamond* (38) is at TNA Admiralty Records (hereafter ADM) 51/1476, Part 7, with detail in the entry for 17 July 1804. The log of *Acasta* (48) is at TNA ADM 51/1485, Part 6, with the capture of the launch recorded on 30 June. Captain John Knight's second chart in his series covering the Bay of Brest recorded the range of enemy shells. There is a copy in the British Library at BL Maps 15383(1).
2. Navy Records Society (hereafter NRS) Vol. 14, J. Leyland (ed.), *Despatches and Letters Relating to the Blockade of Brest*, Vol. I (1899), p. 120.

Introduction

1. Nicholas Rodger provides a masterly overview of this period of naval history in *The Command of the Ocean* (London: Allen Lane, 2004).
2. A.S. Cook, 'Establishing the Sea Routes to India and China: Stages in the Development of Hydrographical Knowledge', in H.V. Bowen et al. (eds), *The Worlds of the East India Company* (Woodbridge: Boydell, 2002), pp. 129–30.
3. G. Edwards (ed.), *Letters from Revolutionary France* (Cardiff: University of Wales Press, 2001), pp. 37–8.
4. Any study of naval administration in this period, including publication of cartographic products and their supply to the fleet, must now start with Roger Knight's *Britain Against Napoleon: The Organisation of Victory 1793–1815* (London: Penguin Books, 2013). Two important doctoral theses remain

unpublished: Andrew Cook's 'An Author Voluminous and Vast: Alexander Dalrymple (1737–1808), Hydrographer to the East India Company and to the Admiralty, as Publisher: A Catalogue of Books and Charts', University of St Andrews (1992) and Adrian Webb's 'The Expansion of British Naval Hydrographic Administration, 1808–1829', University of Exeter (2010).

5. TNA ADM 1/3459, minute dated 7 May 1814.
6. Instruments in use in the period are described by J.A. Bennett in *The Divided Circle: A History of Instruments for Astronomy, Navigation and Surveying* (Oxford: The University Press, 1987).
7. M. Barritt, 'Charts "Sent by the Ever to be Lamented Lord Nelson": Some Reflections on Navigational Practice in the Georgian Royal Navy', in *The Trafalgar Chronicle*, New Series 7 (2022), pp. 60–70.
8. E. Parry, *Memoirs of Rear Admiral Sir W. Edward Parry Kt FRS etc.*, 2nd edn (London: Longman Brown, 1857), p. 25.
9. Factors bearing on the careers of officers and masters are analysed in detail in E. Wilson, *A Social History of British Naval Officers 1775–1815* (Woodbridge: Boydell, 2017).

Chapter 1: Pathfinding for Colonial Warfare

1. TNA ADM 1/1932 Cap H 269, letter dated 18 Dec. 1806.
2. Hurd's biography in J. Marshall, *Royal Navy Biography*, Vol. 1 (London: Longman, Hurst, Rees, Orme, and Brown, 1823), pp. 556–7 is brief, as is that in Commander L.S. Dawson, *Memoirs of Hydrography* (London: Cornmarket Press, 1969), pp. 45–6. His statement of service is preserved at TNA ADM 9/2, no. 202. A few additional details can be gleaned from memorials of his service which he submitted to support claims for greater reward for the post of Hydrographer. These are referenced below. Some transcripts of relevant documents are preserved in UKHO Miscellaneous Letters and Papers (hereafter MLP) 56. Much fresh information is contained in A.J. Webb, *Thomas Hurd, RN & His Hydrographic Survey of Bermuda 1789–97* (Bermuda: National Museum of Bermuda Press, 2016).
3. S.J. Hornsby, *Surveyors of Empire: Samuel Holland, J.F.W. Des Barres and the Making of the Atlantic Neptune* (Montreal and Kingston: McGill-Queen's University Press, 2011), pp. 32–8, 41–5, 147–9.
4. Hurd's work is listed in UKHO MP 36(Ab4ii), 71 and 108; his compilations are at UKHO 284/1 on 5f, 284/2 on Ah2, 289 on 5b and A9448 on 31c, with observations in MP 35(Ab4i), 70–5.
5. TNA ADM 1/3461, Memorial to Board of Admiralty on the conditions of the post of Hydrographer, dated 16 Nov. 1818.
6. TNA ADM 1/487, f. 174.
7. His meticulous log with a full account of the action is at NMM ADM/L/H 115.
8. Hurd's appointment and his survey are discussed in detail by Adrian Webb in *Thomas Hurd, RN & His Hydrographic Survey of Bermuda 1789–97*.
9. TNA Colonial Office (hereafter CO) 37/42/12 p. 3, letter dated 14 Aug. 1789.

10. TNA ADM 6/330; Webb, *Thomas Hurd, RN & His Hydrographic Survey of Bermuda 1789–97*, p. 56.
11. TNA CO 37/44/15, 265.
12. UKHO E19/10 on 5k; J.D. Ware and R.R. Rea, *George Gauld, Surveyor and Cartographer of the Gulf Coast* (Gainsville, FL: University Presses of Florida, 1982), pp. 59–79.
13. TNA ADM 1/493, letter dated 27 May 1795.
14. Rear Admiral Lord Cochrane, quoted in T. Cochrane and H.R. Fox Bourne, *The Life of Thomas, Lord Cochrane, 10th Earl of Dundonald* (London: Richard Bentley, 1869), Vol. II, p. 314.
15. UKHO D8761 on 6a; I am grateful to Adrian Webb, who identified this large and very fragile sheet, a composite of small sheets of tracing paper.
16. TNA ADM 1/493, letter dated 27 May 1795.
17. UKHO MLP 56, papers 22–3, 40–46, 143 and 151–2; M. Lester, 'Vice-Admiral George Murray and the Origins of the Bermuda Naval Base, 1794–96', *The Mariner's Mirror* (henceforth *MM*), 94(3) (August 2008), p. 285; J.J. Colledge, *Ships of the Royal Navy*, Vol. 1: *Major Units* (Newton Abbot: David and Charles, 1969).
18. UKHO MLP 56, papers 148–9; TNA ADM 1/3522, f. 174.
19. NRS 28, C.R. Markham (ed.), *The Correspondence of Admiral John Markham 1801–1807*, letter dated 26 Oct. 1806.
20. Columbine died before statements of service were called for. There is a very brief biographical note in Dawson, *Memoirs of Hydrography*, Part I, pp. 15–16. I am grateful to Mrs R. Roberts for tracking down notes by Sir John Dorington, a descendant of Columbine's sister, published in *Cheltenham Ladies College Magazine*, 1891, pp. 109, 121–3.
21. LMA, Records of the Consistory Court of London, DL/C 181, 83–9; DL/C 284, 134–62.
22. NMM COM 02/63 and 64.
23. Copy at UKHO B260 on Ag4.
24. UKHO A524 on Ag4; e57 on Ag3. The originals of the views are in TNA ADM 344/2516, with another copy of Faden's engraved version at 2517.
25. TNA ADM 1/3522, letter dated 10 Oct. 1807.
26. P. Mackesy, *War Without Victory: The Downfall of Pitt 1799–1802* (Oxford: The University Press, 1984), p. 216.
27. Hood's surveys are at UKHO A269, 282 and 283 on Ah1, and A724 on Ah2.
28. TNA ADM 36/15646, Muster Book No. 13.
29. UKHO MP 46(Ac8) contains a copy passed to William Marsden by Thomas Grenville for the Admiralty's 'Geographic Collection'.
30. TNA ADM 1/324, Q14.
31. Columbine's main plan is at UKHO D709 on Ag4m. A copy of his report is in MP 46(Ac8). Hood's comments are at TNA ADM 1/324, Q18 with a duplicate in CO 295/6.
32. UKHO MP 46(Ac8), 604.
33. TNA ADM 1/3522, 259, 263.
34. Original fair sheet at UKHO s84 on Ag3.
35. Copy at NMM G245:19/13.

36. L.N. Pascoe, 'The Story of the Curator of the Hydrographic Department of the Admiralty 1795 to 1975', unpublished typescript held in UKHO, p. 62.
37. TNA CO 295/19, letter dated 1 Aug. 1808. UCL Legacies of British Slave-ownership, accessed at www.ucl.ac.uk/lbs/estate/view/9752 on 18 June 2018, shows Briarly still registered in 1813.
38. TNA War Office (hereafter WO) 78/900; TNA ADM 1/4379, Pro B 412; TNA CO 295/11, ff. 202–4.
39. *The Register of Shipping for the year 1803*, entry E113; *Lloyd's List*, Tuesday 25 Oct. 1803.
40. *London Gazette*, 8 Oct. 1803.
41. TNA ADM 1/326, Q123 dated 1 Oct. 1805.
42. John Carter Brown Map Collection, Call Number GA 803 1; dimensions are 431cm by 70cm.
43. *Naval Chronicle* (hereafter NC) XV, Part 1 (London: Joyce Gold, 1806), p. 432.
44. BL, Additional Manuscripts (hereafter Add Ms), Windham Papers Vol. XLII, ff. 263–8; Anon., 'Miranda and the British Admiralty, 1804–1806', *The American Historical Review*, 6(3) (1901), pp. 521–2; TNA CO 295/11, f. 204.
45. V.S. Naipaul, *The Loss of El Dorado: A Colonial History* (London: Penguin, 1973), pp. 319, 323–4.
46. TNA CO 295/20, letters dated 18 and 20 Nov. 1807 and 295/19, letter dated 1 Aug. 1808; TNA ADM 1/329, Q64 dated 7 May 1808 and Q117 dated 14 Aug. 1808.
47. TNA ADM/1 2768 Lt B211.
48. TNA ADM 1/328, Q45 dated 14 Apr. 1807.
49. TNA ADM 6/132, 13.

Chapter 2: Pathfinding for an Empire of Trade

1. C.R. Markham, *A Naval Career during the Old War* (London: Sampson Low, 1883), p. 239.
2. TNA ADM 9/3 No. 807.
3. 'Recollections of the British Army', *United Service Journal* (hereafter *USJ*) (1836), p. 485.
4. H. Popham, *A Damned Cunning Fellow* (Tywardreath: Old Ferry Press, 1991), pp. 84–5; Mackesy, *War Without Victory*, pp. 26, 159–60, 163; NRS 59, H.W. Richmond (ed.), *The Private Papers of George, 2nd Earl Spencer*, Vol. IV (1924), pp. 127–8, 238.
5. J. McAleer, *Britain's Maritime Empire: Southern Africa, the South Atlantic and the Indian Ocean, 1763–1820* (Cambridge: The University Press, 2016), pp. 50–2; J. Kinahan, 'The Impenetrable Shield: HMS *Nautilus* and the Namib Coast in the Late Eighteenth Century', *Cimbebasia* 12 (1990), pp. 23–61; the surveys are at UKHO 884 on C and R76, 65 and 66 in Africa Folio 2.
6. BL K.MAR.VI, 1–17 (16 I and II) with original manuscripts at UKHO u7/1–2 on Cu.
7. H. Popham, *A Concise Statement of Facts* (London: John Stockdale, 1805), pp. 19, 26–7; Popham, *A Damned Cunning Fellow*, p. 87.

8. Popham's Red Sea survey work, and that of other Royal Naval personnel, is described in more detail in M.K. Barritt, 'Early Hydrographic Work of the Royal Navy in the Red Sea', *Journal of the Hakluyt Society* (October 2023), accessed at https://hakluyt.com/downloadable_files/Journal/.

9. NMM 912.43(267.5):094 BAR B8409.

10. UKHO 945 on Hg.

11. BL Add MSS 31158, f. 165 dated 30 Oct. 1803; TNA ADM 9/3/807; C. Dixon, 'To walk the quarterdeck: the naval career of David Ewen Bartholomew', *MM*, 79(1) (2013), pp. 58–63; Marshall, *Royal Navy Biography*, Vol. 1, Supplement IV (1830), pp. 444–57.

12. Hansard Index, 1803–30, p. 594.

13. NMM COR/14, 2 and 13 Nov. 1790 et passim and COR/15, 24 Dec. 1792 to 16 Feb. 1793.

14. Rodger, *The Command of the Ocean*, pp. 274–5.

15. Alexander Turnbull Library MS-Papers-6373-46, Journal of Edward Bell, Voyage of HMS *Chatham* to the Pacific Ocean, Vancouver's Expedition 1791–1794, ff. 75–6.

16. W. Bligh, *A Voyage to the South Sea {. . .} in His Majesty's Ship the Bounty, [. . .] an account of the mutiny [. . .] and the subsequent voyage [. . .] in the ship's boat* (London: George Nicol, 1792), pp. 160–2.

17. National Library of Australia MS 5393, Bligh's Notebook and List of Mutineers, 1789, which can be viewed in the library's online digital collections.

18. A.C.F. David, 'The Surveyors of the *Bounty*: A preliminary study' (1982), typescript, limited distribution with copies in UKHO and at BL General Reference Collection X.702/5393, 28–46c, contains a detailed analysis of Heywood's significant output.

19. C. Alexander, *The Bounty: The True Story of the Mutiny on the Bounty* (London: HarperCollins, 2003), p. 65.

20. J. Barrow, *The Mutiny and Piratical Seizure of H.M.S. BOUNTY: with an Introduction by Admiral Sir Cyprian Bridge, G.C.B.* (Oxford: The University Press, 1951 reprint), pp. viii, 196.

21. TNA ADM 107/13, No. 46.

22. Transcript of TNA ADM 1/5330 in Owen Rutter (ed.), *The Court Martial of the Bounty Mutineers* (Toronto, 1931), p. 114.

23. G. Mackaness, *The Life of Vice-Admiral William Bligh RN FRS* (London: Angus and Robertson, 1931), pp. 125, 152, 164.

24. E. Edwards and G. Hamilton, *Voyage of HMS Pandora*, with Introduction and Notes by Basil Thomson (London: Francis Edwards, 1915), pp. 35, 99.

25. Hayward's work is analysed critically by Andrew David in 'Surveyors of the *Bounty*', p. 25.

26. Hayward's sketch survey is UKHO A112 on Ba2, with his rough at B625/1 on Ba3. A copy sent to the Cape of Good Hope is at NMM KEI 5/3. The logs are TNA ADM 51/4437, No. 1, *Diomede*; TNA ADM 51/4457, No. 3, *Heroine*.

27. TNA ADM 36/13516, entries 207 and 208. There is an annotation 'Last MB', indicating that the next book was lost with the ship.

28. TNA ADM 1/168, folio 292A.

29. Copy at BL Maps 147.e.17.(106.), with the manuscript sheets at UKHO 544 on Bb2 and C748/2 and 3 on Af3.
30. BL Maps SEC.13.(910.).
31. TNA ADM 1/168, fos. 561–2, list of appointments, with date of 8 July for Hayward.
32. TNA ADM 1/168, fos. 588–91 and 1/169, fos. 36–7 and 47–9.
33. TNA ADM 36/11751, No. 1489; TNA ADM 1/56, R88, No. 169; NMM KEI 43 contains a copy of Whittle's report, preserved amongst other papers related to hydrographic observations.
34. NMM KEI/5/4; UKHO s45 on Co.
35. Whittle's survey is at UKHO s45 on Co. Pringle's letter is at TNA ADM 1/56 R44 dated 7 May 1797. There are five copies of a fair sheet showing the 'soundings ordered by Rear Admiral Pringle in 1797' and including some extra work. One is at NMM G241:8/5, and four are in the TNA, all signed by Captain G. Bridges of the Royal Engineers (one in WO 78/826, and three in MPHH 1/13, the latter marked 'removed from WO 78/1089'). It seems likely that they were made on Bridges' orders to promulgate the danger of Whittles Rock.
36. TNA ADM 35/605 Entry No. 21; TNA ADM 52/3750 No. 1.
37. TNA ADM 1/56, R88, letter from Pringle dated 27 Nov. 1797.
38. TNA ADM 52/3750; ADM 1/56, R11, Christian, 27 Apr. 1798; ADM 1/169, S8 and ff. 182–3, Rainier, 17 June 1798; ADM 1/57, R8, Rainier, 28 Jan. 1799.
39. NRS 31, R. Vesey-Hamilton and J.K. Laughton (eds), *The Recollections of Commander James Anthony Gardner, 1775–1814* (1906), p. 118.
40. TNA ADM 9/2 No. 292.
41. TNA ADM 1/56, letters R27 and R46; ADM 1/1719; ADM 36/12433; TNA ADM 51/1197 Part 6. The divorce proceedings are in GLRO DL/C182, pp. 179–85; DL/C287, pp. 354–60.
42. TNA ADM 36/15158, Muster Book No. 1; TNA ADM 51/1356, Parts 4–5; NC VI, pp. 250–1.
43. NRS 28, Markham, *The Correspondence*, pp. 163–5, 171, 175. Durban had also served under Captain Markham, now at the Admiralty, with whom Keith corresponded on this proposal.
44. See Mackesy, *War Without Victory*, pp. 84–6 for the long-standing pressure from Dundas, and McAleer, *Britain's Maritime Empire*, pp. 81–2, 104–5 and 144–6 for Popham's arguments.
45. J.D. Grainger, 'The Navy in the River Plate, 1806–1808', *MM*, 81(3) (1995), pp. 293–4; NRS 135, J.D. Grainger (ed.), *The Royal Navy in the River Plate, 1806–07* (1996), pp. 7, 30–3, 51, 105, 246; NMM AGC/8/16, letter dated 13 Sept. 1807.
46. I. Fletcher, *The Waters of Oblivion* (Tunbridge Wells: Spellmount, 1991), p. 25.
47. UKHO s61 on Af3.
48. UKHO s60 and s64 on Af3, B146 on Af2; Old Copy Bundle (hereafter OCB) 547 shows compilation of the eventual Admiralty chart. In the interim, Edmond had communicated his work to Faden, who used it in the second and third editions of his chart originally derived from the Spanish publication.
49. TNA ADM 1/3522, letters dated 1 Aug. 1805 and 10 Oct. 1807, NRS 96, C.C. Lloyd (ed.), *The Keith Papers*, Vol. III (1955), p. 217, letter dated 5 Aug. 1805, and TNA ADM 9/2, p. 394.

50. A. Dalrymple, *A Catalogue of Authors who have written on Rio de la Plata, Paraguay and Chaco* (copy at Bodleian Library Facs.d.95) and *Memoir concerning the Geography of the Countries situated on the Rio De La Plata and on the Rivers falling into it* (copy at Bodleian Library 2098.d.26) were subsequently published in 1807; Cook, 'An Author Voluminous and Vast', p. 177.
51. National Library of Australia MS 43, letter to Lord Grenville dated 6 Oct. 1806.
52. NRS 28, Markham, *The Correspondence*, pp. 228–9.
53. His sounding sheets, containing work from all his deployments to the station, are at UKHO 164/1–2 on Af2.
54. A copy of the abstract and Dalrymple's own memoir on the river are bound together in Bodleian Library 2098.d.26. Later remarks are at UKHO MP 58(Ad5ii). Warner's original surveys are x33 and x35 on Af1 in UKHO, and copies of the Faden chart are at 155 on Af1 and Af2.
55. UKHO MP 36(Ab 4ii); A. Gillespie, *Gleanings and Remarks* (Leeds: B. Dewhurst, 1818), p. 31.
56. TNA ADM 352/287/1; UKHO s64/1 on Af3.
57. NRS 135, Grainger, *The Royal Navy*, p. 297.
58. NRS 135, Grainger, *The Royal Navy*, pp. 288–90, 296; Fletcher, *The Waters of Oblivion*, p. 87; papers, tracings and plans from the campaign are in the Bayntun collection of the Bedfordshire Record Office at DDX 170/7/4.
59. N. Courtney, *Gale Force 10: The Life and Legacy of Admiral Beaufort* (London: Review, 2002), pp. 119–21.
60. UKHO A782/1–8 on Hg and C643/2 and 3 on Af3; NMM NVP/3; TNA ADM 1/3522, letter dated 28 Apr. 1807.
61. Bodleian Library 2098.d.26, pp. 25–6, 28–30.
62. Bodleian Library 2098.d.26, pp. 23–4.
63. UKHO s83/9 and t39 on Af3.
64. UKHO A636 on Af2; UKHO s81 on Af3.
65. TNA ADM 1/3523, letters dated 4, 9 and 27 Apr. 1808.
66. TNA ADM 1/3523, letter dated 31 Mar. 1808; Cook, 'An Author Voluminous and Vast', p. 182. The chart was published on 11 Apr. 1808.
67. See the important analysis in M. Robson, *Britain, Portugal and South America in the Napoleonic Wars: Alliances and Diplomacy in Economic Maritime Conflict* (London: I.B. Tauris, 2011), especially Chapter 5; also J. Davey, 'Atlantic Empire, European War and the Naval Expeditions to South America, 1806–1807', in McAleer and Petley, *The Royal Navy and the British Atlantic World* (London: Palgrave Macmillan, 2016), pp. 162–3, 165–6.
68. T. Fernyhough, *Military Memoirs of Four Brothers* (London: William Sams, 1829), pp. 135–6.
69. UKHO E990 on Af1M.

Chapter 3: Containing the Enemy: The Mediterranean

1. UKHO Outgoing Letter Book (hereafter LB) 1, letter dated 13 Sept. 1815.
2. Barritt, 'Charts "Sent by the Ever to be Lamented Lord Nelson"', pp. 60–70.

3. TNA ADM 1/3523, ff. 154–64; Rear Admiral W.H. Smyth, *The Mediterranean: A Memoir Physical, Historical and Nautical* (London: John W. Parker, 1854), pp. 353–6. In this magisterial volume, Smyth included much biographical material, some of which is not included in the extensive entry in Marshall, *Royal Navy Biography*, Vol. III, Part I, pp. 125–78.

4. Royal Naval Museum Portsmouth (hereafter RNM) MSS 22, *Mediterranean Directions copied from a manuscript folio book belonging to Sir Thomas Troubridge Bart*, annotated as having been examined in the Hydrographical Office on 14 Feb. 1803; RNM MSS 2007.127/1, Letter Book from HMS *Culloden* 1795–7.

5. TNA ADM 36/12006, No. 149; 36/1633, Supernumerary No. 1906; 36/11737–8, No. 1024.

6. *USJ* (1837), Part I, 152; E. Fraser, *The Sailors Whom Nelson Led* (London: Methuen, 1913), p. 203.

7. *Elogia Fúnebre De La Reyna De Las Dos Sicilias María Carlota De Lorena* (Madrid: Imprenta Real, 1814), p. 26.

8. TNA ADM 52/2736, No. 1; W. Soler and A. Ganado, *The Charting of Maltese Waters* (Malta: BDL Publishing, 2013), Chapter 7.

9. A transcription of Nelson's letter, written in Palermo on 2 Apr. 1799, is in a memorial of Briarly composed in 1818 and accessed at http://bibliotecavirtual defensa.es on 19 Dec. 2018.

10. A. Dalrymple, *Memoir concerning the Hydrographical Map of Part of Egypt*, to accompany the chart published by the Hydrographic Office on 25 May 1801, p. 4.

11. NRS 90, Lloyd, *The Keith Papers*, Vol. II (1950), p. 232; TNA ADM 52/3027, *Foudroyant*, 4–7 Mar. 1801.

12. T. Malcomson, 'An Aid to Nelson's Victory? A Description of the Harbour of Aboukir, 1798', *MM*, 84(3), 1998, pp. 291–7.

13. UKHO MP 73(C2), p. 707.

14. UKHO 195 on Rn.

15. NRS 90, Lloyd, *The Keith Papers*, Vol. II, pp. 344, 348; UKHO e13 on Rf.

16. UKHO b2 on 31g.

17. NHB/AL Vu 3.

18. TNA ADM 1/140, N135 and N149; TNA WO1/280, ff. 9–11, 15, 21–6, 35–7.

19. Copy at BL Maps *32806.(4.).

20. TNA ADM 1/411, Part 4, ff. 364–6, 371–4; NMM TYL/1, 105h, letter dated 31 Aug. 1805.

21. R. Knight, *The Pursuit of Victory: The Life and Achievement of Horatio Nelson* (London: Allen Lane, 2005), pp. 444, 465; C. White, *Nelson: The New Letters* (Woodbridge: Boydell, 2005), p. 387; the survey is described in detail in M.K. Barritt, 'Agincourt Sound Revisited', *MM*, 101(2) (2015).

22. TNA ADM 52/1129, Parts 2 and 3; ADM 346/2, 111; UKHO n68 on Med. Folio 4.

23. A.C.F. David, 'Admiral Nelson, Alexander Dalrymple and the Early Years of the Hydrographical Office', *IMCOS Journal*, No. 102 (Autumn 2005), p. 7.

24. H.T. Fry, *Alexander Dalrymple (1737–1808) and the Expansion of British Trade* (London: Frank Cass, 1970), pp. 237–9.

25. TNA ADM 1/3522, letter dated 22 Mar. 1800; A.S. Cook, 'Why Alexandria? Alexander Dalrymple's Experimental Maps of Alexandria of 1801', History of Cartography Athens Conference, 1999.
26. NMM CRK/13/85 dated 16 June 1803, and 13/87 dated 26 Aug. 1803.
27. BL. Add MSS 34932, pp. 200–5, 255–8.
28. Sir N.H. Nicolas, *The Despatches and Letters of Vice Admiral Lord Viscount Nelson* (London: Henry Colburn, 1844–5), Vol. V, pp. 277–8, 19–20.
29. Nicolas, *The Despatches and Letters*, Vol. V, pp. 319–20, 329; TNA ADM 2/923, 65; UKHO o3/2 on Med. Folio 1; o58 on Su.
30. TNA ADM 1/3522, letter dated 10 Oct. 1807.
31. Details from the Court Martial record at TNA ADM 1/5376.
32. T. Campbell and M. Barritt, 'The Representation of Navigational Hazards: The Development of Topology and Symbology on Portolan Charts from the 13th Century Onwards, *Journal of the Hakluyt Society* (December 2020), accessed at https://www.hakluyt.com/journal-of-the-hakluyt-society/.
33. Smyth, *The Mediterranean*, pp. 93, 334.
34. Marshall, *Royal Naval Biography*, Vol. IV, Part II, p. 71.
35. TNA ADM 1/3522, letter dated 28 Feb. 1807.
36. Smyth, *The Mediterranean*, p. 245; UKHO MP 77(C6), pp. 323–5, NMM LBK/66, letter dated 21 Nov. 1806.
37. TNA ADM 51/1522, Part 8; UKHO m99 on Rl.
38. TNA ADM 2/923, 184, p. 208.
39. TNA ADM 51/1518, No. 2; ADM 52/2974 Part 1; BL Add MSS 37268, f. 82.
40. Durban's survey and fair draft are at UKHO n31 and n31a on Ry. Other records include plans of Keith's Reef at 176 on Rg, and n32 and n83 on Med. folio 4. Annotations on n34a record the scrutiny in the Hydrographical Office, and a copy of a first draft of the Admiralty chart at n34b Med. Folio 4 is annotated with further instructions for amendments from Dalrymple dated 30 October, some six weeks after the publication date engraved on the chart.
41. TNA ADM 1/3522, letter dated 23 Dec. 1806; 'Nelson's Reef' is shown on a tracing 'communicated by Captain Codrington' at UKHO n84 on Med. Folio 4.
42. BL Maps C.21.c.15, *List of Admiralty Charts*.
43. In 1821 Beaufort would publish *Memoir of a Survey of the South Coast of Asia Minor, commonly called Karamania*. A copy of this rare book is at BL General Reference Collection Tab.583.a.(2.). Beaufort's fair manuscript for the printer was preserved in the Admiralty Library and is at TNA ADM 7/847.
44. Barritt, 'Charts "Sent by the Ever to be Lamented Lord Nelson"', p. 66.
45. Marshall, *Royal Naval Biography*, Vol. II, Part 2 (1825), p. 845; TNA ADM 51/1518 Part 2.
46. BL Add MSS 34967, pp. 10–11, 43–4 and Add MSS 34919, ff. 193–5; White, *New Letters*, p. 33.
47. TNA WO 1/280, ff. 76, pp. 99–101, 103–4.
48. NRS 92, C.C. Lloyd (ed.), *The Naval Miscellany*, Vol. IV (1952), p. 487; Marshall, *Royal Naval Biography*, Vol. II, Part 2, p. 848. No evidence of such surveys has been found.
49. TNA ADM 2/923, pp. 83–4.
50. BL Add MSS 20189, f. 106; Add MSS 56088, f. 25 and 29.

51. TNA ADM 1/415, letter N 21; TNA ADM 9/2/292; RNM MS 1977/301/100.
52. TNA ADM 29/1, No. 68 contains John King's record of service during the French Revolutionary War.
53. There is a detailed account of this voyage by 'the first regular man of war that ever passed between New Holland and Van Diemen's Land' in Marshall's biography of Captain Johnston, in *Royal Naval Biography*, Supplement Vol. I, Part 1, pp. 170–4. The strategic setting in South America is discussed by Jorge Ortiz-Sotelo and Robert King in '"A Cruize to the Coasts of Peru and Chile": HM Ship *CORNWALLIS*, 1807', *The Great Circle, Journal of the Australian Association for Maritime History*, 32(1) (2010), pp. 35–52.
54. UKHO, g36/1–7 in Tracks Folio 1, NMM NVP/3, p. 282.
55. UKHO LB1, letter dated 5 Feb. 1820. Smyth's commission is recorded at TNA ADM 1/3140, Lt S 132.
56. Marshall, *Royal Naval Biography*, p. 144; TNA ADM 12/161 Heading 57, 8 November 1813.
57. UKHO LB1, annex to letter dated 20 June 1816; also reproduced in Smyth, *The Mediterranean*, pp. 355–6.
58. D. Mack Smith, *A History of Sicily – Modern Sicily after 1713* (London: Chatto & Windus, 1968), p. 339; R. Trevelyan, *Princes under the Volcano* (London: Macmillan, 1972), pp. 11–12, 15–16 and 22–3; Mackesy, *War in the Mediterranean*, p. 399; R. Holland, *Blue-water Empire: The British in the Mediterranean since 1800* (London: Penguin, 2012) also provides excellent strategic context.
59. W.H. Smyth, *Memoir Descriptive of Sicily and its Islands* (London: John Murray, 1824), p. 291.
60. Smyth, *The Mediterranean*, p. 356; a copy of the Neapolitan chart published by Faden in 1806 is at BL Maps K.MAR.V.(62.).
61. Smyth, *Memoir Descriptive of Sicily*, p. 193.
62. Smyth, *Memoir Descriptive of Sicily*, p. 30.
63. M.K. Barritt, '"Willing Assistance, Constantly Rendered": Joint Service Field Survey in Sicily, 1814–1816', *The Ranger: Journal of the Defence Surveyors' Association* (December 2020), pp. 31–8.
64. Smyth, *The Mediterranean*, p. 358. Neither man is mentioned in the memoirs of military maps of the island in The National Archives.
65. Y. Jones, 'Aspects of Relief Portrayal on Nineteenth-Century British Military Maps', *Cartographic Journal*, 11(1) (1974), pp. 20–2; Y. Hodson, *Ordnance Surveyors' Drawings 1789–c1840* (London, 1989), p. 13; P.K. Clark and Y. Jones, 'British Military Map-making in the Peninsular War', unpublished typescript (1974), p. 6.
66. UKHO f35 on Su.
67. UKHO LB1, annex to letter dated 20 June 1816.
68. Smyth, *Memoir Descriptive of Sicily*, p. xiv; UKHO LB 1, No. 30.
69. Smyth, *The Mediterranean*, pp. 356–7.
70. I am grateful to Donata Randazzo for access to the observatory and library and for subsequent contact with the archive of the Naples Observatory.
71. Smyth, *The Mediterranean*, p. 20.
72. Marshall, *Royal Naval Biography*, Vol. III, Part I, p. 144.

Chapter 4: Holding the Centre: Home Waters and Invasion Coasts

1. TNA ADM 1/1232, Cap H 262, letter dated 2 June 1806, TNA ADM 1/3485, memorial dated 14 Apr. 1811, TNA ADM 1/3461, memorial dated 16 Nov. 1818.
2. Knight, *Britain Against Napoleon*, pp. 88 and 255; W.A. Seymour, *A History of the Ordnance Survey* (Folkestone: Dawson, 1980), pp. 24, 50.
3. St Vincent correspondence in NRS 55, D.B. Smith (ed.), *The Letters of Lord St Vincent, 1801–1804*, Vol. I (1921), p. 379 and NRS 61, Smith, *The Letters of Lord St Vincent, 1801–1804*, Vol. II (1926), pp. 379, 409.
4. BL Add MSS 31170, Part I, p. 214, letter dated 29 June 1802.
5. His record of service is at TNA ADM 9/2, No. 353.
6. TNA ADM 1/1992, Cap J75–6; ADM 1/1993, Cap J73–5; UKHO h77 on Dh; UKHO OCB 110.
7. Reports at TNA ADM 1/1993, Cap J77 and J82; log at TNA ADM 51/1509, Part 5; surveys at UKHO l39 on Df and UKHO k96 on Di.
8. TNA ADM 1/542, D935, letter dated 11 June 1804; ADM 1/1993, Cap J77, letter dated 13 July 1804.
9. TNA ADM 1/542, D997, letter dated 29 June 1804.
10. TNA ADM 1/1993, Cap J78, letter dated 26 July 1804.
11. NRS 96, Lloyd, *The Keith Papers*, Vol. III, p. 87.
12. Cook, 'An Author Voluminous and Vast', Vol. III, B993 040731, showing a date of 31 July 1804. It was included in the Chart Committee list of March 1808 but was withdrawn before publication.
13. A. Crawford, *Reminiscences of a Naval Officer during the Late War* (London: Henry Colburn, 1851), Vol. 1, p. 132.
14. M. Flinders, *The Voyage to Terra Australis* (London: G and W Nicol, 1814), Vol. II, p. 96; TNA ADM 1/4880, Pro M 557; V. Cole (ed.) and J. Murray, *The Summer Survey: Log of the Lady Nelson 1801–1802* (Hastings, Victoria: Western Port Historical Society, 2001).
15. TNA ADM 1/1529 Cap B386, undated; TNA ADM 1/4878, Pro M 452, and ADM 1/4880, Pro M 557 and 574.
16. TNA ADM 1/3016, Lt M283–4; ADM 36/16412 and 17435, ADM 35/2475, and ADM 37/1010; ADM 1/3017, Lt M286.
17. TNA ADM 354/223/34, dated 8 July 1806.
18. TNA ADM 1/3016, Lt M288; ADM 1/3017, Lt M288–9; ADM 1/3018, Lt M192–3.
19. TNA ADM 1/3018, Lt M192–5; ADM 2/156.
20. TNA ADM 1/3523, letters dated 2 Nov. 1808 and 23 June and 4 July 1809.
21. TNA ADM 1/3016, Lt M281, and ADM 1/3017, Lt M283, letters dated 20 Jan. and 19 Feb. 1807.
22. A.C.F. David, 'Alexander Dalrymple and the Emergence of the Admiralty Chart', in *Five Hundred Years of Nautical Science 1400–1900* (Greenwich: NMM, 1981), pp. 153–64; Cook, 'An Author Voluminous and Vast', Vol. I, pp. 168–70.
23. UKHO 679 on 12b.
24. TNA ADM 1/1933 Cap H 311 and 312; UKHO MLP 56/151–5, 172–7.

25. UKHO Incoming Letters prior to 1857 (hereafter LP1857), P001 dated 25 Apr. 1831.
26. TNA ADM 1/3522, letter dated 15 June 1805, 174; UKHO 679 on 12b.
27. TNA ADM 1/1930, Cap H 411 dated 4 May 1804 and H 412, dated 26 May; TNA ADM 1/1932, Cap H 263 and 264 dated 28 June 1806; S. Fisher, 'The Origins of the Station Pointer', in *International Hydrographic Review* (hereafter IHR) LXVIII (2) (1991); information from the Museum of Science, Oxford.
28. TNA ADM 1/1933, Cap H 312, letter dated 17 Aug. 1807.
29. TNA ADM 1/3523, letter dated 10 Sept. 1808.
30. Copies at BL Maps K.MAR.V.(14.), 1st (1800) and 2nd (1802) editions, with another copy of the latter at Maps 15383.
31. S. Fisher, 'Captain Thomas Hurd's Survey of the Bay of Brest during the Blockade in the Napoleonic Wars', *MM*, 79(3), pp. 293–304; M.K. Barritt, *Eyes of the Admiralty* (London: NMM, 2008), 45–51, 116–17.
32. NRS 21, Leyland, *Despatches and Letters*, Vol. II (1902), No. 281, dated 23 June 1804.
33. UKHO Original Document (hereafter OD) 507.
34. TNA ADM 1/124, f. 176; NRS 14, Leyland, *Despatches and Letters*, Vol. I, No. 246, letter dated 13 May 1804, p. 319; TNA ADM 1/1930 Cap H, pp. 411–12, letters dated 4 and 26 May 1804; NC XI, p. 492.
35. NP 27 Channel Pilot.
36. TNA ADM 1/1933, Cap H, 310, letter dated 23 July 1807.
37. TNA ADM 51/1476, Part 7 and ADM 52/3597, Part 11, entries for 4, 12 and 17 July 1804.
38. NMM DUC 224:2/18.
39. NRS 14, Leyland, *Despatches and Letters*, Vol. I, No. 237, letter dated 16 Apr. 1804.
40. UKHO MP 106 (De 3).
41. The muster books, in which Hurd is entered in the lists of Supernumeraries for victuals only, are TNA ADM 36/16705 *Diamond*, entry 348 and ADM 36/16770 *Santa Margarita*, entry 221. The relevant logs for *Diamond* are ADM 51/1476, Part 7 and ADM 52/3597, and for *Santa Margarita* ADM 51/1486, Part 8 and ADM 52/3696, Part 23.
42. TNA ADM 52/3699, Part 2, entries for 8–11 Sept. 1804.
43. NRS 21, Leyland, *Despatches and Letters*, Vol. II, No. 323, dated 1 Sept. 1804.
44. TNA ADM 1/1930, Cap H 413, letter dated 13 Sept. 1804.
45. NRS 21, Leyland, *Despatches and Letters*, Vol. II, No. 370, dated 26 Oct. 1804, pp. 104–13.
46. TNA ADM 1/1932 Cap H 262, letter dated 2 June 1806.
47. TNA ADM 1/1932 Cap H 261, letter dated 29 May 1806; Markham, *A Naval Career during the Old War*, p. 239.
48. J.C. Beaglehole, *The Life of Captain James Cook* (London: The Hakluyt Society, 1974), p. 82.
49. TNA ADM 1/1932, Cap H 266 dated 14 Sept. 1806.
50. TNA ADM 1/1932, Cap H 266 dated 14 Sept. 1806.
51. TNA ADM 1/1932, Cap H 265 dated 8 Sept. 1806.
52. NRS 21, Leyland, *Despatches and Letters*, Vol. II, No. 348, dated 23 Sept. 1804.

53. Copy in the Admiralty Library, Portsmouth, UB8.
54. NMM PDW/1.
55. Pascoe, 'Story of the Curator', p. 71.
56. UKHO LB1, letter dated 19 May 1815. George Sidley was Master of the Channel Fleet. He had seen considerable service on the coast of Brittany and in 1814 submitted a survey of the Bay of Brest, Douarnenez Bay, Ushant and the Saints. It has not survived.
57. UKHO LB1, letter dated 19 May 1815.
58. TNA ADM 1/1933 Cap H 310, letter dated 23 July 1807.

Chapter 5: Sea Power Projection: Northern Europe

1. TNA ADM 1/3522, pp. 342–3; Cook, 'An Author Voluminous and Vast', Vol. I, p. 178.
2. BL Add MSS 34934, f. 119, letter dated 26 June 1801.
3. UKHO MP 102(Dc2).
4. TNA ADM 29/1/70; J. Sugden, *Nelson: The Sword of Albion* (London: Bodley Head, 2012), pp. 365–8.
5. The charts were advertised in the short-lived London newspaper *The Porcupine*, No. 3, 1 Nov. 1800.
6. See, for example, D. Pope, *The Great Gamble* (London: Weidenfeld and Nicolson, 1972), p. 356.
7. TNA ADM 52/2761 No. 4; D. Bonner Smith, 'Midshipman W.G. Anderson', *MM*, 15(3) (1929), p. 243.
8. TNA ADM 1/4379 Pro B 412; see also Nelson's letter to St Vincent in Sir N.H. Nicolas (ed.), *The Despatches and Letters*, Vol. IV, p. 499.
9. *Cumloden Papers* (Edinburgh, for private circulation, 1871), p. 21; Nicolas, *The Despatches and Letters*, Vol. V, p. 307; TNA ADM 52/2761 No. 4.
10. Bonner Smith, 'Midshipman W.G. Anderson', p. 247.
11. British Museum 1891,0414.185. Both this and BM 1868,0808.1834 were engraved by S.I. Neele and published by the firm of J. Brydon, as had been his charts of the Mediterranean.
12. Transcript of letter dated 8 Dec. 1801 at Merton Place, accessed at http://bibliotecavirtualdefensa.es.
13. NC V, p. 452.
14. W. James, *Naval History of Great Britain*, Vol. III (London: R. Bentley, 1837), p. 81.
15. Pope, *The Great Gamble*, pp. 502–3; TNA ADM 52/2761, No. 4, 13–16 May 1801.
16. NRS 59, Richmond, *The Private Papers*, Vol. IV, p. 277.
17. NMM CRK/14/65; UKHO MP 101(Dc 1).
18. UKHO C229 on Hm; UKHO MP 102(Dc 2).
19. TNA ADM 6/163; A.N. Ryan, 'The Navy at Copenhagen, 1807', *MM*, 39(3) (Aug. 1953), pp. 201–10.
20. NMM MKH/110, letter dated 26 Mar. 1808.
21. NRS 63, R.C. Anderson (ed.), *The Naval Miscellany*, Vol. III (1927), p. 395.
22. Personal communication from Dr Jakob Seerup, who purchased the chart for the Royal Danish Naval Museum.

23. UKHO MP 101(Dc1) contains remarks from the *Vanguard* and the *Hussar* annotated 'Rec'd Dec 1807 from Lord Gambier by his Secy'.
24. UKHO C263 on Hm.
25. UKHO C262/1 and 2, 263 and 272 on Hm. C272 is his main survey from which BA chart 135 was compiled. Copies of the smaller-scale published charts are at UKHO OCBs 133, 134 and 136, all published on 1 Jan. 1814.
26. NMM COR/15, entry for 28 Dec. 1792.
27. UKHO MP 64 (B4) 622–4; NMM AUS/17.
28. UKHO s50 on Africa f. 2, 789 on Dg and B981 on Og*.
29. UKHO MP 101(Dc1), p. 17.
30. UKHO MP 101(Dc1).
31. UKHO OCB 140.
32. TNA ADM 1/3098 Lt R3 dated 1 Sept. 1809; TNA ADM 37/1531.
33. TNA ADM 1/9, Ha 110 dated 7 Dec. 1809; UKHO NP 19, section 9.33, UKHO OD 103, 19 and 23.
34. UKHO C280 on Hn; NRS 110, A.N. Ryan (ed.), *The Saumarez Papers*, pp. 129, 133, 170, 200, 260.
35. NRS 110, Ryan (ed.), *The Saumarez Papers*, pp. 75–6.
36. C264 on Hn and a plan in MP 101(Dc1).
37. NRS 110, Ryan, *The Saumarez Papers*, pp. 204–12; A.N. Ryan, 'The Melancholy Fate of the Baltic Ships in 1811', *MM*, 50(2) (May 1964), pp. 123–34 and 282; J. Ross, *Memoirs and Correspondence of Admiral Lord Saumarez, from Original Papers in the Possession of the Family* (London: Richard Bentley, 1838), Vol. II, pp. 257–67; TNA ADM 6/353/50.
38. TNA ADM 1/9, Ha 4a, p. 7 verso.
39. TNA ADM 29/1/86; for Cunningham, see Barritt, *Eyes of the Admiralty*, passim.
40. UKHO h1 on Hr.
41. TNA ADM 1/10, Baltic Ha 33, f. 86, memorandum dated 12 July 10. Reeves' directions for Makalito Bay in MP 102(Dc2) confirm that all bearings are magnetic.
42. TNA ADM 12/146, Cut 57.
43. TNA ADM 106/1672, letter dated 22 Apr. 1811.
44. UKHO b85 on Hm.
45. Mackesy, *War Without Victory*, pp. 7, 122–3, 203–4, 225–30.
46. Crawford, *Reminiscences*, Vol. 1, p. 141.
47. TNA ADM 2/827, letter dated 16 Oct. 1803, ADM 1/1529, Cap B385, dated 12 Nov. 1803.
48. UKHO k78/1 on Hv.
49. UKHO MP99(Db1), fos. 697–710.
50. NRS 96, Lloyd, *The Keith Papers*, Vol. III, pp. 79–81.
51. TNA ADM 36/17174, Supernumeraries for Victuals No. 81; TNA ADM 51/1518, entry for 13–14 Apr. 1804.
52. UKHO b83 and i77 on Hv.
53. J. Bew, *Castlereagh: Enlightenment, War and Tyranny* (London: Quercus, 2011), pp. 248–50; James, *Naval History*, Vol. V, pp. 131–9.
54. TNA ADM 1/3987, Précis of papers related to the Scheldt Expedition, 8 and 17.

55. NMM COO/2/B/1, papers of Commodore E.C.R. Owen relating to the Walcheren Expedition, copy of letter dated 3 Aug. 1809.
56. UKHO c53 on 13b.
57. I am grateful to Clifford Jones for consulting the Christ's Hospital Almoner's Minutes (MS 12811/014) for references to George Thomas.
58. LMA MS 12,818A/60 Presentation Paper 139; MS 12,818/12, George Thomas, Entry No. 133.
59. Hartley Library of the University of Southampton MS 45 AO 183, 'The Private Journal of William Mogg', Vol. I, pp. 76–102; L.E. Taverner, 'George Thomas, Master, Royal Navy', *MM*, 36(2) (1950), pp. 117–21.
60. D. Walker and A. Webb, 'The Making of Mr George Thomas RN, Admiralty Surveyor for Home Waters from 1810', *MM*, 104(2) (2013), pp. 211–24.
61. A.G.E. Jones, *Ships Employed in the South Sea Trade 1775–1861*, Vol. 2, Roebuck Society Publication No. 46, pp. 19 and 21, and Parts I–III (Canberra: Roebuck Society, 1986), pp. 22 and 24; J.M. Clayton, *Ships Employed in the South Sea Whale Fishery from Britain: 1775–1815, An Alphabetical List* (Chania: Berforts Group, 2014), p. 90; C.G. Maxworthy, '2011 Churchill Fellowship Report, Precis of Documents in Spanish Archives', pp. 30–8, accessed at www. academia.edu on 7 July 2017.
62. TNA ADM 1/5055, letter dated 30 June 1814.
63. TNA ADM 11/2, no. 193.
64. J.R. Fichter, *So Great a Proffit: How the East Indies Trade Transformed Anglo-American Capitalism* (London: Harvard University Press, 2010), pp. 205–10; James Kirker, *Adventures in China: Americans in the Southern Oceans, 1792–1812* (New York: Oxford University Press, 1970), pp. 25, 29, 65–81.
65. TNA ADM 37/1249, List of Supernumeraries for Victuals Only, No. 971; TNA ADM 51/1595 and 52/3648 No. 12, 8–17 Nov. 1806.
66. TNA ADM 6/185, Record of Academy Royal Scholars, 9 Jan. 1793; TNA ADM 1/1538, letter Cap B340 dated 7 May 1806, and ADM 1/1544, letter Cap B390 dated 12 Feb. 1808.
67. TNA ADM 1/3523, letter dated 26 Apr. 1808, Dalrymple receives approval for the printing of an excellent report from Bouverie.
68. TNA ADM 196/68, No. 242; TNA ADM 35/2327 and 37/1249, No. 556.
69. TNA ADM 55/90.
70. For deployments to protect the Greenland Fishery see M. Barritt, 'In Arctic Waters', in T. Voelcker (ed.), *Broke of the Shannon and the War of 1812* (Barnsley: Seaforth, 2014).
71. TNA ADM 52/3842; TNA ADM 51/1837, Part 4.
72. UKHO 213 on Ah2, published in 1816 as BA chart 278; UKHO A967 on Ah2.
73. TNA ADM 6/165.
74. TNA ADM 106/1694, letter dated 11 Nov. 1818; ADM 37/949, Nos 19106 and 19229; ADM 37/996, No. 52; ADM 37/1614, No. 241.
75. TNA ADM 1/2162, M69 record dated 23 Feb. 1810 and M104 letter dated 20 Mar. 1810 with enclosures.
76. TNA ADM 12/144, Cuts 57 and 68.1.
77. UKHO Surveyors' Letters (henceforth SL) 12a, letters of 12 and 29 Nov. 1832.

78. TNA ADM 1/3987, 40 and 54.
79. Preserved in UKHO MP 100(Db2).
80. UKHO c33 on Hu; Marshall, *Royal Naval Biography*, Supplement Part I (1827), pp. 26–7, 31.
81. UKHO SL 12a, letters dated 14 May, 10 and 23 June, and 8 and 29 Nov. 1832.
82. TNA ADM 106/1687, endorsement on letter dated 7 Apr. 1810.
83. TNA ADM 1/5054, Pro T 383.
84. UKHO 134 on Di and A697 on Of*. See A.H.W. Robinson, *Marine Cartography in Britain: A History of the Sea Chart to 1855* (Leicester: The University Press, 1962) for more information on Thomas's surveys in home waters.
85. His log for the period 27 June 1813 to 27 June 1814 is at TNA ADM 55/79.
86. UKHO SL 12a, letter dated 29 Nov. 1832.
87. UKHO c32 on Hu.
88. UKHO SL 12a, letter dated 29 Nov. 1832.
89. RNM MSS 74.
90. TNA ADM 2/1084, 17 Dec. 1813.
91. UKHO SL 12a, letters dated 14 May, 10 and 26 June and 8 Nov. 1832.

Chapter 6: Sea Power Projection: Iberian Peninsula

1. TNA WO 1/251, pp. 53–4, 239; B.M. de Toy, 'Commanders-in-Chief: Wellington, Berkeley and Victory in the Peninsula', in C.M. Woolgar (ed.), *Wellington Studies II* (Southampton: The University Press, 1999), pp. 197 and 207.
2. NRS 12, Vesey-Hamilton, *The Journals and Letters of Byam Martin*, Vol. II (1902), pp. 404–13.
3. TNA ADM 1/3523, letter dated 12 July 1808.
4. TNA ADM 1/3523, report dated 26 May 1808.
5. BL Maps C.10.d.20, a copy of 'Knight's Mediterranean' Atlas into which the plans have been interleaved.
6. TNA ADM 1/416, N 178 dated 22 June 1810; preface to Faden's edition of Tofiño's *Atlas Marítimo*. There are two copies in the NMM. D1120 527.83(261/262):094 TOF appears to have belonged to one of the two brothers in the Percy family who served in the Royal Navy on the Spanish coast.
7. NMM PRV 40A, letters dated 15 and 17 June with a list compiled by the Captain of the Port.
8. J.L. Bernal, *Breve Noticia de la Labor Científica del Capitán de Navío Don Felipe Bauzá y de Sus Papeles sobre América* (Palma de Mallorca: Imprenta Guasp, 1934), pp. 31–4; F.J. González and L. Martín-Merás, *La Dirección de Trabajos Hidrográficos (1797–1908)* (Madrid: Lunwerg, 2003), pp. 72–5.
9. BL Add MS 51622, ff. 175–6; NMM PRV 42B letter dated 2 Mar. 1810.
10. González and Martín-Merás, *La Dirección de Trabajos Hidrográficos*, p. 74; BL Add MS 51622, f. 211, Bauzá's statement dated 4 Mar. 1824.
11. Bernal, *Breve Noticia de la Labor Científica*, p. 152; A.L. Martínez y Guanter, 'Biografía de Don Felipe Bauzá y Cañas', *Revista General de Marina* (2011), p. 859.
12. NC XXVII, pp. 26–7.

13. A. David et al. (eds), *The Malaspina Expedition 1789–1794*, Vol. I (London: The Hakluyt Society, 2001), p. 322.
14. González and Martín-Merás, *La Dirección de Trabajos Hidrográficos*, p. 73. I am grateful to Richard Smith for drawing my attention to Bauzá's *Portolano*, of which only one copy has been found, held in the Museo Naval Madrid, and for locating Catalá's fair sheets in that museum.
15. A comprehensive search has been conducted in the ADM 1 and 50 series in the TNA, the Purvis Papers (NMM) and the Lynedoch Papers (National Library of Scotland, hereafter NLS), which contain extensive correspondence from Keats.
16. NLS Lynedoch Papers MS 3607, pp. 132–3, 182–3, 188 and 195; Marshall, *Royal Naval Biography*, Supplement Part IV (1830), p. 455.
17. NMM PRV 40B, 21 July 1809.
18. NMM PRV 31, letter dated 11 June; PRV 41B, letters dated 21 May, 5 July and 25 Nov. 1809.
19. NMM PRV 42B, letter dated 26 Feb. 1810.
20. *Revista General de Marina*, Tomo 232, March 1997, 24.608; J. Llabrés Bernal, *Relaciones Históricas de Mallorca*, s XIX, Tomo I (Palma: Antigua Imprenta Soler, 1959), p. 406.
21. TNA ADM 1/417, N286, letter dated 23 Aug. 1810.
22. Smyth, *The Mediterranean*, pp. 149, 175, 353.
23. Marshall, *Royal Naval Biography*, Vol. III, Part 1 (1831), p. 140.
24. NMM LBK/36, order dated 14 July 1809.
25. UKHO 78 on 6g.
26. TNA ADM 1/3523, letters dated 7 July and 3 Aug. 1809. Chart 19 in Volume II of Hurd's *Channel Atlas*, published in 1811, included soundings from Seymour's work.
27. NMM LBK/36, orders dated 15 Apr. 1809, Commander William Daniel of *Jasper* to take soundings upstream of Villa Nova.
28. Michael Nash Collection, Vice Admiral Berkeley papers, report dated 23 July 1809.
29. TNA ADM 1/342, Ma 229, Berkeley to Admiralty, letter no. 473 dated 14 Oct. 1810. Positions of the British craft, and depths along the river, are shown in a small-scale plan submitted by Captain Sir Michael Seymour of *Hannibal* (74) and preserved in UKHP MP 104 De2.
30. TNA ADM 51/2333, No. 1.
31. TNA ADM 6/167 and 11/3, No. 333.
32. Marshall, *Royal Naval Biography*, Vol. II, Part 1 (1824), pp. 225–8.
33. UKHO MP 74 (C3), pp. 160–8.
34. UKHO o92 on Ss.
35. Crawford, *Reminiscences*, Vol. 2, p. 262. The phenomenon was later described by Smyth in *The Mediterranean*, p. 9.
36. UKHO p97 on Med. Folio 1, copy of the chart at BL Maps.SEC.5.(148a).
37. TNA ADM 51/2932 Log No. 3.
38. UKHO p1 on Med. Folio 1.
39. TNA ADM 1/420, N776 letter dated 14 July 1811; F. Whittingham (ed.), *A Memoir of the Services of Lieutenant-General Sir Samuel Ford Whittingham* (London: Longmans, Green, 1868), pp. 144–6.

40. Testimonial of General Whittingham dated 22 Jan. 1816, accessed at http://bibliotecavirtualdefensa.es on 19 Dec. 2018.
41. Capitán de navío don Alejandro Briarly, *Memorias sobre algunas de las causas del abandono y estado deplorable en que se halla la Marina española* (Cádiz: private, 1813).
42. Parish of St Peter's, Dublin, 14 Mar. 1793; St Luke, Chelsea, 1 Jul. 1827.
43. Memorial dated 30 Aug. 1818, accessed at http://bibliotecavirtualdefensa.es on 19 Dec. 2018.
44. UKHO L2209 on Med. Folio 1; Smyth, *The Mediterranean*, p. 354.
45. C.D. Hall, *Wellington's Navy: Sea Power and the Peninsular War 1807–1814* (London: Chatham Publishing, 2004), 182-4.
46. UKHO L2207 on Med. Folio 1.
47. TNA ADM 1/3523, letter dated 7 July 1809.
48. English versions of the charts published by Arrowsmith in 1811 are at BL Maps K.MAR.V.(53.), 19960.(1.) and 19960.(2.). The sailing directions were published by the Admiralty in 1814. I am grateful to Richard Smith for sharing information from his research into Spanish and Portuguese cartography.
49. UKHO 50 on Hz; approval of Crawford's survey is at Note 9 in Franzini's directions; Hall, *Wellington's Navy*, pp. 21–2; the description from Crawford, *Reminiscences*, Vol. 1, p. 50.
50. TNA ADM 29/1/76.
51. J. McLeod, *Voyage of His Majesty's Ship Alceste* (London: John Murray, 1818), pp. 40–1.
52. Bew, *Castlereagh*, pp. 210, 214, 225.
53. Jones, 'Aspects of Relief Portrayal on Nineteenth-Century British Military Maps', pp. 21–2; Seymour, *A History of the Ordnance Survey*, pp. 51–2; B. Jackson, *Military Surveying* (London: W.H. Allen, 1838), p. 93.
54. R.H.P. Smith, 'Peninsular War Cartography: A New Look at the Military Mapping of General Sir George Murray and the Quartermaster General's Department', *Imago Mundi*, 65(2) (2013), p. 237; S.G.P. Ward, *Wellington's Headquarters* (Oxford: The University Press, 1957), pp. 23–5, 59; Jackson, *Military Surveying*, p. x.
55. TNA WO 37/10/15 contains examples.
56. Ward, *Wellington's Headquarters*, pp. 110–11; TNA MR1/167; I.C. Robertson, *Wellington at War in the Peninsula* (Barnsley: Seaforth, 2000), pp. 22–4, 56.
57. They can be found in UKHO MP 103–5.
58. UKHO 156 on Hy is the one surviving sheet of Lockwood's survey.
59. NLS, Murray Archives, Adv.MS.46.2.2, Peninsula 1808–09, pp. 167–8.
60. NLS, Murray Archives, Adv.MS46.10.1, no. 40; I am grateful to Richard Smith for drawing this document to my attention.
61. N.C. XXI, pp. 83–4; Hall, *Wellington's Navy*, p. 72.
62. Michael Nash Collection, Vice Admiral Berkeley papers, letters from McKinley dated 23 Feb., 3 Mar. and 14 June 1809.
63. UKHO m85 on Hg; another sheet, dated 1807, described as showing the inlets of Vigo/Pontevedra and Villagarcia has not survived (m81 in MS Book A).
64. UKHO MP 105(De 2ii), pp. 534–8.

65. Gawthrop's work and its use in updating charts is discussed with that of other practitioners in M.K. Barritt, 'The Charting of Arosa Bay: A Case Study in British Naval Pathfinding in the Peninsular War (1807–1814)', *Imago Mundi*, 75(2) (2023).
66. H. Davies, 'Naval Intelligence Support to the British Navy in the Peninsular War', *Journal of the Society for Army Historical Research* 86 (2008), pp. 37–9.
67. NMM KEI 43; Marshall, *Royal Naval Biography*, Vol. IV, Part II (1835), p. 456 et passim.

Chapter 7: World War: The Americas and the Pacific

1. Some material in this chapter first appeared in the author's 'Pathfinders: Front-line Hydrographic Data-gathering in the Wars of American Independence and 1812', in *The Trafalgar Chronicle, New Series 1* (Barnsley: Seaforth Publishing, 2016), pp. 92–103.
2. TNA ADM 1/506, O22, minute dated 7 Jan. 1814.
3. TNA ADM 1/3522, letters dated 11 June 1805 and 10 Oct. 1807; TNA 29/1/87; NRS 28, Markham, *The Correspondence*, pp. 75–6.
4. UKHO LB1, letters dated 11 July 1816 and 25 Mar. 1818, TNA ADM 12/188, Cut 57/2, 21 Jan. 1818.
5. TNA ADM 1/506, O22.
6. James, *Naval History of Great Britain*, Vol. VI, p. 187; *USJ* (1836), Part III, pp. 25–6.
7. UKHO r38 on Cg, r39 and v 83 on C, with remarks in MP 85(Ca 2), p. 180, MP 87(Ca 4), pp. 674–702, and MP 88(Ca 5), pp. 339–69.
8. See note 2.
9. UKHO B31 on US f1.
10. J. Scott, *Recollections of a Naval Life* (London: Richard Bentley, 1834), Vol. III, pp. 109, 187.
11. Scott, *Recollections of a Naval Life*, pp. 116, 136.
12. Both surveys are in UKHO MP 33(Ab2).
13. Cochrane's report of the operation is at TNA ADM 1/506, ff. 1191–5.
14. UKHO 303 on Ra.
15. UKHO LB1, Nos. 343 and 443. The surveys have not survived. De Mayne's contribution and the coverage of BA Chart 305 are discussed in R. Morrison and R. Hansen, *Charting the Chesapeake* (Hagerstown: Maryland State Archives, 1990), p. 55.
16. TNA ADM 1/503, O 100, f. 557, report from Warren dated 28 May 1813.
17. TNA ADM 51/2401, Part 9; R.J. Barrett, 'Naval Recollections of the Late American War', *USJ* (1841), Part I, p. 462.
18. UKHO p27 on Aa2 Part 5.
19. UKHO 190 on Aa2.
20. UKHO MP 31(Aa1ii), pp. 115–27.
21. UKHO 182 on Aa1 and E432 on Aa2M; TNA MPG 1/60. His survey of the Niagara River up to Queenston is at UKHO p. 23 on Aa1, Part 6.
22. UKHO MP 31(Aa1ii), journal dated 1817, pp. 5–6.

23. UKHO MLP 61, letter dated 5 May 1829.
24. TNA ADM 1/2264 Cap O 271 dated 3 Aug. 1815.
25. TNA ADM 1/2264 Cap O 299 dated 7 Oct. 1815. The survey is at UKHO B718 on 50c, and Vidal's field book showing track and coastline is in UKHO MP 31(Aa1ii), pp. 134–40.
26. E.H. Burrows, *Captain Owen of the African Survey* (Rotterdam: A.A. Balkema, 1979), p. 69.
27. TNA PROB 11/1998/108.
28. UKHO MP 54(Ad1), pp. 501–4.
29. UKHO LB1, letter dated 2 Sept. 1815.
30. TNA ADM 12/188, Cut 57.
31. C.R. Markham, *A Memoir of the Indian Surveys* (London: W.H. Allen, 1878), pp. 14–16, 23.
32. NRS 104, G.S. Graham and R.A. Humphreys (eds), *The Navy and South America 1807–1823*, pp. 72–4, 77, 79–80.
33. NRS 104, Graham and Humphreys, *The Navy and South America*, pp. 86, 90–2; TNA ADM 1/1947 Cap H 210; E.A. Tagart, *A Memoir of the late Captain Peter Heywood RN, with extracts from his Diaries and Correspondence* (London: Effingham Wilson, 1832), pp. 255–71.
34. NRS 104, Graham and Humphreys, *The Navy and South America*, pp. 90, 98–100, 105–6, 128–9, 132–3, 135–7.
35. D. Porter, *Journal of a Cruise made to the Pacific Ocean* (New York: Wiley and Halsted, 1822), Vol. I, pp. 111–14.
36. TNA ADM 352/107.
37. W. Kaye Lamb (ed.), *The Voyage of George Vancouver 1791–1795* (London: The Hakluyt Society, 1984), Vol. II, pp. 781–4; UKHO 446 and 446a on Pu*.
38. UKHO 135 on Pv* is Pipon's, and 584 on Pv is Staines'. The latter is illustrated on p. 131 of M. Blewitt, *Surveys of the Seas: A Brief History of British Hydrography* (London: MacGibbon and Kee, 1957).
39. Marshall, *Royal Naval Biography*, Supplement Part I, pp. 94–105, 388–9; Barrow, *The Mutiny and Piratical Seizure of HMS BOUNTY*, Chapter VIII.
40. TNA ADM 37/3532, Muster Book Nos. 208 and 209.
41. B. Hall, *Extracts from a Journal, written on the coasts of Chili, Peru, and Mexico in the years 1820, 1821, 1822* (Edinburgh: Archibald Constable, 1825), Vol. II, Appendix No. 1, pp. 4–5.
42. Callao (UKHO 115 Ad1, UKHO View Folio 8E, 16), Juan Fernández (UKHO C96 on Pacific Folio 3, with an additional set of views at TNA ADM 344 2255) and Valparaíso (UKHO 119 on Ad1).
43. Hillyar's journal is at NMM MS87/026. Gardiner's journal, edited by J.S. Rieske with an introduction by Andrew Lambert, was published as *Hunting the Essex* (Barnsley: Seaforth, 2013).
44. UKHO 115 and 119 on Ad1 and C96 in Pacific f.3.
45. BA 632 (Angra Pequena) published on 11 Jan. 1828.
46. UKHO x14 on Nx.
47. TNA ADM 1/3459, minute dated 7 May 1814.
48. UKHO d35, with a survey of Ascension Island at d34, both on shelf Cb.
49. UKHO MLP 70.

Chapter 8: Securing an Uneasy Peace

1. TNA ADM 12/179, Heading 57, 12 Oct. 16.
2. G.H. Richards, *A Memoir of the Hydrographical Department of the Admiralty* (London, 1868), private collection, pp. 8–9; Dawson, *Memoirs of Hydrography*, Part I, pp. 99–101, and Part II, p. 3.
3. A. Day, *The Admiralty Hydrographic Service 1795–1919* (London: HMSO, 1967), pp. 34–44; C.I. Hamilton, *The Making of the Modern Admiralty: British Naval Policy-Making 1805–1927* (Cambridge: The University Press, 2011), pp. 44–51 and 55; Pascoe, 'The Story of the Curator', p. 7; Becher's notes in UKHO MLP 107 and UKHO MLP 5, Item 1; Webb, 'The Expansion of British Naval Hydrographic Administration', pp. 28–31.
4. BL Add MSS 35302, p. 171.
5. TNA ADM 106/1687, letters and papers dated 16 and 23 Jan. 1817.
6. W. Laird Clowes, *The Royal Navy: A History from the Earliest Times to the Present*, Vol. VI (London: Sampson Low, Marston & Co., 1901), pp. 233–4.
7. TNA ADM 51/3489, No. 6.
8. TNA ADM 51/3489, No. 6.
9. UKHO B200 and A992 on Af2.
10. The original surveys are at UKHO 899 on Co and s36 on Cn.
11. UKHO E433 on Rf.
12. UKHO MP 46(Ac 8), pp. 376–8.
13. James, *Naval History of Great Britain*, Vol. V, pp. 204–6; *Gentleman's Magazine*, Vol. LXXIX (1809), pp. 866–7.
14. TNA ADM 6/132, clerk's note on inside cover dated 14 Dec. 1809, NMM ADM 354/233, letter dated 7 Sept. 1808, TNA ADM 106/1677, letter dated 14 Dec. 1809.
15. TNA CO 267/25, letter dated 26 Dec. 1809.
16. University of Illinois, Chicago, Sierra Leone Collection, Box 2, Folder 11, ff. 1–2, letter dated 27 Dec. 1809. I am very grateful to Valerie Harris, Associate Special Collections Librarian, for providing a transcript of this letter.
17. TNA ADM 1/4716 Pro H 1003, letter dated 17 Nov. 1815.
18. UKHO 897 on Cg.
19. TNA ADM 1/1812, Cap F 204, p. 4.
20. UKHO LP1857 C, No. 16; UKHO s37 on Cg.
21. UKHO r47 on Cg; UKHO r43 on Ch.
22. UKHO r48 on Ch.
23. UKHO LB1, Nos. 275 and 278.
24. UKHO B105 Ce.
25. *USJ* (1836), Part III, p. 26.
26. The manuscript survey is at UKHO A422 on Ck; there is a copy of the published chart at BL Maps 64625(1).
27. TNA ADM 12/184.
28. UKHO MLP 82 shows that 1819 was the peak year for allocations during Hurd's tenure of office, with 10 chronometers allocated to Arctic parties, 23 to Admiralty Surveyors, and 57 to captains in the fleet.

29. See, for example, F. Fleming, *Barrow's Boys* (London: Granta, 1998), pp. 35 and 38. For a very balanced review of the controversy, see C.I. Jackson's introduction to the third volume in the Hakluyt Society's publication of *The Arctic Whaling Journals of William Scoresby the Younger*, Series III, Vol. 21 (2009), pp. xxvii–xxxv.
30. Marshall, *Royal Navy Biography*, Vol. III, Part I (1831), pp. 83–94; the *Dictionary of Canadian Biography* [online] gives a good summary of Buchan's two inland expeditions. Survey sheets from that made in 1819 are at UKHO 285 on Ah2.
31. UKHO w18 and w42 on Hk. Ross's report to Hope on the return convoy is at TNA ADM 7/801, p. 85, dated 22 Oct. 1814.
32. Parry, *Memoirs of Rear Admiral Sir W. Edward Parry*, p. 68.
33. NMM MS 63/003, letter dated 25 Jan. 1819.
34. J. Ross, *Observations on a Work, Entitled 'Voyages of Discovery and Research within the Arctic Regions', by Sir J. Barrow: Being a Refutation of the Numerous Misrepresentations Contained in that Volume* (Edinburgh and London: W. Blackwood and Sons, 1846), footnote to p. 19.
35. Ross, *Observations on a Work*, p. 30, and *A Letter to John Barrow Esq. on the Subject of the Polar Expedition or The Reviewer Reviewed by A Friend to the Navy* (London: James Ridgway, 1819), p. 10; the passage in J. Barrow's *A Chronological History of Voyages into the Arctic Regions* (London: John Murray, 1818) occurs on pp. 366–70.
36. The Hartley Library, University of Southampton, MS 45 AO 183, 'The Private Journal of William Mogg', Vol. I, p. 74.
37. M.K. Barritt, 'Captain Jonathon Foulerton, Elder Brother', *Trinity House Fraternity Review 2021*, pp. 98–9.
38. M.K. Barritt, 'Lieutenant Thomas Evans, Mr George Thomas and the Survey of Liverpool', *MM*, 108(2) (2022), pp. 216–33.
39. TNA ADM 1/3523, letter dated 13 June 1809.
40. NMM MRK/104/51–3.
41. M.K. Barritt, 'Surveying the Islands: Captain Martin White RN and the Hydrography of the Channel', in C. Partridge, J. de Préneuf and A. Lambert (eds), *The Channel Islands in Anglo–French Relations, 1689–1918* (Woodbridge: Boydell and Brewer, 2024).
42. UKHO 820 on Ps.
43. TNA ADM 1/3458, letters dated 1 and 6 July 1812.
44. TNA ADM 1/2712, Cap W30; ADM 1/228, K91; ADM 1/2713, Cap W283 and W300; ADM 1/1230, A181; ADM 1/2715, Cap W204 and W365.
45. NMM ADM 359/36B correspondence dated 4 Apr., 4 and 24 Aug., 1 Sept., 25 Oct. and 26 Nov. 1816.
46. The Hydrographic Instructions for this survey are at TNA ADM 1/3460, dated 18 Feb. 1817. The spelling of the ship's name varies, but that adopted here was used invariably in White's records.
47. TNA ADM 344/1210–22, UKHO w54 on 9ck and w53 on Ba2.
48. TNA ADM 12/186, Heading 57, Minute of 1 Dec. 1818.
49. TNA ADM 12/179, Heading 57, Minute of 12 Oct. 1816, referring to Hurd's letter of 7 May 1814; UKHO MLP 70.
50. TNA ADM 1/1566, Cap B25 and 46.

51. UKHO B120 on Cb and B120a in Africa Folio 7.
52. UKHO MP 106(De 3).
53. UKHO MP 87(Ca 4), pp. 260 onwards and 520–615. His narrative of the first deployment is at TNA ADM 55/88.
54. T. Boteler, *Narrative of a Voyage of Discovery to Africa and Arabia: Performed in His Majesty's Ships, Leven and Barracouta, from 1821 to 1826, under the Command of Capt. F. W. Owen, R. N* (London: Richard Bentley, 1835), pp. 7–8.
55. George, son of John and Helen Bartholomew of Baldridge House, Dunfermline.
56. TNA ADM 1/3460, dated 4 Dec. 1817.
57. TNA ADM 12/184, Heading 57, Admiralty 4 Dec. 1817; UKHO MLP 6, No. 5.
58. TNA ADM 80/156, letter 4.
59. TNA ADM 80/157, letters 6, 30, 31, 33, 35; UKHO D775–6 on Ag6, D780 on Ag6 and E247 on Ag4.
60. UKHO LB1, letters 354–5, 383.
61. UKHO OD 512.
62. TNA ADM 80/157, letter 42.
63. UKHO D791/1–4 on Ag6.
64. UKHO LB1, letters dated 19 Feb. and 28 Apr. 1819.
65. UKHO Minute Book (MB) 1, f. 39, dated 19 Apr. 1826; Dawson, *Memoirs of Hydrography*, Part I, pp. 125–6.
66. UKHO LB1, letter dated 20 June 1816 is Hurd's recommendation that a ship be allocated for the Mediterranean survey.
67. Smyth, *The Mediterranean*, p. 369; V. Valerio, 'Landscapes and Charting in the Nineteenth Century: Neapolitan-Austrian and English Cooperation in the Adriatic Sea', in *Mappae Antiquae, Liber Amicorum Günter Schilder* ('t Goy-Houten: HES & De Graaf Publishers, 2007), p. 473.
68. TNA ADM 1/3459, minute dated 7 May 1814.

Postscript: A 'Great Maritime Nation'

1. Anon., *Charting the Seas in Peace and War* (London: HMSO, 1947), p. 10.
2. TNA ADM 1/3458, dated 14 Apr. 1811, and 3461, dated 16 Nov. 1818.
3. *USJ*, Vol. I, p. 290.
4. U. Lamb, 'The London Years of Felipe Bauzá: Spanish Hydrographer in Exile, 1823–34', *The Journal of Navigation*, 34 (1981), pp. 319–40.
5. *Libros manuscritos de asientos*, Archivo Naval Cartagena; Royal Geographical Society, Supplementary Papers, Vol. III (London, 1893), p. 439.
6. A. Briarly, *Observaciones sobre la posibilidad y necesidad de mejorar la navegación del Río Guadalquivir* (Sevilla: Imprenta de D. Josef Hidalgo, 1814) and *Plano del Corte del Borrego*, 1816; BL 9180.dd.3.(7.).
7. *USJ* (1837), Part I, p. 152.
8. Carmen Fernández Álvarez, 'Francisco Fernández Golfín, los años del exilio (1823–1831)', accessed at https://dialnet.unirioja.es/descarga/articulo/4573744.pdf; *Festejos de la Ciudad de Palma* (Palma de Mallorca: Imprento Guasp, 1833), p. 45.

9. His promotions are recorded in successive issues of *Guía Política y Militar* and later *Estado Militar de España*, published by the Imprenta Real.
10. UKHO SL 12a, undated memorial, probably rendered in 1831.
11. UKHO SL 12b, letters dated 2 Dec. 1846 and 1 Mar. 1847.
12. The figures for 1823 have been compiled from the ship's muster books. The comparative figures from other years are taken principally from the record of activity in Dawson's *Memoirs of Hydrography*. There is a list of the services of surveying officers of the ranks of lieutenant and midshipman, to January 1833, in UKHO MLP 20, Folder 1, Item 2. It gives cumulative time, but not dates of service. The figure in the table with the biggest variation is the bearing of lieutenants in 1829.
13. Robinson, *Marine Cartography in Britain*, p. 10.
14. B.J. Sulivan, 'A Proposal for Organising a Scientific Corps of Naval Officers', 1858; a copy of this paper has not been located, but some of its content is included in Appendix E of H.N. Sulivan (ed.), *Life and Letters of the Late Admiral Sir Bartholomew James Sulivan K.C.B. 1810–1890* (London: John Murray, 1896).
15. Sulivan, *Life and Letters*, pp. 126, 417, 240.
16. Sulivan, *Life and Letters*, pp. 123–4.
17. Dawson, *Memoirs of Hydrography*, Part II, p. 180; A. Lambert, *The Crimean War: British Grand Strategy Against Russia, 1853–56* (Abingdon: Routledge, 2016), pp. 4, 108 et passim, 316.
18. Day, *The Admiralty Hydrographic Service*, p. 85.
19. R.O. Morris, *Charts and Surveys in Peace and War: The History of the Royal Navy's Hydrographic Service 1919–1970* (London: HMSO, 1995), pp. 125–8.
20. UKHO Hydrographic Department jacket H 2/57, letter dated 13 Feb. 1957; relevant reports of proceedings in jacket H 7468/56.
21. See R. Harding, 'Sailors and Gentlemen of Parade: Some Professional and Technical Problems Concerning the Conduct of Combined Operations in the Eighteenth Century' and P. Mackesy, 'Problems of an Amphibious Power: Britain Against France, 1793–1850', both reprinted in R. Harding (ed.), *Naval History 1680–1850* (Aldershot: Ashgate, 2006).
22. A.V. Swain, 'Rapid Environmental Assessment Al Faw 2003', *The Ranger: Journal of the Defence Surveyors' Association*, 3(1) (2010), pp. 68–75.

Bibliography

Manuscript Sources and Other Archive Material

The endnotes contain details of item and folio or page numbers from the following series:

The National Archives, Kew (TNA)

ADM 1: Admiralty Board in-letters
ADM 1/3522–3: Correspondence of the Hydrographer to the Admiralty and the Admiralty Chart Committee
ADM 2: Admiralty Board out-letters
ADM 3: Admiralty Board minutes
ADM 6: Service records, registers, returns and certificates
ADM 7: Miscellanea
ADM 9: Survey returns of officers' services
ADM 11: Officers' service records
ADM 12: Admiralty Board indices and digests
ADM 29: Officers' and ratings' service records
ADM 35: Ships' pay books
ADM 36 and 37: Ships' muster books
ADM 50: Admirals' journals
ADM 51: Captains' logs
ADM 52: Masters' logs
ADM 55: Logs of exploring vessels (available online)
ADM 80: Letter books of Admirals Keats (141) and Popham (156–7)
ADM 106: Navy Board in-letters from masters
ADM 107: Navy Board passing certificates of lieutenants
ADM 196: Officers' service records

BIBLIOGRAPHY

ADM 344: Admiralty: Hydrographic Department: Coastal and riverine views
ADM 346: Admiralty: Hydrographic Department: Ships' remark books
ADM 352: Admiralty: Hydrographic Department: Original surveys
ADM 354: Navy Board: Bound out-letters
CO 37: Colonial Office and predecessors: Bermuda, original correspondence
CO 295: Colonial Office and predecessors: Trinidad, original correspondence
HO 28: Home Office, Admiralty correspondence
MPG 1: Maps and plans extracted to flat storage from various series of records of the Colonial Office
MPHH 1: Maps and plans extracted from War Office to extra-large flat storage
MR 1: Public Record Office: Maps and plans extracted to rolled storage from various departments
PROB 11: Probate records: Will registers
WO 1: War Department: In letters and papers
WO 37: War Office: Intelligence Branch of QMG in Spain: Papers
WO 78: War Office and predecessors: Maps and plans

The British Library (BL)

Additional Manuscripts:
20189, Lowe Papers
31158 and 31168–70, St Vincent Papers
34919, 34930, 34932, 34934–6, 34966–7 and 34981, Nelson Papers
35302, Barrow Bequest; autograph copy of Barrow's autobiographical memoir
37268, Ball Papers
37883, Windham Papers
51622, Holland Papers
56088, Lowe Papers

The Alexander Turnbull Library

MS-Papers-6373-46, Journal of Edward Bell

Bedfordshire Record Office

DDX 170/7/4 Bayntun collection

The John Carter Brown Map Collection

GA 803 1, Briarly chart

The London Metropolitan Archives (LMA) / Greater London Record Office (GLRO)

DL/C: Records of the Consistory Court of London
MS 12818, 12818A: Christ's Hospital presentation papers
MS 12876/6–7: Christ's Hospital register of children discharged and apprenticed, 1777–1815
MS 30.338: Christ's Hospital Royal Mathematical School register of boys apprenticed to ship's masters

BIBLIOGRAPHY

The National Library of Australia

MS 43, Dalrymple letter
MS 5393, Bligh's Notebook and List of Mutineers (available online)

The Naval Historical Branch (Admiralty Library) (NHB/AL) and National Museum of the Royal Navy (RNM) Portsmouth

Portfolio F 21: Plans of Basque roads
RNM MSS 22: *Mediterranean Directions copied from a manuscript folio book belonging to Sir Thomas Troubridge Bart*
RNM MSS 74: *A Nautical Description of the Banks, Shoals and Channels at the mouths of the River Scheld* [sic] with sailing directions, by Mr George Thomas
RNM MSS 2007.127/1: Letter book from HMS *Culloden*, 1795–97

The National Library of Scotland

Lynedoch Papers, MS 3607
Murray Archives, Adv.MS.46.2.2, Peninsula 1808–09
Murray Archives, Adv.MS46.10.1, maps and charts

The National Maritime Museum (NMM)

ADM/BP: Navy Board: Unbound out-letters (catalogued under TNA ADM 359)
ADM/L: Lieutenants' logs
AGC: Manuscript documents acquired singly
AUS 17: Papers of Francis William Austen
COO/2–3: Cochrane Collection (Owen Papers)
COM/1–2: Columbine Papers
COR 14, 15: Cornwallis Papers
CRK: Philipps-Croker Collection
DUC: Duckworth Papers
G Series: Miscellaneous manuscript surveys
GREN: Grenville Papers
KEI: Keith Papers
LBK/36: Berkeley letter books
LBK/66: Longstaff letter book
MKH: Hood family papers
MRK: Markham Papers
MS 87/026: Journal of Captain Hillyar
NVP 3: Book of Nautical Remarks
PDW 1: Whitshed Papers
PEN 224: Penrose Papers
PRV: Purvis Papers

The Hartley Library, University of Southampton

MS 45 AO 183: 'The Private Journal of William Mogg'

BIBLIOGRAPHY

United Kingdom Hydrographic Office (UKHO)

Curator's Catalogue A (Book A): the first manuscript catalogue of holdings in the
 Hydrographic Office, with their item and shelf or folio numbers
Incoming Letters prior to 1857 (LP1857) batched alphabetically
Miscellaneous Letters and Papers by File No. (MLP)
Miscellaneous Papers (MP), including Remark Books
Minute Books (MB)
Original Documents (OD)
Outgoing Letter Books (LB)
Surveyors Letters, Incoming (SL)

Printed Sources

Primary

The British Library

Maps 15383: Knight's Charts of the Bay of Brest, 2nd edn (1802)
Maps C.10.d.20: Knight's Charts of the Mediterranean
Maps C.21.c.15: List of Admiralty Charts
Maps K.MAR.V.(14.): Knight's Charts of the Bay of Brest, 1st (1800) and 2nd
 (1802) edns
Maps K.MAR.V.(53.), 19960: Franzini's directions for the coast of Portugal
Maps K.MAR.VI.(1–17.): Red Sea charts
Maps SEC.5: Mediterranean charts

The British Museum, Department of Prints and Drawings

1868,0808.1834: Briarly on the Battle of Copenhagen
1891,0414.185: Briarly's plan of the Battle of Copenhagen

The Bodleian Library, Oxford

5 DELTA 195–203: Dalrymple's plans, charts and memoirs
Facs.d.95 and 2098.d.26: Dalrymple publications related to the River Plate

The Admiralty Library, Portsmouth

UB8: Book of remarks for the Western Station, contains a copy of Captain Thomas
 Hurd's *A Nautical Description of the Bay of Brest with indications for its navigation;
 also for A NEW CHANNEL into the FOUR*, London, 1809
Vb 9II: *Baltic Seas – Directions and Remarks for the better navigating those seas, as
 made and collected by various Naval Officers in the course of service during the years
 1808 & 1809* published by Ballintine and Byworth in 1811
Vk 5: *The Mediterranean Atlas*, published by Captain Thomas Hurd, Hydrographer
 to the Admiralty Board
Vq 30: Charts and plans in the Western Mediterranean produced by the HO in
 1803–19 (15 folded sheets in a case)

Vu 3: Lord Keith's atlas of *Charts and Plans in the Mediterranean, including the navigation from the English Channel to the Straits of Gibraltar*
Vy 3: Charts of the North Sea and Baltic
Vy 4: Captain John Knight's four charts of the Bay of Brest, 2nd edn published by Faden in 1802

The National Maritime Museum

527.83(46):094 TOF: Tofiño de San Miguel, Brigadier Don Vicente, trans. J. Dougall, *España Maritima or Spanish Coasting Pilot*, London, 1812
912.43(267.5):094 BAR B8409: Bartholomew coastal views in the Red Sea
912.44(26:46)'17':094: *Atlas Marítimo de España*, Madrid, 1789
D 8513/2: *Channel Atlas*

UKHO

Old Copy Bundles (OCB): generally comprehensive series of the successive printed states of every British Admiralty chart
Pilots or Sailing Directions (NP)

The Navy Records Society (NRS)

Vols 12 and 24: Vesey-Hamilton, R. (ed.). *The Journals and Letters of Admiral of the Fleet Sir Thomas Byam Martin, 1773–1854*, Vols I and II (1898 and 1902)
Vols 14 and 21: Leyland, J. (ed.). *Despatches and Letters Relating to the Blockade of Brest*, Vols I and II (1899 and 1902)
Vol. 28: Markham, C.R. (ed.). *The Correspondence of Admiral John Markham 1801– 1807* (1904)
Vol. 31: Vesey-Hamilton, R. and J.K. Laughton. *The Recollections of Commander James Anthony Gardner, 1775–1814* (1906)
Vol. 39: Laughton, J.K. (ed.). *Letters and Papers of Charles, Lord Barham, 1758– 1813*, Vol. III (1910)
Vols 55 and 61: Smith, D.B. (ed.). *The Letters of Lord St Vincent, 1801–1804*, Vols I and II (1921 and 1926)
Vol. 59: Richmond, H.W. (ed.). *The Private Papers of George, 2nd Earl Spencer*, Vol. IV (1924)
Vol. 62: Perrin, W.G. (ed.). *Letters and Papers of Admiral Viscount Keith*, Vol. I (1927)
Vol. 63: Anderson, R.C. (ed.). *The Naval Miscellany*, Vol. III (1927)
Vols 90 and 96: Lloyd, C.C. (ed.). *The Keith Papers*, Vols II and III (1950 and 1955)
Vol. 92: Lloyd, C.C. (ed.). *The Naval Miscellany*, Vol. IV (1952)
Vol. 98: Hughes, E. (ed.). *The Private Correspondence of Admiral Lord Collingwood* (1957)
Vol. 104: Graham, G.S. and R.A. Humphreys (eds). *The Navy and South America 1807–1823* (1962)
Vol. 110: Ryan, N.A. (ed.). *The Saumarez Papers: Selections from the Baltic Correspondence 1808–1812* (1968)
Vol. 135: Grainger, J.D. (ed.). *The Royal Navy in the River Plate, 1806–07* (1996)

BIBLIOGRAPHY

Vol. 138: Lavery, B. (ed.). *Shipboard Life and Organisation, 1731–1815* (1998)
Vol. 141: Morriss, R. (ed.). *The Channel Fleet and the Blockade of Brest* (2001)
Occasional Publication 1: Syrett, D. and R.L. Di Nardo (eds), *The Commissioned Sea Officers of the Royal Navy 1660–1815* (1994)

The Hakluyt Society

Second Series:
Vols 163–6: Kaye Lamb, W. (ed.). *The Voyage of George Vancouver 1791–1795*, Vols I–IV (1984)
Third Series:
Vols 8, 11, 13: David, A. et al. (eds). *The Malaspina Expedition 1789–1794*, Vols I–III (2001, 2003, 2004)
Vols 12, 20 and 21: Jackson, C.I. (ed.). *The Arctic Whaling Journals of William Scoresby the Younger*, Vols I–III (2003, 2008, 2009)

Secondary

Alexander, C. *The Bounty: The True Story of the Mutiny on the Bounty* (London: HarperCollins, 2003)
Andrewes, W.J.H. (ed.). *The Quest for Longitude* (Harvard: The University Press, 1993)
Anon. 'Recollections of the British Army', *United Service Journal* (1836)
Anon. 'Miranda and the British Admiralty, 1804–1806', *The American Historical Review*, 6(3) (1901)
Anon. *Charting the Seas in Peace and War* (London: HMSO, 1947)
Barrett, R.J. 'Naval Recollections of the Late American War', *United Service Journal* (1841), Part I
Barritt, M.K. *Eyes of the Admiralty* (London: National Maritime Museum, 2008)
Barritt, M.K. 'In Arctic Waters', in T. Voelcker (ed.), *Broke of the Shannon and the War of 1812* (Barnsley: Seaforth, 2014)
Barritt, M.K. 'Agincourt Sound Revisited', *The Mariner's Mirror*, 101(2) (2015)
Barritt, M.K. 'Pathfinders: Front-line Hydrographic Data-gathering in the Wars of American Independence and 1812', in *The Trafalgar Chronicle, New Series 1* (Barnsley: Seaforth Publishing, 2016)
Barritt, M.K. 'An Offshore Hydrographic Survey by the Royal Navy in 1798', *The Mariner's Mirror*, 103(4) (2017)
Barritt, M.K. '"Willing Assistance Constantly Rendered": Joint Service Field Survey in Sicily, 1814–1816', *The Ranger: Journal of the Defence Surveyors' Association* (December 2020)
Barritt, M.K. 'Captain Jonathon Foulerton, Elder Brother', *Trinity House Fraternity Review 2021*
Barritt, M.K. 'Lieutenant Thomas Evans, Mr George Thomas and the Survey of Liverpool', *The Mariner's Mirror*, 108(2) (2022)
Barritt, M.K. 'Charts "Sent by the Ever to be Lamented Lord Nelson": Some Reflections on Navigational Practice in the Georgian Royal Navy', in *The Trafalgar Chronicle*, New Series 7 (2022)
Barritt, M.K. 'The Charting of Arosa Bay: A Case Study in British Naval Pathfinding in the Peninsular War (1807–1814)', *Imago Mundi*, 75(2) (2023)

BIBLIOGRAPHY

Barritt, M.K. 'Early Hydrographic Work of the Royal Navy in the Red Sea' (October 2023), *Journal of the Hakluyt Society*, accessible at https://hakluyt.com/downloadable_files/Journal/

Barritt, M.K. 'Surveying the Islands: Captain Martin White RN and the Hydrography of the Channel', in C. Partridge, J. de Préneuf and A. Lambert (eds), *The Channel Islands in Anglo–French Relations, 1689–1918* (Woodbridge: Boydell and Brewer, 2024)

Barrow, J. *A Chronological History of Voyages into the Arctic Regions* (London: John Murray, 1818)

Barrow, J. *The Mutiny and Piratical Seizure of HMS BOUNTY* (London: John Murray, 1831)

Beaglehole, J.C. *The Life of Captain James Cook* (London: The Hakluyt Society, 1974)

Bennett, J.A. *The Divided Circle: A History of Instruments for Astronomy, Navigation and Surveying* (Oxford: The University Press, 1987)

Bernal, J.L. *Breve Noticia de la Labor Científica del Capitán de Navío Don Felipe Bauzá y de Sus Papeles sobre América* (Palma de Mallorca: Imprenta Guasp, 1934)

Bew, J. *Castlereagh: Enlightenment, War and Tyranny* (London: Quercus, 2011)

Blewitt, M. *Surveys of the Seas: A Brief History of British Hydrography* (London: MacGibbon and Kee, 1957)

Bligh, W. *A Voyage to the South Sea {. . .} in His Majesty's Ship the Bounty, [. . .] an account of the mutiny [. . .] and the subsequent voyage [. . .] in the ship's boat* (London: George Nicol, 1792)

Bonner Smith, D. 'Midshipman W.G. Anderson', *The Mariner's Mirror*, 15(3) (1929)

Boteler, T. *Narrative of a Voyage of Discovery to Africa and Arabia: Performed in His Majesty's Ships, Leven and Barracouta, from 1821 to 1826, under the Command of Capt. F. W. Owen, R. N* (London: Samuel Bentley, 1835)

Burrows, E.H. *Captain Owen of the African Survey* (Rotterdam: A.A. Balkema, 1979)

Campbell, T. and M. Barritt. 'The Representation of Navigational Hazards: The Development of Topology and Symbology on Portolan Charts from the 13th Century Onwards' (December 2020), *Journal of the Hakluyt Society*, accessible at https://hakluyt.com/downloadable_files/Journal/

Cavell, S.A. *Midshipmen and Quarterdeck Boys in the British Navy, 1771–1831* (Woodbridge: Boydell, 2012)

Clark, P.K. and Y. Jones. 'British Military Map-making in the Peninsular War', unpublished typescript, 1974

Clayton, J.M. *Ships Employed in the South Sea Whale Fishery from Britain: 1775–1815, An Alphabetical List* (Chania: Berforts Group, 2014)

Close, C. *The Early Years of the Ordnance Survey* (Newton Abbot: David & Charles, 1969)

Cochrane, T. and H.R. Fox Bourne. *The Life of Thomas, Lord Cochrane* (London: Richard Bentley, 1869)

Cole, V. (ed.) and J. Murray. *The Summer Survey: Log of the Lady Nelson 1801–1802* (Hastings, Victoria: Western Port Historical Society, 2001)

Colledge, J.J. *Ships of the Royal Navy*, Vol. 1: *Major Units* (Newton Abbot: David & Charles, 1969)

Colnett, J. *A Voyage to the S. Atlantic and Round Cape Horn into the Pacific Ocean* (London: printed for the author, 1798)

Cook, A.S. 'An Author Voluminous and Vast: Alexander Dalrymple (1737–1808), Hydrographer to the East India Company and to the Admiralty, as Publisher: A Catalogue of Books and Charts', unpublished PhD thesis comprising volumes I–III, St Andrews, 1992

Cook, A.S. 'Why Alexandria? Alexander Dalrymple's Experimental Maps of Alexandria of 1801', History of Cartography Athens Conference, 1999

Cook, A.S. 'Establishing the Sea Routes to India and China: Stages in the Development of Hydrographical Knowledge', in H.V. Bowen et al. (eds), *The Worlds of the East India Company* (Woodbridge: Boydell, 2002)

Corbett, J.S. *The Campaign of Trafalgar* (London: Longmans, Green, 1910)

Courtney, N. *Gale Force 10: The Life and Legacy of Admiral Beaufort* (London: Review, 2002)

Crawford, A. *Reminiscences of a Naval Officer during the Late War* (London: Henry Colburn, 1851)

Dalrymple, A. *Collection of Nautical Memoirs and Journals* (London: William Ballintine, 1806)

Dalrymple, A. *A Catalogue of Authors who have written on the Rio de la Plata, Paraguay and Chaco* (London: Ballintine & Law, 1807)

Dalrymple, A. *Memoir Concerning the Geography of the Countries situated on the Rio de la Plata and on the Rivers falling into it* (London: Ballintine & Law, 1807)

Dalrymple, A. *Case of Alexander Dalrymple, Late Hydrographer to the Admiralty, 31 May 1808* (London: Ballintine & Law, 1808)

Davey, J. 'The Advancement of Nautical Knowledge: The Hydrographical Office, the Royal Navy and the Charting of the Baltic Sea, 1795–1815', *Journal for Maritime Research*, 13(2) (2011)

Davey, J. *The Transformation of British Naval Strategy: Seapower and Supply in Northern Europe, 1808–1812* (Woodbridge: Boydell, 2012)

Davey, J. *In Nelson's Wake: The Navy and the Napoleonic Wars* (London: Yale University Press, 2017)

David, A.C.F. 'A Provisional Catalogue of Logs, Journals, Documents, Letters, Record Copies of Books and Pamphlets Published by the Hydrographic Department and Held in its Archives', unpublished typescript (1974)

David, A.C.F. 'Alexander Dalrymple and the Emergence of the Admiralty Chart', in *Five Hundred Years of Nautical Science 1400–1900* (Greenwich: National Maritime Museum, 1981)

David, A.C.F. 'The Surveyors of the *Bounty*: A preliminary study of the hydrographic surveys of William Bligh, Thomas Hayward and Peter Heywood and the charts published from them', unpublished typescript (1982)

David, A.C.F. 'Admiral Nelson, Alexander Dalrymple and the Early Years of the Hydrographical Office', *IMCOS Journal*, No. 102 (Autumn 2005)

David, A.C.F. 'Anglo-Spanish Cooperation in Hydrography, Navigation and Nautical Astronomy, 1788–1834', in L. Martín-Merás (ed.), *Navigare Necesse Est: Estudios de Historia Marítima en honor de Lola Higueras* (Gijón: Fundación Alvargonzález, 2008)

Davies, H. 'Naval Intelligence Support to the British Army in the Peninsular War', *Journal of the Society for Army Historical Research*, 86 (2008)

Dawson, L.S. *Memoirs of Hydrography* (London: Cornmarket Press, 1969)

Day, A. *The Admiralty Hydrographic Service 1795–1919* (London: HMSO, 1967)

De Toy, B.M. 'Commanders-in-Chief: Wellington, Berkeley and Victory in the Peninsula', in C.M. Woolgar (ed.), *Wellington Studies II* (Southampton: The University Press, 1999)

Dixon, C. 'To Walk the Quarterdeck: The Naval Career of David Ewen Bartholomew', *The Mariner's Mirror*, 79(1) (2013)

Edgell, J. *Sea Surveys* (London: HMSO, 1948)

Edwards, E. and G. Hamilton. *Voyage of HMS Pandora*, with introduction and notes by Basil Thomson (London: Francis Edwards, 1915)

Edwards, G. (ed.). *Letters from Revolutionary France* (Cardiff: University of Wales Press, 2001)

Fernyhough, T. *Military Memoirs of Four Brothers* (London: William Sams, 1829)

Fichter, J.R. *So Great a Proffit: How the East Indies Trade Transformed Anglo-American Capitalism* (London: Harvard University Press, 2010)

Fisher, S. 'The Origins of the Station Pointer', *International Hydrographic Review* Vol. LXVIII (2) (1991)

Fisher, S. 'Captain Thomas Hurd's Survey of the Bay of Brest during the Blockade in the Napoleonic Wars', *The Mariner's Mirror*, 79(3) (1993)

Fleming, F. *Barrow's Boys* (London: Granta, 1998)

Fletcher, I. *The Waters of Oblivion: The British Invasion of the Rio de la Plata, 1806–1807* (Tunbridge Wells: Spellmount, 1991)

Flinders, M. *The Voyage to Terra Australis* (London: G. and W. Nicol, 1814)

Franzini, M.M. *Roteiro das Costas de Portugal* (Lisbon: Imprenta Regia, 1812)

Fraser, E. *The Sailors Whom Nelson Led* (London: Methuen, 1913)

Fry, H.T. *Alexander Dalrymple (1737–1808) and the Expansion of British Trade* (London: Frank Cass, 1970)

Gardiner, A. and J.S. Rieske (ed.). *Hunting the Essex* (Barnsley: Seaforth, 2013)

Gardiner, R. (ed.). *Nelson Against Napoleon: From the Nile to Copenhagen, 1798–1801* (London: Chatham, 1997)

Gardiner, R. (ed.). *The Campaign of Trafalgar 1803–1805* (London: Chatham, 1997)

Gardiner, R. (ed.). *The Victory of Seapower: Winning the Napoleonic War 1806–1814* (London: Chatham, 1998)

Gardiner, R. (ed.). *The Naval War of 1812* (London: Chatham, 1998)

Gillespie, A. *Gleanings and Remarks* (Leeds: B. Dewhurst, 1818)

González, F.J. and L. Martín-Merás. *La Dirección de Trabajos Hidrográficos (1797–1908)* (Madrid: Lunwerg, 2003)

Grainger, J.D. 'The Navy in the River Plate, 1806–1808', *The Mariner's Mirror*, 81(3) (1995)

Hall, B. *Extracts from a Journal, written on the coasts of Chili, Peru, and Mexico in the years 1820, 1821, 1822* (Edinburgh: Archibald Constable, 1825)

Hall, C.D. *Wellington's Navy: Sea Power and the Peninsular War 1807–1814* (London: Chatham Publishing, 2004)

Hamilton, C.I. *The Making of the Modern Admiralty: British Naval Policy-Making 1805–1927* (Cambridge: The University Press, 2011)

Harding, R. (ed.). *Naval History 1680–1850* (Aldershot: Ashgate, 2006)

Herschel, J.F.W. (ed.). *The Admiralty Manual of Scientific Enquiry* (London: John Murray, 1849)

Hodson, Y. *Ordnance Surveyors' Drawings 1789–c1840* (London: British Library, 1989)

Holland, R. *Blue-water Empire: The British in the Mediterranean since 1800* (London: Penguin, 2012)

Hornsby, S.J. *Surveyors of Empire: Samuel Holland, J.F.W. Des Barres and the Making of the Atlantic Neptune* (Montreal and Kingston: McGill-Queen's University Press, 2011)

Howgego, R. *The Historical Encyclopedia of Atlantic Vigias: A Complete Guide to the Known Nautical Hazards and Dangers, 1700–1900* (London: I.B. Tauris, 2015)

Howse, D. *Greenwich Time and the Discovery of Longitude* (Oxford: The University Press, 1980)

Jackson, B. *Military Surveying* (London: W.H. Allen, 1838)

James, W. *Naval History of Great Britain*, 6 vols (London: R. Bentley, 1837)

Jones, A.G.E. *Ships Employed in the South Sea Trade 1775–1861* (Canberra: Roebuck Society, 1986)

Jones, Y. 'Aspects of Relief Portrayal on Nineteenth-Century British Military Maps', *Cartographic Journal*, 11(1) (1974)

Kinahan, J. 'The Impenetrable Shield: HMS *Nautilus* and the Namib Coast in the Late Eighteenth Century', *Cimbebasia* 12 (1990), pp. 23–61

Kinahan, J. *By Command of their Lordships* (Windhoek: Namibia Archaeological Trust, 1992)

Kirker, J. *Adventures in China: Americans in the Southern Oceans, 1792–1812* (New York: Oxford University Press, 1970)

Knight, R. *The Pursuit of Victory: The Life and Achievement of Horatio Nelson* (London: Allen Lane, 2005)

Knight, R. *Britain Against Napoleon: The Organization of Victory 1793–1815* (London: Allen Lane, 2013)

Knight, R. *Convoys: The British Struggle Against Napoleonic Europe and America* (London: Yale University Press, 2022)

Laird Clowes, W. *The Royal Navy: A History from the Earliest Times to the Present* (London: Sampson Low, Marston & Co., 1897–1903)

Lamb, U. 'The London Years of Felipe Bauzá: Spanish Hydrographer in Exile, 1823–34', *The Journal of Navigation*, 34 (1981)

Lambert, A. *The Challenge: Britain Against America in the Naval War of 1812* (London: Faber & Faber, 2012)

Lambert, A. *The Crimean War: British Grand Strategy Against Russia, 1853–56* (Abingdon: Routledge, 2016)

Lester, M. 'Vice Admiral George Murray and the Origins of the Bermuda Naval Base, 1794–96', *The Mariner's Mirror*, 94(3) (August 2008)

Lewis, M. *A Social History of the Navy, 1793–1815* (London: George Allen & Unwin, 1960)

Lewis, M. *The Navy in Transition* (London: Hodder & Stoughton, 1965)

Light, K. *The Saving of an Empire: The Journey of Portugal's Court and Capital to Brazil, 1808* (Ely: Melrose Books, 2009)

Mackaness, G. *The Life of Vice-Admiral William Bligh RN FRS* (London: Angus & Robertson, 1931)

Mackesy, P. *The War in the Mediterranean, 1803–1810* (London: Longman, 1957)

Mackesy, P. *Statesmen at War: The Strategy of Overthrow, 1798–1799* (London: Longman, 1974)

Mackesy, P. *War Without Victory: The Downfall of Pitt 1799–1802* (Oxford: The University Press, 1984)

Mackesy, P. *British Victory in Egypt, 1801* (London: Routledge, 1995)

Mackesy, P. 'Problems of an Amphibious Power: Britain Against France, 1793–1850', in R. Harding (ed.), *Naval History 1680–1850*

Malcomson, T. 'An Aid to Nelson's Victory? A Description of the Harbour of Aboukir, 1798', *The Mariner's Mirror*, 84(3) (1998)

Markham, C.R. *A Naval Career during the Old War: Being a Narrative of the Life of Admiral John Markham* (London: Sampson Low, 1883)

Markham, C.R. *A Memoir of the Indian Surveys* (London: W.H. Allen, 1871)

Marshall, J. *Royal Navy Biography*, 12 vols (London: Longman, Hurst, Rees, Orme, and Brown, 1823–35)

Martínez y Guanter, A.L. 'Biografía de Don Felipe Bauzá y Cañas', *Revista General de Marina* (2011)

McAleer, J. *Britain's Maritime Empire: Southern Africa, the South Atlantic and the Indian Ocean, 1763–1820* (Cambridge: The University Press, 2016)

McAleer, J. and C. Petley (eds). *The Royal Navy and the British Atlantic World, c. 1750–1820* (London: Palgrave Macmillan, 2016)

McCarthy, J. *That Curious Fellow: Captain Basil Hall, RN* (Dunbeath: Whittles Publishing, 2011)

McLeod, J. *Voyage of His Majesty's Ship Alceste* (London: John Murray, 1818)

Morris, R.O. *Charts and Surveys in Peace and War: The History of the RN Hydrographic Service 1919–1970* (London: HMSO, 1995)

Morrison, R. and R. Hansen. *Charting the Chesapeake* (Hagerstown: Maryland State Archives, 1990)

Munch-Petersen, T. *Defying Napoleon: How Britain Bombarded Copenhagen and Seized the Danish Fleet in 1807* (Stroud: Sutton Publishing, 2007)

Naipaul, V.S. *The Loss of El Dorado: A Colonial History* (London: Penguin, 1973)

Naval Chronicle (London: Joyce Gold, 1799 onwards)

Nicolas, N.H. (ed.). *The Despatches and Letters of Vice Admiral Lord Viscount Nelson* (London: Henry Colburn, 1844–5)

O'Byrne, W.R. *A Naval Biographical Dictionary* (London: John Murray, 1849)

Ortiz-Sotelo, J. and R. King. '"A Cruize to the Coasts of Peru and Chile": HM Ship *CORNWALLIS*, 1807', *The Great Circle, Journal of the Australian Association for Maritime History*, 32(1) (2010)

Oxford Dictionary of National Biography (Oxford, 2004)

Parkinson, C.N. *War in the Eastern Seas, 1793–1815* (London: George Allen & Unwin, 1954)

Parry, E. *Memoirs of Rear Admiral Sir W. Edward Parry Kt FRS etc.*, 2nd edn (London: Longman Brown, 1857)

Parry, W.E. *Three Voyages for the Discovery of a North-West Passage from the Atlantic to the Pacific, and Narrative of an attempt to reach the North Pole* (London: Harper & Brothers, 1844)

Pascoe, L.N. 'The Story of the Curator of the Hydrographic Department of the Admiralty 1795 to 1975', unpublished typescript held in UKHO

Pocock, T. *Stopping Napoleon: War and Intrigue in the Mediterranean* (London: John Murray, 2004)

Pocock, T. *Breaking the Chains: The Royal Navy's War on White Slavery* (London: Chatham, 2006)

Pope, D. *The Great Gamble* (London: Weidenfeld and Nicolson, 1972)

Popham, H. *A Damned Cunning Fellow* (Tywardreath: Old Ferry Press, 1991)

Popham, H.R. *A Concise Statement of Facts* (London: J. Stockdale, 1805)

Porter, D. *Journal of a Cruise made to the Pacific Ocean* (New York: Wiley and Halsted, 1822)

Ralfe, J. *The Naval Biography of Great Britain* (London: Whitmore & Fenn, 1828)

Richards, G.H. *A Memoir of the Hydrographical Department of the Admiralty* (London, 1868), private collection

Ritchie, G.S. *The Admiralty Chart* (London: Hollis Carter, 1967)

Robertson, I.C. *Wellington at War in the Peninsula* (Barnsley: Seaforth, 2000)

Robinson, A.H.W. *Marine Cartography in Britain: A History of the Sea Chart to 1855* (Leicester: The University Press, 1962)

Robson, M. *Britain, Portugal and South America in the Napoleonic Wars: Alliances and Diplomacy in Economic Maritime Conflict* (London: I.B. Tauris, 2011)

Rodger, N.A.M. *The Command of the Ocean* (London: Allen Lane, 2004)

Ross, J. *A Voyage of Discovery, made under the orders of the Admiralty, in His Majesty's Ships Isabella and Alexander, for the purpose of exploring Baffin's Bay, and enquiring into the probability of a North-West Passage* (London: John Murray, 1819)

Ross, J. *A Letter to John Barrow Esq. on the Subject of the Polar Expedition or The Reviewer Reviewed by A Friend to the Navy* (London: James Ridgway, 1819)

Ross, J. *Memoirs and Correspondence of Admiral Lord de Saumarez, from Original Papers in the Possession of the Family* (London: Richard Bentley, 1838)

Ross, J. *Observations on a Work, Entitled 'Voyages of Discovery and Research within the Arctic regions', by Sir J. Barrow: Being a Refutation of the Numerous Misrepresentations Contained in that Volume* (Edinburgh and London: W. Blackwood & Sons, 1846)

Rutter, O. (ed.). *The Court Martial of the Bounty Mutineers* (Toronto, 1931)

Ryan, A.N. 'The Navy at Copenhagen, 1807', *The Mariner's Mirror*, 39(3) (Aug. 1953)

Ryan, A.N. 'The Melancholy Fate of the Baltic Ships in 1811', *The Mariner's Mirror*, 50(2) (May 1964)

Sainty, J.C. *Office-Holders in Modern Britain IV, Admiralty Officials 1660–1870* (London: The University Press, 1975)

Scott, J. *Recollections of a Naval Life* (London: Richard Bentley, 1834)

Seymour, W.A. (ed.). *A History of the Ordnance Survey* (Folkestone: Dawson, 1980)

Smith, D.M. *A History of Sicily – Modern Sicily after 1713* (London: Chatto & Windus, 1968)

Smith, R.H.P. 'Peninsular War Cartography: A New Look at the Military Mapping of General Sir George Murray and the Quartermaster General's Department', *Imago Mundi*, 65(2) (2013)

Smyth, W.H. *Memoir Descriptive of Sicily and its Islands* (London: John Murray, 1824)

Smyth, W.H. *The Mediterranean: A Memoir Physical, Historical and Nautical* (London: John W. Parker & Son, 1854)

BIBLIOGRAPHY

Smyth, W.H. *The Sailor's Word Book* (London: Blackie & Son, 1867)

Soler, W. and A. Ganado. *The Charting of Maltese Waters* (Malta: BDL, 2013)

Sugden, J. *Nelson: A Dream of Glory* (London: Jonathan Cape, 2004)

Sugden, J. *Nelson: The Sword of Albion* (London: Bodley Head, 2012)

Sulivan, H.N. (ed.). *Life and Letters of the late Admiral Sir Bartholomew James Sulivan K.C.B. 1810–1890* (London: John Murray, 1896)

Swain, A.V. 'Rapid Environmental Assessment Al Faw 2003', *The Ranger: Journal of the Defence Surveyors' Association*, 3(1) (2010)

Tagart, E.A. *A Memoir of the late Captain Peter Heywood RN, with extracts from his Diaries and Correspondence* (London: Effingham Wilson, 1832)

Taverner, L.E. 'George Thomas, Master, Royal Navy', *The Mariner's Mirror*, 36(2) (1950)

Taylor, E.G.R. *The Mathematical Practitioners of Hanoverian England 1714–1840* (Cambridge: The University Press, 1966)

Trevelyan, R. *Princes under the Volcano* (London: Macmillan, 1972)

Vale, B. *A Frigate of King George: Life and Duty on a British Man-of-War* (London: I.B. Tauris, 2001)

Valerio, V. 'Landscapes and Charting in the Nineteenth Century: Neapolitan-Austrian and English Cooperation in the Adriatic Sea', in *Mappae Antiquae Liber Amicorum Günter Schilder* ('t Goy-Houten: HES & De Graaf Publishers, 2007)

Voelcker, T. *Admiral Saumarez versus Napoleon* (Woodbridge: Boydell, 2008)

Walker, D. and A. Webb. 'The Making of Mr George Thomas RN, Admiralty Surveyor for Home Waters from 1810', *The Mariner's Mirror*, 104(2) (2018)

Ward, P.A. *British Naval Power in the East 1794–1805: The Command of Admiral Peter Rainier* (Woodbridge: Boydell, 2013)

Ward, S.G.P. *Wellington's Headquarters* (Oxford: The University Press, 1957)

Ware, J.D. and R.R. Rea. *George Gauld, Surveyor and Cartographer of the Gulf Coast* (Gainsville, FL: University Presses of Florida, 1982)

Webb, A.J. 'The Expansion of British Naval Hydrographic Administration, 1808–1829', unpublished PhD thesis, University of Exeter, 2010

Webb, A.J. *Thomas Hurd, RN & His Hydrographic Survey of Bermuda 1789–97* (Bermuda: National Museum of Bermuda Press, 2016)

White, C. *Nelson: The New Letters* (Woodbridge: Boydell, 2005)

Whittingham, F. (ed.), *A Memoir of the Services of Lieutenant-General Sir Samuel Ford Whittingham* (London: Longmans, Green, 1868)

Wilson, E. *A Social History of British Naval Officers 1775–1815* (Woodbridge: Boydell, 2017)

Winfield, R. *British Warships in the Age of Sail, 1793–1817* (London: Seaforth, 2005)

Winfield, R. *British Warships in the Age of Sail, 1714–1792* (London: Seaforth, 2007)

Woodman, R. *The Victory of Seapower: Winning the Napoleonic War 1806–1814* (London: Chatham, 1998)

Woodman, R. *Neptune's Trident: A History of the British Merchant Navy, Volume One* (Stroud: History Press, 2008)

Index

Aboukir Bay
  battle and hydrographic information
      60–2
Adam, Charles, Captain Royal Navy
  operations and surveys on the coast
      of Catalonia 138
Admiralty, Board of
  encouragement of hydrographic
      data-gathering 66–7, 103, 115,
      129–30
  Mediterranean strategy 64–5
Adriatic theatre of operations 66, 71,
      74
Adventure Bank 191
Africa, West Coast
  RN operations and surveys 174–9
Agincourt Sound 65–6
Alicante, survey of 141
Andaman Islands 39
Antigua 24
anti-slavery operations by Royal Navy
      and associated surveys 174–9
Antwerp, as French naval base 118–19
Archangel
  John Ross's survey of 180
Arctic
  protection of whale fishery and
      surveys 122
  discovery voyages 179–81

Army, British, *see* Royal Engineers;
      Royal Staff Corps
Arosa (Arousa), Ría de 146
Arrowsmith, charts published by 51,
      70, 110, 142 n. 48
astronomy
  definitions 203–13
  practice of in RN surveys 9, 12, 17,
      24–7, 38, 41, 43, 53–4, 59–60,
      62, 68–71, 77–9, 109, 132,
      160–1, 179–80, 184–6, 188–90
Atkinson, Thomas, Master Royal Navy
  service in Mediterranean and
      surveys 60, 62, 66–7, 71
  service in Baltic and surveys 103,
      107–8
Austen, Francis, Captain Royal Navy
  background and education 11–12
  serves under Cornwallis in East
      Indies 109
  surveys including operations in
      Baltic 109–10

Bahama Islands 188–9
Ball, Sir Alexander, Rear Admiral,
      Governor of Malta, 69
Baltic Sea
  navigational challenges 103, 106
  campaign of 1801 103–8

INDEX

campaign of 1807 103, 107–9
subsequent RN operations and
surveys 109–15
Banks, Sir Joseph
champions hydrographic
practitioners from the Royal
Navy 43
Barnett, Edward, Midshipman Royal
Navy
serves with De Mayne 189
Barrow, Sir John, Second Secretary to
the Board of Admiralty 170
on mutiny in *Bounty* 42
tribute to Columbine 176–7
promotion of exploration 179–80
Bartholomew, David, Captain Royal
Navy
career in merchant service and entry
to Royal Navy 36
service with Home Popham in Low
Countries and Red Sea 38–9
earns enmity of St Vincent 38
service and survey work in Plate
Estuary 52–7
service and surveys in Indian Ocean
and Persian Gulf in *Sapphire*
36, 185
service at Cádiz 133–4
commands *Erebus* in Virginia
campaigns 155–6
doubts prospects in 1815 185
appointment as Admiralty Surveyor
amongst Atlantic Islands 185
operations in *Leven* 185–7
survey orders and records 186
schooling of junior officers 186–7
death of 187
Bauzá, Felipe, Capitán de Fragata,
Assistant Director of Spanish
Hydrographic Office
response to French invasion in 1809
and support to British forces at
Cádiz 131–3
publishes *Portolano de las Costas de la
Península de España* in 1813
132–3
Baynton, Benjamin, Lieutenant Royal
Navy 139

Bayntun, Henry, Captain Royal Navy
53–4
Beaufort, Francis, Captain Royal
Navy
surveys in the Indian and Atlantic
Oceans in the *Woolwich* 54
surveys in the Plate Estuary 54
survey on coast of Karamania 70,
201
as Hydrographer 4, 56, 195–6
Beautemps-Beaupré, Charles-François
7
Becher, Alexander, Lieutenant Royal
Navy
education 161
on Lakes Frontier Survey 161
with Bartholomew in *Leven* 187
with Hall in *Conway* 167
Beltt, Jeremiah, Master Royal Navy
master of *Penelope*, Captain William
Broughton, off Scheldt Estuary
117–18
surveys in Baltic 112–13
lost in *St George* 113
Benin, Bight of 177
Berkeley, Sir George Cranfield,
Admiral
commands in Lisbon and supports
Wellington 136–7
appointed High Admiral of the
Portuguese Navy 142
Berlenga, Islands 142
Bermuda
strategic importance of 18–20, 22
inhabitants as seamen and pilots 20
shipyards 22
Hurd Channel 20–1
Grassy Bay 21
Ireland Island 21–2
Biafra, Bight of 177
Bickerton, Sir Richard, Rear Admiral
commands *Sybil* in West Indies and
encourages Lieutenant
Columbine 24
second in command in
Mediterranean 65
orchestrates campaign of surveys
during Peace of Amiens 65–6

Bligh, William, Captain Royal Navy
and officers in *Bounty* 40–5
commands *Glatton* at Copenhagen
81
in charge of Hydrographical Office
during Dalrymple's
indisposition 84, 117
tasked for wartime surveys 117
Bolton, Sir William, Captain Royal
Navy
advocates occupation of Walcheren
119
surveys 118–19
Bonifacio, Strait of 65
Bouverie, The Hon. Duncombe
Pleydell, Captain Royal Navy
commands *Medusa* in Plate
expedition 121–2
and career of George Thomas
122–3
Brady, Patrick, Master Royal Navy
surveys in *Phoebe* in Pacific 166–7
surveys on south west coast of
Africa 167
Brazil
Royal Navy and escort of Portuguese
fleet to Brazil 115, 142
RN surveys in Brazilian waters
162–3, 173
Brest
dangers in approaches 1–4, 91–2
charts of Bay of Brest 89–90, 98–9
Briarly, Alexander, Master then Acting
Lieutenant Royal Navy
entry to Royal Navy and service and
surveys in Mediterranean 61–2,
105
service and surveys in Baltic 104–6
St Vincent and Briarly 30, 105
Nelson and Briarly 62, 104–6
surveys and operations in Trinidad
and Venezuela 29–33
end of career in Royal Navy 33
at Cádiz 134
enters service in navy of Spain 134
fits out transports for Anglo-Sicilian
force bound for Spain 140
later career and death 140–1, 193–4

'British National Standard' of
cartography and teaching at
Staff College 143
Broughton, William, Captain Royal
Navy
service and surveys on the Dutch
coast 117–18
Bryden, Robert, Acting Master Royal
Navy, survey by 159
Buchan, David, Commander Royal
Navy
experience and appointment for
Arctic exploration 179
Burlings, *see* Berlenga

Cadaqués, and survey of 138–9
Cádiz 65
British assistance to defend in
1809–10 132–5
charts and survey of 130, 135
Callao, British surveys of 165–7
Canada
surveys after the Seven Years War
16–17
operations and surveys on the Great
Lakes frontier 152, 157–61
Cape Verde Islands
surveys of 185–7
Catalá, Francisco, Teniente de Navío,
Spanish Navy
surveys by 132–3, 139, 141
Catalonia, coast of, and RN surveys
138–40
Catchup Sands, entry to the Tagus 143
Ceuta 65
Chaguaramas 25–6
Chapman, William, Master Royal Navy
Admiralty Surveyor 86, 181
Channel Atlas, The 97–8
Channel Islands, surveys of 152, 182–4
chart supply 6–7, 10, 103, 107, 109,
127, 130, 136–7, 142, 151
Chart Committee of the Admiralty
establishment and members of 35–6,
52, 99, 174, 188
recommends supply of charts by
Tofiño 130
scrutiny of surveys 61, 88

Chesapeake Bay, operations and
surveys 153–7
Chile 49, 73, 164
Chillingsworth, Thomas, Master Royal
Navy
surveys in Canada 160
China, RN operations and surveys
41–2, 46
Christ's Hospital, *see* Royal
Mathematical School
chronometers
issue of 9, 71, 152, 179
use of in surveys 9, 38, 41, 70–1,
152–3, 162, 186, 207
Clarence, Duke of 126
Cochrane, Sir Alexander, Vice Admiral
in Trinidad 30–3
operations on Spanish coast in 1803
145, 152
employs Anthony Lockwood in
West Indies 152
attachment of surveyors to squadron
in North America 152
Cockburn, Sir George, Rear Admiral
campaign on rivers of Virginia
153–5
conveys Napoleon to exile at
St Helena 168
Collier, Sir George, Captain Royal
Navy
senior officer on the west coast of
Africa 177
death of 178–9
Collingwood, Cuthbert, Lord, Vice
Admiral
on dangers in approaches to Brest 3,
89
critical of Rear Admiral John
Knight 65
commends William Durban 71
Colnett, James, Captain Royal Navy 82
Columbine, Edward, Captain Royal
Navy
early life and career 11, 22–4
service and surveys in *Sybil*, Captain
Richard Bickerton 24
commands *Ulysses*, guard-ship for
Trinidad 24–5, 72
surveys Trinidad 25–9
grasp of operational significance and
priorities 26–7
on Chart Committee 33, 35–6
appointments on West Coast of
Africa 174
death of 176
tributes to 28, 176–7
papers in National Maritime
Museum 12, 27
compasses
azimuth compass 9, 118, 153, 203,
213
miner's compass 2, 92, 209
Continental System, Napoleon's 7, 56,
75, 151
Cook, James, Captain Royal Navy 7
in North America 16
commends brig rig for survey vessels
96
Copenhagen
battle in 1801 103–7
British attack in 1807 108–9
Cornwallis, William, Commodore
(later Admiral)
commander-in-chief East Indies,
and encouragement of surveys
39
personal involvement in survey
operations 39
protégés 39, 109
and the survey of the approaches to
Brest 93–6
Corunna, operations and surveys at
144–5
Crawford, James, Master Royal Navy,
surveys by 142–3
Crichton, George, Lieutenant Royal
Navy
early career and surveys in Persian
Gulf 162
surveys on Brazilian coast 162
later life 162
Croker, John Wilson, First Secretary to
the Admiralty 13
support for Hurd 169
influence on Hydrographical Office
169–70

INDEX

Croque Harbour, Newfoundland 122
Crozier, Francis, Midshipman Royal
        Navy
    service in *Briton* with Captain
        Staines 165
Cudlip, James, Master Royal Navy,
        survey by 154
Cunningham, Charles, Captain Royal
        Navy
    commands *Clyde* and encourages
        hydrographic data-gathering 114
Cutfield, William, Commander Royal
        Navy 187

Dalrymple, Alexander, Hydrographer
        to the Board of Admiralty
    activity and publications as
        Hydrographer to the East
        India Company 6, 41, 66
    appointed Hydrographer to the
        Board of Admiralty 6, 24
    relationship with the Naval Lords
        66–7, 68–9, 82, 127
    publishes first Admiralty charts 6,
        67, 103
    supplies charts and publications for
        RN operations 52, 66–7, 103,
        107–9
    recommends employment of officers
        on survey 52, 54, 82, 87
    commends and publishes their work
        21, 22, 24, 28, 41, 44, 46, 51–2,
        54, 12–15
    and appointment of a Chart
        Committee 35–6, 99
    supersession by Hurd 33, 36, 99
Danzig 111
De Mayne, Anthony, Master Royal
        Navy
    service and survey in Baltic in 1807
        152
    surveys on the west coast of Africa
        153
    surveys during operations on the
        coast of the USA in 1814 153–5
    as Admiralty Surveyor in the
        Bahamas and at Jamaica 188–9,
        194

Denham, Henry Mangles,
        Midshipman Royal Navy 185,
        195
Des Barres, J.F.W., Colonel
    need for correction of errors in his
        charts 152
Detroit 161
Deurloo Channel 119, 123–5
Donnelly, Ross, Captain Royal Navy,
        surveys 51
Douglas, James, Master Royal Navy,
        surveys by 162
Dover, Strait of, surveys 82–4
Dundas, Henry, Lord Melville,
        Secretary of State for War
    President of the Board of Control of
        the East India Company 37
    support for, and employment of,
        Home Popham 37
Dundas, Robert Saunders, Viscount
        Melville, First Lord of the
        Admiralty
    secures resources during post-war
        recession 170
    support for Hydrographer and
        Admiralty Surveyors 73, 96, 185
Durban, William, Captain Royal Navy
    education and early career, service at
        Cape of Good Hope 48–9
    earns interest of Lord Keith 49
    surveys of Lampedusa and of the
        Skerki Bank 68–71
    assists in surveys around Sardinia 65
    employment in *Ambuscade* in the
        Mediterranean 71–2
Durnford, Edward Philip,
        Midshipman Royal Navy
    service in *Leven* and marked talent
        187

East India Company, Honourable
    and government strategy 37, 46
    Secret Committee 37
    and RN support against pirates in
        Persian Gulf 171
East Indies station
    strategy 39
    surveys 40–2, 44–6

Edmonds, Joseph, Commander then
    Captain Royal Navy
  protégé of Home Popham 35
  surveys in the Mediterranean 63
  surveys in the Plate Estuary 51–2
education, mathematical 17
  curricula in Scotland and England
    compared 11–12, 84, 179
Egypt
  British operations in 1800–1 37,
    62–3
  British expedition in 1807 63–4
Elphinstone, George Keith, Viscount
    Keith, Admiral
  operations, and encouragement of
    surveys, at the Cape of Good
    Hope in 1795 47–8
  commander-in-chief in
    Mediterranean 62–4
  encouragement of hydrography
    47–9, 63, 66, 68–9, 82–4, 138
  commander-in-chief North Sea and
    Downs 49, 82
English Channel
  surveys of 82–7, 182–5
Esquerques, see Skerki Bank
Evans, Thomas, Lieutenant Royal
    Navy, surveys by 182

Faden, charts and sailing directions
    published by 24, 28–9, 52, 90,
    75 n. 60, 88, 90, 122, 130 n. 6
Falmouth 30, 87, 96
False Bay 47
Fane, Francis, Captain Royal Navy 139
Fernando Po, surveys of 177
Finlaison, William, Commander Royal
    Navy, surveys by 177–8
Finland, Gulf of, surveys in 110,
    111–12
Fitzmaurice, Lewis, Master Royal
    Navy
  surveys during expedition to River
    Congo 179
Fletcher, Robert, Master Royal Navy,
    surveys by 122
Flinders, Matthew, Captain Royal
    Navy

Atlas to *A Voyage to Terra Australis*
    44
Australian surveys brought back to
    England by John Murray 84
  manuscript surveys in The National
    Archives 201
Flushing 117
  importance to Napoleon and
    destruction during expedition
    of 1809 118–19, 124
Foulerton, John, Captain, Elder
    Brother of Trinity House 181
France
  responsibility for hydrography in 6,
    196
Franklin, John, Captain Royal Navy
    180
Franzini, Marino Miguel, Major
    Portuguese Royal Corps of
    Engineers
  employed by Admiral Berkeley 142
  judgments on RN surveys 142
Frazer, George, Acting Second Master
    Royal Navy
  early career with Bartholomew 187
Funchal, Madeira 185, 187
Fundy, Bay of
  importance of settlement in, and
    surveys of 16

Galapagos Islands
  surveys of 164
Gambier, James, Lord, Admiral
  commodore in North America in
    1771, with Hurd under his
    command 17
  commands 1807 expedition to
    Copenhagen 103, 107–9
Gardiner, Allen, Midshipman Royal
    Navy
  with Captain Hillyar in *Phoebe* in
    Pacific 166
Gauld, George, Surveyor
  surveys off Florida 20
Gawthrop, Peter, Master Royal Navy
  surveys on coasts of Iberia 143,
    146–7
Gooch, William, astronomer 164

Gould, Davidge, Captain Royal Navy 61

Graham, Thomas, Lieutenant General, at Cádiz 132–5

Graves, Sir Thomas, Vice Admiral 90

Graves, Thomas, Midshipman Royal Navy
service with William Henry Smyth 190
subsequent service in the Mediterranean 190

Great Belt, surveys of 103, 107–9, 152

Hagan, Robert, Lieutenant Royal Navy, survey by 177–8

Hall, Basil, Captain Royal Navy
voyage and observations in *Conway* 165, 167, 209
views on hydrography 165

Hall, Robert, Commodore
senior officer, Straits of Messina 73, 79
Naval Commissioner Great Lakes 159

Hallowell, Benjamin, Captain later Rear Admiral
knowledge of Mediterranean and gathering of hydrographic intelligence 63, 139
at siege of Alexandria in 1807 63

Hamilton, William, Master Royal Navy, survey by 148

Hancock, John, Captain Royal Navy 118, 124

Hawaiian Islands
RN surveys in 189

Hayward, Thomas, Lieutenant Royal Navy
background 11, 42–3
with Bligh in *Bounty* and Edwards in *Pandora* 43–4
survey at Trincomalee 44–5
command of *Swift*, survey in Banda Sea, lost at sea 45–6

Hepburn, John, Master Royal Navy, survey 63–4

Hergest, Richard, Lieutenant Royal Navy, survey by 164–5

Hewett, William, Lieutenant then Commander Royal Navy 195
education and early career 162–3
as Admiralty Surveyor in the North Sea 163, 194

Heywood, Peter, Captain Royal Navy
background 11
with Bligh in *Bounty* 40, 42
career and surveys on East Indies station 40–2, 46, 154
and James Horsburgh 41
service and surveys in the Plate Estuary in 1806 52, 54–6
senior officer on River Plate 1814 163–4
support for John Ross 180

Hillyar, James, Captain Royal Navy
journal, charts and views from Pacific in 1814 165–7

Hislop, Sir Thomas, Lieutenant Governor of Trinidad 30–2, 140

Holbrook, George, Master Royal Navy
appointed to *Sydney* 181

Holland, Henry Richard Vassall Fox, 3rd Baron 131

Holland, Samuel, Major
surveys in North America 16

Honolulu, RN survey at 189

Hood, Sir Samuel, Vice Admiral
commodore in Trinidad and support of *Columbine* 25–7

Horizontal Sextant Angle Resection 9, 21, 85, 87, 118, 206, 210

Horsburgh, James, Hydrographer to the East India Company
Directions for sailing to and from the East Indies 41

Howe, Richard, Earl Howe, Admiral of the Fleet, First Lord of the Admiralty
operations during the War of American Independence and support for Thomas Hurd 18

Hurd, Thomas, Captain Royal Navy, Hydrographer to the Board of Admiralty

early career 17
service and surveys in North
America 17–18
survey of Bermuda 18–22
fair sheets and chart of Bermuda
15–16, 22
promoted to Captain 81
employed on surveys on the
Channel coast of England
87–8
survey of the Bay of Brest and
lessons from 1–4, 88–100
on Chart Committee 35, 61, 99
appointed Hydrographer 36
and constraints of establishment of
Hydrographical Office 145
implements improved chart supply to
the Fleet 127, 130, 136, 142–6
values work of foreign counterparts
130, 136
supports appointment of surveyors
to theatres of war 114–15,
151–2
assessment of incoming
hydrographic data 59–60, 67,
114–15, 123, 136
urges formation of a cadre of
hydrographic practitioners 4, 9,
11–12, 100, 115, 127, 151, 169,
195
looks for higher skills amongst
hydrographic practitioners 59,
114–15, 154, 195
recommendations for and influence
on employment on Admiralty
surveys 86, 100, 114–15, 152–3,
181–2, 189, 192, 194–5
reports on competence of personnel
in survey ships and parties 123,
179, 195
administration of chronometers and
instruments 160, 179
Annual Reports to Board of
Admiralty 191
his death and subsequent tributes
192
Hydrographer to the Board of
Admiralty

remit and authority 6, 10
scrutiny of incoming data 59–60,
66–7, 69, 107, 136
influence on and approval of
appointments to survey vessels
162–3, 181
Hydrographer's Annual Report 191
Hydrographical Office
establishment and facilities 6, 151
receipt of surveys 107, 109, 114, 170,
176, 180

Île de France 47
Inshore Squadron off Brest 88–90, 93
Interior Survey, Royal Military
Surveyors and Draftsmen of 143

Jamaica 188
Jeremie Bay 65
Jervis, John, Earl St Vincent, Admiral
of the Fleet, First Lord
experience in Mediterranean and
priority for hydrographic
data-gathering 66
tribute to Hurd's survey of Bermuda
22
relationships with hydrographic
practitioners 30, 33, 38, 71,
81–2, 89–90, 104
Johnstone, James, Commander then
Captain Royal Navy
surveys during Pacific voyages of
Colnett and Vancouver 82, 164
service in West Indies 82
recommended by Sir Joseph Banks
for employment making
surveys 82
surveys for Lord Keith on North
Sea and Downs station 82–4
Alert commissioned for his survey
work 84
Juan Fernández 165, 167
Jupiter's satellites, observation of
eclipses 160, 188, 206

Kattegat, surveys 109, 112, 115
Keats, Sir Richard Goodwin, Rear
then Vice Admiral

senior officer in Great Belt 152
senior officer off Cádiz 133–5
Keith, Viscount, Admiral, *see*
        Elphinstone, George
Keith's Reef 69–70, *see also* Skerki
        Bank
Kelly, Benedictus Marwood, Captain
        Royal Navy, surveys by 177
King, Philip Parker, Lieutenant
        Royal Navy and surveys by 168,
        201
King, William, Captain Royal Navy
        and surveys by 51
Kingston, Jamaica 188
Kingston, Ontario 160
Kirby, William, Master Royal Navy
        surveying in the Mediterranean 65
Knight, Sir John, Rear Admiral
    early career in North America 89
    protégé of Samuel Hood 63–4
    publishes small scale charts and
        charts for the Mediterranean
        64
    surveys in the Bay of Brest 2, 89–90,
        96
    appointed Flag Officer Gibraltar,
        operations in 1805 64–5
    contribution to hydrography and
        charting 63–4, 89–90, 96, 99

Laborde, Alexandre de, adviser to
        Napoleon, in Spain 131
Labrador 122
Lakes Frontier Survey, Canada
        157–61, 168
Lampedusa 69
Lash, James, Master Royal Navy,
        survey 111
Leeke, Henry, Commander Royal
        Navy 177
Leghorn 79
Lennock, George, Commander Royal
        Navy, survey 124
Little, William, Master's Mate 63
Lisbon 126, 129
    surveys of 136–7, 142
    measurements at the Observatory
        186

Liverpool, surveys of approaches 125,
        182, 185
Lockwood, Anthony, Master Royal
        Navy
    survey of Corunna and approaches
        144–5, 152
    survey in Channel Islands 152
    surveys in West Indies and North
        America 152
    difficult relationship with Hurd 152
Lyon, George Francis, Commander
        Royal Navy
    commands *Hecla* in Arctic 181
Lys, Matthew, Lieutenant Royal Navy,
        survey by 173

McKinley, George, Captain Royal
        Navy 142–3, 146–7
Magnetic variation 212–13
Malcolm, Charles, Captain Royal
        Navy
    career and encouragement of surveys
        162–3
Malcolm, Pulteney, Captain Royal
        Navy then Rear Admiral
    encourages Heywood in East Indies
        40
    flag officer during Chesapeake
        campaign 154
Malden, Charles, Lieutenant Royal
        Navy
    early career and service with
        William Henry Smyth in the
        Mediterranean 189
    subsequent service and surveys 189
Malta
    RN operations and surveys 62, 64,
        69, 74
Mann, Thomas, Master Royal Navy
    surveys in the Mediterranean 63–4
Markham, John, Rear Admiral
    service with Keith in War of
        American Independence and in
        Mediterranean 66
    on Board of Admiralty and support
        for Dalrymple 36, 66
    identifies and encourages
        employment of skilled

hydrographic practitioners 49
n. 43, 52
support for Hurd 15, 96
patronage as MP for Portsmouth 182
Marmaris Bay, survey of 63
Marquesas Islands
base for Captain David Porter USN
164
RN surveys at 164–5
Martin, Thomas Byam, Captain Royal
Navy
encouragement of hydrographic
data-gathering 110–11
liaison with Lord Wellington in
Spain 130
as Comptroller of the Navy and
support for Hurd 170
Mason, Francis, Captain Royal Navy
soundings in the Plate Estuary 51
surveys in the waters of the Low
Countries 118, 123
commands *Fisgard* and encourages
George Thomas 123
Masters Royal Navy
Admiralty instructions for
navigational reports 8
contribution to hydrographic
data-gathering 7, 9, 26, 41, 47,
60–3, 93, 103–8, 111–15, 122,
123–6, 136–8, 142–3, 144–8,
152–7, 159–60, 166–7, 171–4,
179, 188–9
appointments to survey vessels 170
Mediterranean Sea
inadequate charting for British Fleet
60
theatre of highest number of surveys
by RN 202
Melville, Viscount, *see* Dundas
Mendoza de Rios, Joseph, Captain
Spanish Navy
resident in England and contact
with Hydrographer 130
Miranda, Francisco de, General
31–3
Mogg, William, Clerk Royal Navy
service with George Thomas and
journal 120–1

and George Lyon 181
Montagu, Sir George, Admiral 123
Moore, John Hamilton,
Practical Navigator 8
Moore, Thomas, Master Royal Navy 111
Morris, Charles, Master Royal Navy,
survey by 154, 156
Moubray, Richard Hussey, Captain 67
Mowat, Henry, Lieutenant Royal Navy
operations and surveys in *Canceaux*
in North America 17
Mudge, William, Major General 17, 181
Mudge, William, Lieutenant then
Commander Royal Navy
service with Martin White and with
Bartholomew in *Leven* 186–7
subsequent career 187
Murray, George, Rear then Vice
Admiral
survey experience with George
Gauld 20
in command on North America
station 19
and Hurd's survey of Bermuda 20–2
Murray, George, Rear Admiral
commands forces deployed to River
Plate 52–3
Murray, George, Major-General
Quartermaster General (QMG) in
Peninsular War 144, 146
Murray, John, Lieutenant Royal Navy
background and Scottish education
84
surveys in Australia 84
appointment as Maritime Surveyor
85
surveys on the South Coast of
England 85–6
draws criticism of the Hydrographer
86
later career 86

Naples 60, 62, 71, 73–4, 79
*Nautical Almanac and Tables Requisite,
The* 118, 206–7, 209
Neapolitan collaboration with the
Royal Navy in surveys of the
Adriatic 190

INDEX

Nelson, Horatio, Viscount, Vice
Admiral
campaign of the Nile 61–2
campaign of Copenhagen 103–6
commander-in-chief Mediterranean
65–7, 69
commends William Durban 71
encourages hydrographic survey 62,
67
and the Hydrographical Office 67
Newfoundland, 17, 43, 100, 122, 168,
179
Ney, Peter, Master Royal Navy, survey
147 (Figure 31)

Ordnance Board and Royal Naval
surveys 82, *see also* Interior
Survey; Trigonometrical Survey
Otter, Henry, Captain Royal Navy
196
Owen, Edward, Commodore
encouragement and support of
survey work 124, 126, 160
Senior Officer of squadron in
southern North Sea 124
commander-in-chief Great Lakes
159
Owen, William Fitzwilliam, Captain
Royal Navy
expedition to Java in 1811 160
in charge of Lakes Frontier Survey
160–1
survey of African coast 161, 187
Owen, Richard, Midshipman
serves with De Mayne 189

Pakenham, Edward, Captain, Royal
Navy 45–6
Palamos, survey of 139
Palermo 68, 77
Observatory 74, 77–8
Parker, Alexander, Master RN 107
Parker, Sir Hyde, Admiral
commands in Baltic in 1801 107
Parry, William Edward, Lieutenant
then Captain Royal Navy
service as midshipman and surveys
11, 180

commands *Alexander* in Ross's
Arctic expedition of 1818 180
as Hydrographer 169
Patuxent, River, survey of 154–5
Pearl Lochs (Pearl Harbor) 189
Penetanguishene, Georgian Bay,
Canada 159
Peninsular War in Spain and Portugal
course of 129
military surveys during 143–4
Penrose, Sir Charles Vinicombe, Vice
Admiral
enters Royal Navy through the
Royal Naval Academy 20
commands *Cleopatra* at Bermuda
and reports on Hurd's survey
20
commands naval forces supporting
advance into southern France
10, 148
commander-in-chief Mediterranean,
and support for William Henry
Smyth 189
Persian Gulf
surveys 36, 171, 202
Peru 121, 164
Piazzi, Giuseppe, Abbaté, Astronomer
at Palermo 77–9
Pipon, Philip, Captain Royal Navy
commands *Tagus* in Pacific 165
Plate Estuary
British operations in 1806 49–56,
122
intelligence from in 1814 163
surveys of 51–5
Popham, Sir Home Riggs, Captain
then Rear Admiral
education and early career 36–7
surveys on west coast of Africa 37
operations and survey in Red Sea
37–9, 71
expedition to Cape of Good Hope
49
South America and expedition to
River Plate 31, 49, 52–3, 56
expedition to Scheldt in 1809 119,
124
on Chart Committee 33, 35

encouragement and training of officers in hydrography 35–6, 38, 52, 159
senior officer on the north coast of Spain 147
correspondence with Hydrographer 188
flag officer in Jamaica 188–9
Port of Spain, Trinidad 25, 28–32
Porter, David, Captain US Navy
command of *Essex* in Pacific 164–5
Portugal
operations in 1806–13 128–9, 136–8, 142–3
secrecy surrounding official charts and hydrographic data 142
personnel involved in hydrography 6
small number of charts passed to British 142
Poyntz, Newdigate, Lieutenant Royal Navy, survey by 159
Prince of Wales Island 37
Príncipe, Ilha do, surveys of 177
Puget, Peter, Captain Royal Navy
service in Inshore Squadron off Brest 90, 98
commands Advanced Squadron at Copenhagen in 1807 108
Purvis, John Child, Rear then Vice Admiral
commands squadron off Cádiz 130–4
receives Spanish charts and views 130

Quebec 17

Rainier, Lieutenant John Spratt 45
Rainier, Peter, Vice Admiral, commander-in-chief, East Indies 39–47
encouragement of surveys 39–40, 44–5
'Rapid Environmental Assessment' 60, 114–15, 127, 136, 147–8, 198 n. 22
Recife, operations and surveys at 173
Red Sea, and surveys 37–8, 162–3, 171
Reeves, James, Master Royal Navy

survey in Baltic and recommendation as Surveying Master 113–15
Remarks and Remark Books 12, 92
Revenue Service
cutters used in surveys by the Royal Navy 82, 86–7, 96
Rio de Janeiro 43, 121
Robertson, George, Captain, Royal Navy 43
Robertson, James, Headmaster of the Royal Academy, Portsmouth
Elements of Navigation 8–9
Robinson, Charles Gepp, Commander, Royal Navy 195
Roompot, surveys of 119, 124, 126
Rosas, survey of 139
Ross, John, Commander then Captain Royal Navy
education and early career 12, 48, 111, 179
service and surveys in Baltic 111
survey in the White Sea 180
expedition to Canadian Arctic in 1818 179–80
records examined in the Admiralty 180
Royal Engineers
Surveyors 76–7, 143
Royal Mathematical School at Christ's Hospital 9, 12
RN personnel educated there 12, 119–20, 162
Royal Navy
reductions in ships and personnel in 1815 169
statistics of surveys and practitioners during French Revolutionary and Napoleonic Wars 200–2
post war operations in the Mediterranean 173–4, 189–91
Royal Naval Academy, Portsmouth 9
officers educated at 12, 20, 161, 166
Royal Staff Corps
formation, training and deployment in Iberian Peninsula campaign 143–4
assistance in survey of Sicily 76–7

Royer, Charles, Lieutenant Royal Navy
  service and surveys in the
    Mediterranean 67
Ryves, George Frederick, Captain
    Royal Navy
  survey of 'Agincourt Sound' 65–6

St Helena 48
  survey of 168
Saintes, battle of the, 12 April 1782 18
Santa Cruz, Tenerife 185
Santander, and surveys of 147–8
Sardinia, and surveys of 60, 65, 70
Saumarez, James, First Baron de
    Saumarez, Admiral
  commander-in-chief Baltic 109, 111
  proposal for a Surveying Master
    113–15
  and John Ross 111, 179–80
Scheldt, Estuary
  hydrographic challenges and RN
    surveys 117–19, 123–6
  expedition of 1809 118–19, 124,
    126–7
Scotland
  educational system and preparation
    of hydrographic practitioners
    11–12
Setubal, survey of 136
Seymour, Joseph, Master Royal Navy,
    survey by 136–8
Seymour, Sir Michael, Captain Royal
    Navy 137 n. 29
Shillibeer, John, Lieutenant Royal
    Marines
  survey drawn by 165
  account of call of Briton at Pitcairn
    Island 165
ships, American merchant
  Harry and Jane 121
ships, French Navy
  L'Orient 62
ships, Revenue Service
  Hunter 82
  Ranger 96
ships, Royal Naval
  Acasta 1
  Active 67

Adventure, see Aid
Africa 53
Agincourt 65
Aid 189–90
Aimable 118
Alert 84
Algerine 115
Amazon 107
Ambuscade 71–2
Amelia 153
Ariel 111
Arrow 118
Athenien 68, 70
Audacious 61–2, 104
Barfleur 136–7
Baracouta 187
Beagle (1820) 165
Beagle (1967) 198
Bellerophon 113
Bellona 104–6
Blonde 189
Bounty, armed ship 40–3
Briton 165
Cambrian 139
Canceaux 17
Caroline, tender 47–8
Centaur 66, 108
Clyde 114
Comet 61
Confiance 159
Conflict 96, 100
Congo 179
Conway 167
Countess of Elgin 126
Culloden 61
Crocodile 176
Daedalus, storeship 164
Dalrymple 197
Dedaigneuse 40–1, 46
Defence 113
Diadem 51–3
Diamond 1–2, 93–4
Diomede (1781) 44–5
Diomede (1798) 51, 54
Dispatch 109
Doris 173
Earnest 110
Elephant 109–10

INDEX

Euphrosyne 47
Fairy 163
Fisgard 118–19, 123, 125
Fleche, La 123
Fox 40–1, 162
Fox, cutter 118, 183
Gleaner 125
Glatton 81
Hecate 198
Hecla 181
Heroine 45
Hydra 41
Impregnable 125
Investigator 125–6, 181
Invincible 138
Kite 107
Leven 185–7
Leveret 152
Lively 142, 146
Magnificent 3, 90, 92–3
Mariner 110
Marlborough 154
Medusa 121–3
Monarch 47
Montagu 89–90, 166
Montreal 160
Netley 159
Pallas 63
Pandora (1779) 43–4
Pandora (1813) 154
Penelope 117
Phoebe 165
Pigmy, cutter 182
Polyphemus 52, 56, 107
Protector, gun-brig 54
Protector, survey ship 163
Queen 64
Rattler 118, 123, 143, 154
Raven 119, 124
Resistance 46
Resolution 20
Resolution, cutter 23
Revenge 174
Rhin 162
Rodney 141
Roebuck 137, 198
Romney 38, 143
Royal Oak 154

St George 106–7, 112–13
Saldanha, Dutch prize 48
Santa Margarita 93–4
Sapphire 36, 185
Scylla 79
Shamroc 184
Sorlings 85–6
Sphinx 48
Suffolk 41
Swift 45–6
Sybil 23–4
Sydney 181
Tartar 177
Termagant 65
Thalia 104, 122
Theseus 62
Tremendous 47
Ulysses 25, 27, 72
Undaunted 138–9
Vanguard 62
Vengeance 107–8
Victory 66, 71
Vulcan 41
Vulture 182
Weazle 48, 65, 68–71
Wolverine 118
Woolwich, store-ship 54, 130
ships, Southern Whale Fishery
    Commerce 120–1
ships, Spanish Navy
    Archimedes 54
    Escorpion 132
ships, transport service
    Ellice 68
    Walker 51
ships, US Navy
    Constitution 178
    Essex 164, 166
shipwrecks
    statistics 3
    Skerki Bank and *Athenien* 68–9
Sicily
    strategic importance of 60, 65, 68, 73
    navigational dangers in approaches
        to the Sicilian Channel 68–70,
        73–4
Sidley, George, Master RN, survey by
    99

Simon's Bay 47

Skerki Bank 68–70

Skyring, William, Midshipman Royal
Navy
serves in *Briton* in Pacific 165

Slater, Michael Atwell, Lieutenant
then Commander Royal Navy
service with Smyth in
Mediterranean, and subsequent
service 190

slave trade, RN patrols to combat
174–9

Smith, Sir William Sidney, Rear then
Vice Admiral
flag officer in Mediterranean 1806, 68
urges action to aid slaves in North
African states 173

Smyth, William Henry, Lieutenant
then Commander Royal Navy
early life and entry to Royal Navy
72–3
service off Cádiz and elsewhere on
Spanish coast 134–5, 140–1
earns approval of Hurd 59, 100
appointed Admiralty Surveyor in
the Mediterranean 61, 11–12
surveys in Sicilian waters 73–9
good relationships with British and
Sicilian communities in Sicily
74–5
with allied fleet at Algiers 173
collaborative work in Adriatic with
Austrian and Italian surveyors
190
assistants in *Aid* 189–90
survey methodology 76–9, 190–1
'Mediterranean Smyth' 189–90
later life 169, 193

Sounding, conduct of 4, 8, 10, 17, 21,
41–2, 53–5, 63–4, 69–70, 76–7,
83–5, 90–5, 104–10, 112–13,
126, 136, 139, 153–7, 161,
171–2, 177–8, 190–1, 207–8

South America
British commercial interest in 31–2,
56–7
Royal Naval operations 49–56, 73,
163–7, 173

South America station of Royal
Navy 56, 173

Southern Whale Fishery 120, 164

Spain
allied to France 46, 121
invasion by Napoleon 129
hydrography in 6, 130–3

Spence, Graham, Admiralty Surveyor
surveys and retirement 87, 125
critical of Hurd 87

Spratt, Thomas, Captain Royal Navy
in Mediterranean and Black Sea 196

Squire, James, Master Royal Navy,
surveys by 107, 115

Staines, Sir Thomas, Captain Royal
Navy
operations in Pacific 164–5
encouragement of hydrography 165

station pointer 74, 87–8, 126, 206

Stirling, Charles, Rear Admiral
commands squadron on the River
Plate 49

Strachan, Sir Richard, Rear Admiral
commander-in-chief, North Sea
station 119, 123

strategy
sea power strategy of British
Government 5

Strode, Edward Master Royal Navy
at Aboukir Bay 25, 63
with Columbine in Trinidad 25–6
survey during 1807 Copenhagen
expedition 108–9

Suez 37, 197

Sulivan, Bartholomew James, Captain
Royal Navy
views on the Surveying Service
196

surveying/surveys
definitions 203–13
statistics for surveys conducted by
RN personnel during the wars
and to 1823 7, 200–2
survey process
control 1–4, 8–10, 17, 25–6, 41–2,
54, 69–71, 85–6, 87, 93–4,
117–18, 126, 136, 146–7, 153,
160–1, 174, 184, 186, 203–13

sounding 4, 8, 10, 17, 21, 41–2,
53–5, 63–4, 69–70, 76–7, 83–5,
90–5, 104–10, 112–13, 126,
136, 139, 153–7, 161, 171–2,
177–8, 190–1, 207–8
tidal observations 93, 125, 135,
146, 155, 182–3, 186, 194,
211
records 12, 25–7, 62, 85, 91–3,
184–6, 204–5
Surveying Service, Royal Naval
proposed by Thomas Hurd 4, 81,
100, 169–70
bearing in 1823, 1829 and 1839 195
importance of front-line operations
in wartime 196–7
operations in WW2 and
subsequently 197–8
surveyors
hydrographic practitioners,
background and education
11–12
Admiralty 9, 36, 72, 86, 148, 155,
181, 185, 190, 201
Sweden
British anchorages and trading posts
111–12
danger of embargo of British ships
112
Sykes, John, Captain Royal Navy,
survey 124

Tagus river and estuary, and surveys of
136–8, 142–3
Tarragona 138
Tayler, Joseph Needham, Captain
Royal Navy, and survey 148
Tello, José Espinosa, in London 132
Thomas, George, Master Royal Navy
early life and education at Christ's
Hospital 119–20
indentured to Southern Whale
Fishery 120–1
circumstances of entry to the Royal
Navy 121–2
service in *Medusa* 122
qualifies as Master and joins *Fisgard*
122–3

surveys of Scheldt Estuary in
Fisgard and later 123–6
surveys as Admiralty Surveyor 125,
181, 194–5
survey at Liverpool and clash with
Lieutenant Thomas Evans
182
dissatisfaction at status 194
Thomas, Richard, Captain Royal Navy
138–9
Thoms, George, Master Royal Navy
survey on Chesapeake 154
survey at St Helena 168
Thornton, Mr, pilot and survey off
Dutch coast 118
Tidal observations 93, 125, 135, 146,
155, 182–3, 186, 194, 211
Tipu Sultan 40, 47
Tobago 72
Tofiño de San Miguel, Vicente,
Brigadier Royal Navy of Spain,
surveys of Spanish coast 130–2, 138,
146
denied access to Portuguese coast
142
Atlas Marítimo 135, 141
Torres Vedras, lines of 137–8
Toulon 60, 65–6
Trafalgar, campaign of 60, 65–6
Trigonometrical Survey of Great
Britain
in coastal counties 81–2, 87
Trincomalee, survey of 44–5
Trinidad
strategic significance 25, 32
surveys 24–9
Trinity House, Board of
examination of masters for the
Royal Navy 7, 120, 123
Tripoli 71
Troubridge, Sir Thomas, Rear
Admiral
service in Mediterranean and
collection of hydrographic data
61, 66
on Board of Admiralty 66
passes hydrographic data to
Dalrymple 66, 69

encouragement of Dalrymple and system of supply of charts to the Fleet 66–7

Tuckey, James Hingston, Commander Royal Navy and expedition to River Congo 179

Turner, Richard, Master Royal Navy collection of manuscript plans 130

United States of America war with Britain in 1812–14 150–67

Ushant archipelago 1–3, 88–99

Valdés, Cayetano, Lieutenant General, Spanish Navy 134–5

Valparaíso 73, 165–7

Vancouver, George, Captain Royal Navy
  expedition and account 82, 134, 164–5
  officers who had served with him 7, 56, 82, 90, 122, 124, 164

Venezuela 30–2

Vidal, Alexander, Lieutenant (later Captain) Royal Navy
  early career and service with Owen in Canada 160–1
  service with Bartholomew in *Leven* 187
  subsequent career 187, 195

Vigias 185, 213

Vigo 146

Walcheren 117
  expedition of 1809 118–19, 123–4

Wales, William, Mathematical Master at Christ's Hospital 43, 119–20, 179

Walker, William, Master Royal Navy, surveys by 137–8, 173–4

Warner, John, Master Royal Navy, survey by 52

Weir, Duncan, Master Royal Navy surveys in Indian Ocean and East Indies 41

Wellington, Arthur Wellesley, 1st Duke 33, 129–30, 132, 136–8, 142–4

West Indies surveys by Edward Columbine 23–9

Whale Rock 185

Whidbey, Joseph, Master Royal Navy surveys during 1809 expedition to the Scheldt 124
  superintendent of construction of Plymouth breakwater 56

White, Martin, Lieutenant then Captain Royal Navy
  background and early career 182
  renders survey work from Channel Islands and earns interest of Hydrographer 182–3
  commands *Fox* cutter for Channel Islands surveys 183
  Shamroc commissioned for surveys in English Channel and Approaches 184–5

Whittle, Daniel, Lieutenant Royal Navy
  surveys and chart of False Bay 47
  carries despatches to India and is lost on return voyage 47–8

Wielingen Channel 117

Wilberforce, William 174, 176

Willis, John, Master Royal Navy, surveys 122

Young, Sir William, Admiral 124–5